Eat Light

The Healthy, Satisfying Way to Lose & Keep Off Weight Complete with Recipes & Menus

HPBooks

Susan Brown Deeming holds a bachelor's degree in Food Science from Iowa State University and a doctorate in Biochemistry and Nutrition from the University of Arizona. She taught Nutrition and Food Science at the University of Wisconsin— Stout and the University of Arizona. Since receiving her degrees, she has worked continually to broaden her food skills. She is currently media representative for the Oregon Dietetic Association.

While working with a physician in Tucson, Arizona, Sue did diet counseling. She currently writes a monthly column, Diet Right! for The Oregonian, a Portland, Oregon paper. She also writes a food preservation column during canning season.

Sue and husband Bill, are founders of The Author's Kitchen, located in Portland, Oregon. This company provides educational and promotional materials on food, recipe development and nutritional consultation for businesses interested in promoting good health. In conjuction with The Author's Kitchen, Sue has taught several nutrition seminars by demonstrating foods, recipes and menus rather than dwelling only on the principles of biochemistry.

CONTENTS

ANOTHER BEST-SELLING VOLUME FROM HPBooks

Publisher: Rick Bailey; Executive Editor: Randy Summerlin; Editorial Director: Elaine R. Woodard; Editor: Carroll P. Latham; Art Director: Don Burton; Book Design: Leslie Sinclair; Managing Editor: Cindy Coatsworth; Typography: Michelle Carter; Director of Manufacturing: Anthony B. Narducci; Food Stylist: Carol Flood Peterson; Photography: deGennaro Associates; Special thanks go to Brooke Harvey Oriental Porcelain Inc., of Palos Verdes Estates, CA, for loan of cover props and props on pages 77, 93, 107 and 113.

Published by HPBooks, a Division of HPBooks, Inc.
P.O. Box 5367, Tucson AZ 85703 602/888-2150
ISBN 0-89586-351-0
Library of Congress Catalog Card Number 85-82162
© 1985 HPBooks, Inc. Printed in the U.S.A.
3rd Printing

Cover Photo: Day 21 Menu, 1500 Calories Dinner, clockwise from top left: Champagne Jelly, page 125; mixed salad greens; parsleyed rice; California Vegetable Medley, page 112; Chicken Monterey, page 112.

Eat-Right—Eat-Light

Over one-third of the population is overweight. If you are overweight but enjoy food and want to know how to eat well and wisely while losing weight, then this is the book for you!

This is not a book of short cuts or miracles. The key to any weight-loss is **YOU.** If you're willing to make yourself stay with this program, success can be yours. You'll not only look better, but you'll feel better, too!

Common sense tells you there aren't any magic formulas or foods that make weight disappear. If you're overweight, you probably have some eating habits that need to be changed. It's not food that's bad for us, but the way we prepare it, the amount we eat and sometimes the type of food we eat.

The way to change bad eating habits is to deliberately, consciously, do something to improve your habits and do it over and over again. This program will help you change your habits.

With this weight-loss plan, you can start to lose weight today—this very minute! There are no calorie charts to memorize, no diet meals to plan—unless you want to plan your own meals—and no complicated lists of do's and don'ts.

In Section I, *Sensible-Weight-Loss Plan,* you'll evaluate whether you are overweight, how much you should lose and about how long it will take to lose the weight. Study Section I and become familiar with the menus I've provided.

Diets that limit the foods you eat—or take you off certain foods—don't teach you how to eat when you've reached your goal. Using this program, you will find that all types of foods can be included in a weight-loss diet. You will learn (1) to eat well and wisely by following the planned menus provided, (2) how to avoid overeating and (3) how to limit high-calorie sweets and fats now and when you reach your target weight.

You'll enjoy this easy-to-follow plan. I not only give you menus, but also recipes for many of the entrees. Meals are an adventure of taste experiences.

The *Sensible-Weight-Loss Menus,* beginning on page 14, contain 21 days of breakfasts, lunches and dinners at 1000-, 1200- and 1500-calories per day. Each meal is interesting, nutritionally balanced and uses foods from your local supermarket. No special shopping is required.

There is also a set of *Time-Saver Weight-Loss Menus,* page 114. They include simple foods that require no recipes. The meals are easy to prepare with little fuss or bother. These time-saver menus are flexible enough to fit into anyones' lifestyle. The whole family will enjoy these meals. Simply increase serving sizes or add extra bread or dessert for the non-dieters.

Over 100 recipes give exciting choices, such as Graham Waffles & Apricot Syrup, sliced Canadian bacon and skim milk for breakfast; Gazpacho-Yogurt Cooler, Seafood-Citrus Salad with Lime Dressing and French bread with margarine for lunch; and London Broil, baked potato, steamed broccoli and Marinated-Cucumber Salad for dinner with Honey-Rum Yogurt for dessert. Imagine eating all that food and staying within 1000 calories!

In addition to the recipes given with the menus, there is a chapter of delicious but low-calorie dessert recipes. Who would think you could have Choco-Banana Smoothie (a milkshake), Orange Sherbet or Cappuccino Mousse while you're on a diet?

If all you want to do is lose weight, read and study this book through page 125. Use the menus and recipes and you'll lose weight. To keep the weight off, I suggest you read on through Sections II and III.

Section II, *Weight-Management System,* will help you learn to manage your weight whether you want to lose or maintain. Study this section to learn how to use the system for planning nutritionally balanced meals that include many of your favorite foods and still keep calories low. As you use this system, you'll have more control over your diet whether you are losing weight or keeping it off.

With the Weight-Management System, you'll learn to recognize meals that fit into your weight-control program—even while dining out. A restaurant meal or dinner with friends need not be a diet-breaker. Compare your meal with the exchanges allowed, and order accordingly. See pages 12 and 131 for more information on dining out.

You'll also learn to plan your own nutritionally balanced meals using a step-by-step process. New, healthier eating habits and the use of the Weight-Management System are the keys to creating a maintenance plan that keeps the weight off.

Section III, *Weight-Maintenance Recipes,* contains delicious calorie-trimmed weight-maintenance recipes. They are prepared using cooking techniques that don't add unnecessary calories. You'll enjoy some rich, high-calorie ingredients used in small amounts to enhance flavor. There are recipes for Snacks & Light Meals, Salads & Vegetables, Main Dishes and Maintenance Desserts.

Sensible-Weight-Loss Plan

_____Section I

WHO SHOULD USE THIS PLAN?

If you have less than 30 pounds of excess weight to lose and have the determination and patience to stay with a weight-loss plan, then this plan is designed for you. The menus and recipes are suitable for any adult who wants to lose weight.

If you want to lose _more_ than 30 pounds, use this plan, but do it with the help of a registered dietitian, doctor or weight-control group. They can give you the personal support and encouragement needed when a longer time is required to reach your target weight.

Children and adolescents who are still growing have special nutritional needs. For them, determining a calorie level that will support growth and energy needs requires the professional help of a registered dietitian or doctor. They have the know-how to adjust the Sensible-Weight-Loss Menus to meet these special needs.

Pregnancy is not the time to lose weight. A pregnant woman needs enough nutritious food to feed herself and her baby. The amount of weight gained during pregnancy can be controlled, but only under medical supervision.

BEFORE BEGINNING YOUR DIET

Overweight is a risk factor linked with several serious medical problems, such as heart disease, diabetes, gall-bladder disease and hypertension. To learn what your personal health situation is, I suggest—**consult your physician before starting any weight-loss program.** If you haven't had a physical examination within the last three years, this is a good time to have one. Because many health problems are related to age, a physical examination is particularly important as you get older.

HOW MUCH WEIGHT DO YOU NEED TO LOSE?

Your weight normally fluctuates two to four pounds from day to day, so a weight range is more realistic than a single-pound number. Once you have reached the middle of your weight range, see how you look and feel. Do you need to lose more or regain some of the weight?

There are several ways to determine your best weight. One way is to compare your height and weight to height-and-weight tables based on statistical averages. **These averages do not and are not meant to establish an "ideal" weight for any individual.** The tables are valuable only as guidelines for determining your target weight.

To use height-and-weight tables:
• Weigh yourself in light clothing and shoes with one-inch heels. A balance-type scale with a beam and movable weight is more accurate than a bathroom scale. If a bathroom scale is all you have, check its accuracy by weighing a ten-pound bag of flour. Adjust the weight reading, if necessary. Record your weight and save it for later use.
• Measure your height in the same shoes. Record your height. Now evaluate your frame size by measuring your elbow width. See Table A, *Medium-Body Frame for Men & Women,* opposite. From this table, you can determine if you have a small, medium or large frame. The table shows only medium-frame measurements. If you have a large or small body frame, your elbow width will be larger or smaller than that given in the table.
• Find your height and frame size in Table B or C, *Height*

Many of the lunches can be taken as brown-bag lunches. Seafood-Stuffed Artichokes, page 111, makes an especially tasty lunch.

& Weight for Men or *Height & Weight for Women,* page 9. If your weight falls within the range given for your height and weight, you may need only to firm up your muscles.

Another way to determine how much weight to lose is to compare your weight at age 25 to what you now weigh. Find your desirable-weight range on Table B or C. This is your target.

If you were not overweight and your weight at age 25 was within your desirable range, that weight is a reasonable one for you now. To determine how much you need to lose by this method, subtract your age-25 weight from your present weight.

Body-Fat Measurement—Usually, an overweight person has excess body fat, but not always. Trained athletes with highly developed muscles can weigh more than the average in weight charts and yet not have excess fat. The opposite is also possible. You could be within your weight range and have too much body fat.

The most accurate method to determine body-fat is to be weighed while suspended in water. This method is expensive and is often used to weigh athletes in training.

Excess body fat is usually deposited at places on the body that can be measured by a simple *skinfold measurement.* This test measures the amount of fat under the skin and estimates the amount of total body fat. Dietitians, physicians and exercise physiologists have the tools and expertise to perform this test. The test is reliable and usually inexpensive.

You can do a simple *pinch test* at home that is similar to a skinfold measurement. The pinch test is done on women on the abdomen over the hip bone and the under side of the upper arm, half way between the shoulder and elbow. On men, pinch the rib cage just under the bottom rib and on the arm in the same place as for women.

Pinch up a layer of skin and fat between your first finger and thumb without including the underlying muscle. Make sure the finger and thumb are parallel to each other. Measure the distance between your finger and thumb. If the measurement is over one inch, you have too much body fat.

Determine Your Body Frame by Elbow Width

The following gives a simple procedure for approximating your frame size. Extend your arm and bend the forearm upward at a 90-degree angle. Keep the fingers straight and turn the inside of your wrist toward the body. Place the thumb and the first finger of your other hand on the two prominent bones on either side of your elbow. Being careful to keep your finger and thumb the correct distance apart, measure the space between with a ruler or tape measure. Compare this measurement with the measurements shown below.

For the most accurate measurement, have a nutritionist, exercise physiologist or physician measure your elbow width with calipers.

Table A Medium-Body Frame for Men & Women*

Height (in 1-inch heels)	Elbow Width (inches)	Height (in 1-inch heels)	Elbow Width (inches)
	MEN		WOMEN
5' 2'' - 5' 3''	2-1/2'' - 2-7/8''	4' 10'' - 4' 11''	2-1/4'' - 2-1/2''
5' 4'' - 5' 7''	2-5/8'' - 2-7/8''	5' 0'' - 5' 3''	2-1/4'' - 2-1/2''
5' 8'' - 5' 11''	2-3/4'' - 3''	5' 4'' - 5' 7''	2-3/8'' - 2-5/8''
6' 0'' - 6' 3''	2-3/4'' - 3-1/8''	5' 8'' - 5' 11''	2-3/8'' - 2-5/8''
6' 4''	2-7/8'' - 3-1/4''	6' 0''	2-1/2'' - 2-3/4''

Source: Metropolitan Life Insurance Co. Courtesy of the Metropolitan Life Insurance Co., New York, Copyright 1983.

*This table lists the elbow measurement for men and women of medium frame at various heights. Measurements smaller than those listed indicate a small frame while larger measurements indicate a large frame.

Measuring body fat doesn't tell you the number of pounds to lose, but by repeating this technique occasionally during your diet, you can see your progress. Once you can pinch less than an inch, you have lost your excess body fat and should feel and look better.

Using the information above, evaluate your weight in light of your own body build. Set some realistic weight goals for yourself. This might be to stay with the plan and not deviate, exercise every day, lose one to two pounds per week, or get down enough to wear the suit you wore to your graduation or wedding.

HOW DO YOU LOSE WEIGHT?

The answer is simple—eat fewer calories than your body needs for its daily functions—and increase your activities. Calories are a measure of the energy value of food and the energy needed by the body. When more calories are taken into the body than are used, the extra calories are stored in the form of fat and your weight increases. As you diet and exercise, the body is forced to rely on its stored calories for the extra fuel it needs. As the fat is used, weight will drop.

Body fat has a caloric value of about 3500 calories per pound. Therefore, in order to lose one pound of body fat, you must eat 3500 fewer calories than your body uses. To lose ten pounds, you must cut out 35,000 calories!

If you eat 500 fewer calories each day for seven days—that adds up to 3500 calories—you'll lose one pound. If you eat 1000 fewer calorie each day for seven days—a 7000-calorie deficit—you'll lose two pounds!

But the body needs more than just calories. If calories were all our bodies needed, we could just stop eating. Or we could eat 1000 calories of ice cream each day. However, many essential nutrients, such as protein and vitamin C should be provided daily.

If the body doesn't get the nutrients it needs, your health is threatened. Because of this, dietitians and physicians recommend that you don't lose more than one to two pounds a week. **If your goal is to lose ten pounds, plan to take five to ten weeks to lose the weight.**

By going on a complete fast and not eating at all or eating less than 1000 calories a day, the weight may come off quickly, but much of the loss will be water, along with valuable body protein needed to maintain body tissue, organs and muscles. The damage done in this semi-starvation state doesn't justify the benefits of quick weight loss.

How Many Calories Do You Need?—Energy needs for individuals are different based on age, sex, weight and the types and amounts of physical activity engaged in. However, healthy adults require about 15 calories per pound of body weight each day for normal activities. That doesn't include strenuous physical activities that work up a sweat.

Determine your calorie requirement by multiplying your target weight by 15. Don't use your current weight if you are overweight. For example, an overweight woman whose target weight is 110 pounds requires about 1650 calories to balance her normal activities (110 pounds x 15 calories per pound = 1650 calories).

In order to lose weight at a rate of one pound per week, she needs to cut out 500 calories and increase activity slightly. She shouldn't try to lose any faster or she may endanger her health. She should choose a 1000- or 1200-calorie diet (1650 calories less 500 calories = 1150 calories).

A diet of less than 1000 calories is not recommended. Women of average height can usually lose weight gradually and safely on a 1000- or 1200-calorie diet. Men and tall women can be successful with 1200- or 1500-calorie diets.

If a man's desirable weight is 165 pounds, he needs 2475 calories per day (165 pounds x 15 calories = 2475 calories). By reducing his calorie intake to 1500 calories per day and increasing activity slightly, he should be able to lose about two pounds per week.

INCREASE PHYSICAL ACTIVITY

To reduce body fat without losing important lean tissue, a balanced, low-calorie diet along with exercise is a must. If all you do is cut down on the amount of food you eat, the body will compensate by conserving energy.

Exercising does not increase the appetite! Actually, moderate exercise decreases appetite as well as increases the calories used *throughout* the day.

If you find yourself thinking about food, take a walk or put on a record or video tape and dancercise for awhile. The exercise will take your mind off food and help control your appetite.

The benefits of exercise can last for hours. I'm an early morning runner. After a brisk workout, I feel fresh and invigorated and can launch into my day with enthusiasm. You may prefer a midday workout or evening exercise. Find out when your best exercise time is, then exercise regularly.

If you haven't been exercising, the exercise plan mentioned below will start you toward improved cardiovascular fitness, too. If you are already involved in a cardiovascular fitness program, continue with it.

Set aside 30 minutes for exercise at least every other day. Regular moderate activity is always more beneficial than occasional intense activity. Continue to exercise the entire 30-minute period even if you have to slow down.

Exercise should increase your breathing rate and pulse and should work up a sweat, but it should also be reasonably comfortable. If you are gasping for breath or exhausted before 30 minutes is up, you are exercising too hard. Slow down. Find a pace that can be maintained the entire time.

Height & Weight for Men
According to Body Frame, Ages 25-59

Weight in Pounds (In Indoor Clothing)*

HEIGHT (In 1-inch heels) Feet Inches	SMALL FRAME	MEDIUM FRAME	LARGE FRAME
5' 2"	128-134	131-141	138-150
5' 3"	130-136	133-143	140-153
5' 4"	132-138	135-145	142-153
5' 5"	134-140	137-148	144-160
5' 6"	136-142	139-151	146-164
5' 7"	138-145	142-154	149-168
5' 8"	140-148	145-157	152-172
5' 9"	142-151	148-160	155-176
5' 10"	144-154	151-163	158-180
5' 11"	146-157	154-166	161-184
6' 0"	149-160	157-170	164-188
6' 1"	152-164	160-174	168-192
6' 2"	155-168	164-178	172-197
6' 3"	158-172	167-182	176-202
6' 4"	162-176	171-187	181-207

Table C

Height & Weight for Women
According to Body Frame, Ages 25-59

Weight in Pounds (In Indoor Clothing)*

HEIGHT (In 1-inch heels) Feet Inches	SMALL FRAME	MEDIUM FRAME	LARGE FRAME
4' 10"	102-11	109-121	118-131
4' 11"	103-113	111-123	120-134
5' 0"	104-115	113-126	122-137
5' 1"	106-118	115-129	125-140
5' 2"	108-121	118-132	128-143
5' 3"	111-124	121-135	131-147
5' 4"	114-127	124-138	134-151
5' 5"	117-130	127-141	137-155
5' 6"	120-133	130-144	140-159
5' 7"	123-136	133-147	143-163
5' 8"	126-139	136-150	146-167
5' 9"	129-142	139-153	149-170
5' 10"	132-145	142-156	152-173
5' 11"	135-148	145-159	155-176
6' 0"	138-151	148-162	158-179

*Indoor clothing weighing 5 pounds for men and 3 pounds for women.
Source: Metropolitan Life Insurance Co. Courtesy of the Metropolitan Life Insurance Co., New York, Copyright 1983.

My husband, Bill, and I enjoy jogging for our daily exercise.

Measure food carefully until you learn the amount by looking at it on the plate. Measuring cups, measuring spoons and small scales on which to weigh some foods are necessary utensils.

The "no pain, no gain" theory of exercise has no place in your diet-exercise program.

Choose an activity you enjoy and can look forward to, such as a brisk walk, jog, walk-jog combination, riding a bike or swimming laps. In addition, increase activity in your daily routine. Use the stairs instead of the elevator. Park away from where you are going so you can walk—then walk briskly. For errands within walking distance, walk don't drive.

Start slowly with your exercise program. The first day, walk one mile at a quick but comfortable pace. If it takes 30 minutes to walk the mile, you are walking at a two-miles-per-hour rate. Gradually over three or four weeks, increase your pace—and the distance covered—without increasing the time. Set a goal of walking 3.5 miles per hour or 1-3/4 miles in 30 minutes. If you are able to start your exercise program walking 3.5 miles per hour, work in some jogging or carry a backpack to increase energy used.

Walking at a 3.5-mile-per-hour pace for 30 minutes, four days a week, uses about 3500 calories in six weeks. At that rate, eight pounds could be lost in a year by walking alone!

For bicycling on either a stationary or rolling bike, follow the same plan. Start at a speed that is comfortable for 30 minutes, then gradually increase your speed.

You can lose weight without exercising, but it is slower. Plus you lose the benefits of improved fitness and increased vitality. Regular exercise is the only way to keep weight under control for a lifetime. Don't let yourself get away with not exercising. The benefits are too valuable to pass up.

Plan to continue your exercise program after reaching your desired weight. It has been shown that people who diet and exercise, and then continue to exercise after leaving the diet, are more likely to keep the weight off than are those who don't exercise regularly.

Artificial Sweeteners

Controversy still surrounds the use of artificial sweeteners. There is question of the potential risk to frequent users over extended periods of time. In addition, there is no evidence that use of artificial sweeteners actually aids weight loss.

Use of artificial sweeteners has risen dramatically in the last 5 years, but so has the weight problem. The recipes and menus in this book do not use artificial sweeteners or products that contain artificial sweeteners. *If you would like a sweeter taste to the recipes, use your own judgment in adding an artificial sweetener.* Use of diet soft drinks and sweeteners for tea or coffee is also left to your discretion. See Non-Caloric Beverages, page 13.

Tips for Successful Weight Loss

● *Eat only the amount of each food listed* for the 1000-, 1200- or 1500-calorie diet you choose to follow. A larger serving means extra calories and less weight loss.

● *Take the time to measure or weigh each serving.* The serving size may not be what you're used to having. Using the same size plates, cups and bowls at each meal will help you "see" how much a serving is by its size in relation to the dish. Once you can look at food on the plate and know that it is 1/2 cup fruit, 1/2 cup rice or 2 ounces meat, you can eliminate measuring each serving.

● *Eat everything that is listed in the menu.* Each menu is nutritionally balanced. Some substitutions are given in the menus so if you don't have one item on hand, you can use something else. Make substitutions, but don't leave out any foods. If a mid-afternoon or evening snack is important, save a part of lunch or dinner to eat later.

● *Don't skip meals.* If time is short, have a simple meal from the Time-Saver Weight-Loss Menus, page 114. If you aren't hungry, serve part of the meal and save some for a snack later. Skipped meals often lead to an out-of-control appetite before the next meal. Regular meals help control appetite and prevent overeating.

● *Watch out for extra calories.* If you are used to adding sugar to your cereal or cream or cream substitute to coffee, see what the menu allows. Do not spread butter or margarine on bread unless specified in the menu. These extra calories add up.

● *Don't let hunger build up.* If you prefer smaller meals more frequently, divide the three meals in the menu into six small meals. For some people, this helps control appetite. But don't add extra foods not listed in the day's menu.

● *Make diet meals something special.* On a sensible-weight-loss program, you aren't simply trying to avoid food. You're learning how to eat in a way to manage your weight.

● *Take time to set the table and sit down.* Standing in the kitchen will make you feel that a snack is all you can have. Eating on the run leaves the feeling of not eating at all.

● *Serve meals attractively.* Garnish the plates with fresh herbs or part of the recipe ingredients. Serve foods on interesting and sometimes unusual dishes.

Using pretty paper plates, have a picnic on the patio or in front of the fireplace. Another time, serve fruit in stemmed glasses with club soda poured over, garnished with mint leaves for an elegant finish to a meal.

● *Keep yourself satisfied by doing activities you enjoy,* but avoid activities usually accompanied by eating. *Before eating something not on your diet, ask yourself if you really want that food or are you looking for something to do.* Boredom and habit are the two most common reasons for overeating.

● *Weigh yourself no more than every three or four days.* Wear light clothing and shoes. If you are keeping with the plan, the pounds will come off!

● *Drink at least six glasses of water every day.* Water rinses waste materials from the body and also helps control appetite by filling the stomach. Add a thin slice of lime, lemon or orange to perk up a glass of ice water. Flavored mineral waters are especially nice and have no calories. I find their carbonation especially refreshing.

Garnished foods are appealing. By rows from top: carrot spiral; French cornichon fan; cucumber slices with scalloped edges; radish spiral; onion brush; lime curl or twist; orange-peel knot, curl, slivers; radish rose; lemon or orange curls or slices.

Fresh-herb garnishes add color. Herbs above by rows from top left: celery leaves, mint, parsley, dill weed, cilantro, thyme, rosemary, basil, water cress.

WHAT TO EXPECT

Don't expect overnight miracles, even though you may lose rapidly at first. During the first week of your diet, you'll lose a lot of water. After that, the body will balance itself and not lose water and pounds so rapidly.

You may reach a plateau in your weight loss. If the plan doesn't seem to be working anymore, don't give up! Water in the body is readjusting to less body fat. Continue to exercise regularly—and stay with the plan. You'll soon begin another gradual loss.

If you go ten days to two weeks without losing weight, you may need to reduce calories in the diet further or increase physical activity. If you are already following the 1000-calorie diet, try increasing activities. If there still is no weight loss, consult a registered dietitian to help balance calories, nutritional needs and activities.

On hectic days when time or energy are short, don't throw out the diet for take-out pizza. Let the *Time-Saver Weight-Loss Menus* come to the rescue. If you make substitutions, make them for the same meal—breakfast for breakfast, lunch for lunch or dinner for dinner.

Continue to use the 21 menus or the Time-Saver Weight-Loss Menus until you reach your goal or learn how to create your own diet menus using the Weight-Management System, page 126.

Sack Lunches—Most of the lunches can be carried to work, especially if there is a microwave oven available for reheating. When a menu doesn't have a lunch for packing, substitute a sandwich or salad from the Time-Saver Weight-Loss Menus.

Dining Out—Dining out doesn't have to mean breaking the diet. Make a game of planning ahead what you will and won't eat. When others order cocktails, order a club soda with a slice of lime for yourself. For an appetizer, have a salad with lemon or vinegar as a dressing, or a broth-type soup, not a creamed soup or chowder. Soup is ideal when eating out. It takes time to eat and is filling without adding many calories.

When dining out, order broiled or baked chicken and have the skin removed, or order broiled or poached fish. If you like ethnic foods, most Chinese stir-fried dishes are acceptable. Avoid deep-fried items. Italian spaghetti with a plain tomato or clam sauce will be low in calories, too. At a Mexican restaurant, avoid the chips and dishes with lots of cheese. Choose one taco, a taco salad with a tomato-salsa dressing only, or one chicken enchilada with lots of lettuce and salsa on the side.

Remember that restaurant serving sizes are usually larger than your diet plan allows. Judge what your serving size should be. Eat only that amount. Leave everything else on your plate.

Alcoholic Beverages

Severely limit alcoholic beverages. Not only are they extra calories, but alcohol stimulates the appetite and may prompt you to overeat. Instead of an alcoholic drink, make a cocktail of fruit juice and club soda with a twist of lemon or lime for an evening relaxer.

An occasional 12-ounce bottle of low-alcohol beer or a four-ounce glass of low-alcohol wine can be worked into your diet program. Account for the calories in the beer or wine by eliminating 2 teaspoons of margarine or oil during that day.

Alcoholic beverages used in small amounts as flavorings add very few calories but enhance full, rich tastes. When cooked, the alcohol itself is burned off leaving only the flavor.

Non-Caloric Beverages

The Sensible-Weight-Loss Menus do not include or exclude non-caloric beverages with meals. The use of non-caloric beverages is up to the dieter. They can be included at anytime without effecting the daily exchange requirements. The choice of beverage is up to you.

Black coffee and tea have no calories, but caffeine may be of concern. Decaffeinated coffee and herb teas offer another non-caloric option.

Artificially sweetened soft drinks have few if any calories and can be considered non-caloric beverages. See Artificial Sweeteners, page 10. An alternative to artificially sweetened soft drinks is carbonated mineral water or club soda. Some mineral waters are now lightly flavored with fruit or citrus essence. Those flavored with fruit juice are not non-caloric drinks.

Water is a non-caloric beverage. *It is important, especially when losing weight, to drink 6 to 8 glasses of water each day.* A glass of ice water with a slice of lemon is very refreshing either alone or with a meal.

Now You Have All the Parts

You now have all the parts you need to successfully lose weight with this diet plan.

— You know what your current weight is.
— You know how many pounds you are going to lose.
— You have chosen the Sensible-Weight-Loss Plan you want to use. You'll use the menus and recipes, pages 14 to 113. Or, plan your own menus using the Plan-a-Meal Worksheet, page 129, a Plan-a-Meal Weight-Loss Guide, page 128, and the Food-Exchange Lists, pages 134 to 139.
— You are ready to begin your exercise routine.

Sensible-Weight-Loss Menus & Recipes

The menus and recipes in this section were developed to help you lose weight and learn new eating habits so you don't gain back unwanted pounds. Drinking diet meals or eating a limited number of foods doesn't show you how to eat once the weight is lost.

These menus and recipes encourage good eating habits that can become a life-long tool for managing weight. The recipes following each menu leave you with no calories to look up or keep track of. All you have to do is follow the suggested serving size.

The menus contain a wide variety of foods from family favorites to simple one-dish meals including intriguing ethnic specialties. Each menu is complete in itself and does not depend on the other 20 menus. You can follow the 21 *Sensible-Weight-Loss Menus* until you reach your target weight, or skip those days or meals that don't appeal to you.

Prepare the menus in order or skip around, choosing your favorites first or saving them for last. You can also repeat menus as often as you like. The 21 menus merely give you a variety of choices. ■

Day 1

1000-Calorie	1200-Calorie	1500-Calorie
Breakfast		
1 serving Fruit Compote* **or** 1/3 cup fruit cocktail in extra-light syrup over 1/2 cup cooked oatmeal **or** other cooked cereal 1 serving Spicy Eggnog*	1 serving Fruit Compote* **or** 1/3 cup fruit cocktail in extra-light syrup over 1 cup cooked oatmeal **or** other cooked cereal 1 serving Spicy Eggnog*	1 serving Fruit Compote* **or** 1/3 cup fruit cocktail in extra-light syrup over 1 cup cooked oatmeal **or** other cooked cereal 1 serving Spicy Eggnog*
Lunch		
1 serving Tomato Sipper* **or** 1/2 cup (4 oz.) tomato juice 1 serving Tuna Bagelwich* 12 red or green grapes 1 cup (8 oz.) skim milk **or** 1 cup plain low-fat yogurt	1 cup canned tomato soup prepared with skim milk 1 serving Tuna Bagelwich* 12 red or green grapes	1 cup canned tomato soup prepared with skim milk 1 serving Tuna Bagelwich* 1/2 bagel topped with 1 tablespoon Neufchâtel cheese 12 red or green grapes
Dinner		
1 small serving Apple-Ham Strips* 1/2 cup whipped sweet potatoes **or** winter squash with 1 teaspoon diet margarine 1/4 cup cut green beans cooked with 1/4 cup sliced red onion 3 (1-inch) angel-food-cake cubes 1 serving Lemon Yogurt, page 118	1 small serving Apple-Ham Strips* 1/2 cup whipped sweet potatoes **or** winter squash with 1 teaspoon diet margarine 1/2 cup cut green beans cooked with 1/2 cup sliced red onion 5 (1-inch) angel-food-cake cubes 1 serving Lemon Yogurt, page 118	1 large serving Apple-Ham Strips* 1/2 cup whipped sweet potatoes **or** winter squash with 1 teaspoon diet margarine 1/2 cup cut green beans cooked with 1/2 cup sliced red onion 5 (1-inch) angel-food-cake cubes 1 serving Lemon Yogurt, page 118

* Recipe follows.

Fruit Compote

Top this fruit mixture with one tablespoon cinnamon-flavored yogurt for a tasty dessert.

1 cup water
1 orange-spice tea bag
1/2 (8-oz.) pkg. mixed dried fruit
1 (16-oz.) can sliced peaches packed
   in extra-light syrup

1 teaspoon cornstarch
2 cups partially thawed frozen,
   unsweetened raspberries, strawberries
   or blackberries

In a medium saucepan, bring water to a boil; add tea bag. Remove from heat; let tea steep 5 minutes. Remove and discard tea bag. Place dried fruit in a medium bowl. Pour tea over fruit; let stand 30 minutes. Drain soaked fruit, reserving tea in a medium saucepan. Drain peaches; add syrup to reserved tea. Add drained peaches to soaked fruit. Stir cornstarch into tea mixture until dissolved. Stir constantly until mixture comes to a boil and thickens. Let cool 15 minutes. Add cooled thickened mixture and berries to dried-fruit mixture; stir gently. Cover tightly; refrigerate until served, up to 7 days. Serve cold or reheat only amount desired over low heat until warm. Makes 16 (1/4-cup) servings.

1 serving (1/4 cup) = 1 fruit, 42 calories

Spicy Eggnog

An old-fashioned fluffy eggnog everyone will enjoy.

1 pint skim milk (2 cups)
1/2 teaspoon vanilla extract
1/8 teaspoon ground cinnamon

2 egg whites, room temperature
1-1/2 teaspoons sugar
Freshly grated nutmeg, if desired

In a small saucepan, heat milk over medium heat until small bubbles form around edge of pan. Stir in vanilla and cinnamon; set aside. Beat egg whites until foamy. Gradually beat in sugar; beat until glossy soft peaks form. While stirring gently, slowly pour hot milk mixture into egg-white mixture. Pour eggnog into 2 drinking glasses; sprinkle nutmeg over each serving, if desired. Serve warm. Makes 2 servings.

1 serving = 1 milk, 1 meat, 115 calories

Tomato Sipper   *Photo on page 17.*

Look for picante sauce in the Mexican-food area of your supermarket.

1 (12-oz.) can tomato juice
1/2 (10-1/2-oz.) can condensed beef broth
1/2 cup water

1 tablespoon lemon juice
1 teaspoon Worcestershire sauce
1 tablespoon picante sauce, if desired

In a small saucepan, combine all ingredients. Bring to a boil over medium heat; reduce heat to low. Cover; simmer 10 minutes. Serve hot in soup bowls or mugs. Or, to serve cold, cool to room temperature; cover and refrigerate 2 hours or up to 7 days. Serve in mugs or small drinking glasses. Makes 5 (1/2-cup) servings.

1 serving (1/2 cup) = 1 vegetable, 25 calories

Tuna Bagelwich

Wine vinegar accents the tuna flavor without adding calories.

2/3 (3-oz.) pkg. Neufchâtel cheese,
  room temperature
1 tablespoon buttermilk or skim milk
1/8 teaspoon dried dill weed
Dash of garlic salt
1 (6-3/4-oz.) can tuna packed in water,
  drained
1 green onion, sliced

2 tablespoons sliced pimento-stuffed olives
1 tablespoon red-wine vinegar
2 (3-inch-diameter, 1-1/2-inch-thick)
  pumpernickel bagels or onion bagels
4 iceberg-lettuce or Bibb-lettuce leaves
4 cherry tomatoes

In a small bowl, beat cheese and buttermilk or skim milk until smooth. Stir in dill weed and garlic salt. In another small bowl, combine tuna, green onion and olives. Sprinkle vinegar over tuna mixture; toss with a fork to distribute. Cut bagels in half horizontally; toast cut sides. Place 1 bagel half, toasted-side up, on each of 4 plates. Spread 1/4 of cheese mixture over toasted side of each bagel half. Top each with a lettuce leaf. Spoon 1/4 of tuna mixture over lettuce on each bagel half. Keeping slices together and not cutting all the way through, thinly slice cherry tomatoes from bottom to top. Fan slices of 1 cherry tomato on top of each sandwich. Makes 4 servings.

---

1 serving = 2 meat, 1 bread, 1/2 fat, 200 calories

Apple-Ham Strips

Apple and mild-flavored mustard complement the ham.

1 tablespoon plus 1-1/2 teaspoons regular
  margarine
3/4 cup chopped onion
2 medium Rome Beauty apples or
  other baking apples (3 per lb.)

3 tablespoons Dijon-style mustard or
  other prepared mustard
1/3 cup unsweetened apple juice
12 oz. cooked lean center-cut ham

In a medium nonstick skillet or a skillet coated with nonstick vegetable spray, melt margarine over medium-high heat. Add onion; sauté until soft. Meanwhile, peel, core and slice apples. Stir mustard, apple slices and apple juice into sautéed onions. Bring to a boil; reduce heat until mixture barely simmers. Cover; simmer 10 minutes. Cut ham into 12 equal strips. Add ham strips to apple mixture. Simmer 10 minutes longer. Sauce should be slightly thickened. If sauce is too thin, remove cover and let mixture boil several minutes. **For 1000- or 1200-Calorie Menus (small serving),** place 2 ham strips and 1/2 cup apple mixture on each plate. **For 1500-Calorie Menu (large serving),** place 4 ham strips and 1/2 cup apple mixture on each plate. Spoon any leftover apple mixture and ham into a container with a tight-fitting lid. Cover tightly; refrigerate up to 3 days. To serve, reheat in a skillet or a microwave. Spoon 1/2 cup hot apple mixture onto a plate. Add appropriate number of ham strips for a small or large serving as directed above. Makes 6 small servings or 3 large servings.

---

1 small serving (2 ham strips, 1/2 cup apple mixture) = 2 meat, 1 fruit, 1/2 fat, 180 calories
1 large serving (4 ham strips, 1/2 cup apple mixture) = 4 meat, 1 fruit, 1/2 fat, 290 calories

---

1000-Calorie Lunch, clockwise from top: Tomato Sipper, page 15, with celery stirrer; skim milk; fresh green grapes; Tuna Bagelwich.

Day 2

1000-Calorie	1200-Calorie	1500-Calorie
	Breakfast	
1 small serving Graham Waffle & Apricot Syrup* **or** 1 Graham Waffle with 1 tablespoon reduced-calorie pancake syrup (60 calories/2 tablespoons) 1 oz. sliced Canadian bacon **or** lean ham, grilled 1 cup (8 oz.) skim milk	1 large serving Graham Waffles & Apricot Syrup* **or** 2 Graham Waffles with 1-1/2 tablespoons reduced-calorie pancake syrup (60 calories/2 tablespoons) 2 teaspoons diet margarine 1 oz. sliced Canadian bacon **or** lean ham, grilled 1 cup (8 oz.) skim milk	1 large serving Graham Waffles & Apricot Syrup* **or** 2 Graham Waffles with 1-1/2 tablespoons reduced-calorie pancake syrup (60 calories/2 tablespoons) 2 teaspoons diet margarine 1 oz. sliced Canadian bacon **or** lean ham, grilled 1 cup (8 oz.) skim milk
	Lunch	
1 serving Gazpacho-Yogurt Cooler* **or** 1/4 cup (2 oz.) tomato juice stirred into 1/2 cup plain low-fat yogurt, seasoned with salt, pepper and hot-pepper sauce 1 serving Seafood-Citrus Salad with Lime Dressing* 1 (1/2-inch-thick) French-bread slice 1 teaspoon diet margarine	1 serving Gazpacho-Yogurt Cooler* **or** 1/4 cup (2 oz.) tomato juice stirred into 1/2 cup plain low-fat yogurt, seasoned with salt, pepper and hot-pepper sauce 1 serving Seafood-Citrus Salad with Lime Dressing* 2 (1/2-inch-thick) French-bread slices 2 teaspoons diet margarine	1 serving Gazpacho-Yogurt Cooler* **or** 1/4 cup (2 oz.) tomato juice stirred into 1/2 cup plain low-fat yogurt, seasoned with salt, pepper and hot-pepper sauce 1 serving Seafood-Citrus Salad with Lime Dressing* 2 (1/2-inch-thick) French-bread slices 2 teaspoons diet margarine
	Dinner	
1 small serving London Broil* 1 small potato (4 to 5 per lb.), baked 2 teaspoons diet margarine 1/2 cup steamed broccoli, seasoned with lemon pepper 1 serving Marinated-Cucumber Salad* **or** 1/4 medium cucumber, sliced, drizzled with 2 teaspoons reduced-calorie salad dressing (25 calories/tablespoon) 3/4 cup fresh or frozen unsweetened strawberries 1 serving Honey-Rum Yogurt, page 117	1 small serving London Broil* 1 small potato (4 to 5 per lb.), baked 2 teaspoons diet margarine 1 cup steamed broccoli, seasoned with lemon pepper 1 serving Marinated-Cucumber Salad* **or** 1/4 medium cucumber, sliced, drizzled with 2 teaspoons reduced-calorie salad dressing (25 calories/tablespoon) 3/4 cup fresh or frozen unsweetened strawberries 1 serving Honey-Rum Yogurt, page 117	1 large serving London Broil* 1 medium potato (3 to 4 per lb.), baked 2 teaspoons diet margarine 1 cup steamed broccoli, seasoned with lemon pepper 1 serving Marinated-Cucumber Salad* **or** 1/4 medium cucumber, sliced, drizzled with 2 teaspoons reduced-calorie salad dressing (25 calories/tablespoon) 3/4 cup fresh or frozen unsweetened strawberries 1 serving Honey-Rum Yogurt, page 117

* Recipe follows.

Graham Waffles & Apricot Syrup

Refrigerate leftover Apricot Syrup to use in Apricot Yogurt, Day 4, page 28.

1/2 cup sifted all-purpose flour
1-1/2 teaspoons baking powder
1/2 teaspoon baking soda
1/4 teaspoon salt

1/2 cup graham flour or whole-wheat flour
1 egg, separated
1 cup buttermilk
1 tablespoon regular margarine, melted

Apricot Syrup:
14 dried apricot halves
6 tablespoons unsweetened pineapple juice
1-1/2 cups boiling water
1-1/4 teaspoons cornstarch

1/2 cup cold water
1 teaspoon lemon juice
1 tablespoon plus 1 teaspoon honey

Prepare Apricot Syrup; keep warm. Preheat waffle iron according to manufacturer's directions. In a sifter, combine all-purpose flour, baking powder, baking soda and salt. Sift into a medium bowl. Stir in graham flour or whole-wheat flour. In another medium bowl, beat egg yolk. Stir in buttermilk and margarine. Add flour mixture to egg mixture. Stir only until flour is moistened; batter will be lumpy. Beat egg white until soft peaks form. Fold beaten egg white into waffle batter. Spoon about 1/3 cup waffle batter onto hot waffle iron. Bake until waffle is golden brown. Bake remaining batter, 1/3 cup at a time. Serve immediately with warm Apricot Syrup. **For 1000-Calorie Menu (small serving),** place 1 waffle on each plate. Top each serving with 1/4 cup syrup. **For 1200- or 1500-Calorie Menus (large serving),** place 2 waffles on each plate. Top each serving with 1/2 cup syrup. Cool leftover waffles. Wrap in plastic wrap or place in a plastic bag. Refrigerate until served, up to 3 days. To reheat, warm under a preheated broiler or in a toaster. Makes 6 (5-inch) waffles, 6 small servings or 3 large servings.

To make Apricot Syrup, place apricot halves in a small saucepan; add pineapple juice. Pour 1-1/2 cups boiling water over fruit. Cover; let stand 20 minutes. In a blender or food processor fitted with a metal blade, puree soaked apricot mixture. Return puree to saucepan. In a small bowl, combine cornstarch and 1/2 cup cold water. Stir cornstarch mixture, lemon juice and honey into apricot puree. Stir constantly over medium heat until mixture comes to a boil and thickens slightly. Reduce heat; keep warm until served. Pour any leftover syrup into a container with a tight-fitting lid. Cover tightly; refrigerate up to 5 days. Makes about 3 cups.

---

1 small serving (1 waffle, 1/4 cup syrup) = 1 bread, 1/2 fruit, 1 fat, 139 calories
1 large serving (2 waffles, 1/2 cup syrup) = 2 bread, 1 fruit, 2 fat, 278 calories
1 waffle = 1 bread, 1 fat, 116 calories
1/4 cup syrup = 1/2 fruit, 23 calories

Marinated-Cucumber Salad

Because of marinating, the radishes will give a pinkish tinge to the salad.

1/3 cup rice vinegar or white-wine vinegar
1/4 cup water
1 tablespoon vegetable oil
1/4 teaspoon salt
1/8 teaspoon pepper
1 teaspoon sugar
1 medium cucumber (2 per lb.), peeled,
  thinly sliced

1/2 small onion (5 per lb.), thinly sliced
1/2 cup thinly sliced red radishes
  (about 4 medium radishes)
2 tablespoons chopped fresh cilantro
  or parsley
4 red-leaf-lettuce leaves

In a medium container with a tight-fitting lid, combine vinegar, water, oil, salt, pepper and sugar. Cover tightly; shake vigorously 15 seconds. Add cucumber, onion, radishes and cilantro or parsley. Gently stir vegetables in dressing to coat with marinade. Cover tightly; refrigerate at least 4 hours or up to 2 days. To serve, place a lettuce leaf on each of 4 salad plates or in 4 salad bowls. Use a slotted spoon to lift cucumber mixture from dressing. Spoon 1/4 of cucumber mixture onto each lettuce-lined plate or bowl. Discard dressing left in container. Makes 4 servings.

---

1 serving = 1/2 vegetable, 1/2 fat, 46 calories

London Broil

Ask the butcher to cut an extra-thick steak for you.

1 (1-1/4-lb.) boneless beef-round
  top-round steak, cut 1 inch thick
2 tablespoons olive oil
1/2 cup red wine
1 garlic clove, minced
1 tablespoon finely chopped onion

1/2 teaspoon pepper
1/4 teaspoon salt
1 bay leaf
1/4 teaspoon dried leaf oregano
1/4 teaspoon dried leaf basil

Trim any visible fat from steak. In a casserole dish or shallow container with a tight-fitting lid, combine remaining ingredients for a marinade. Place steak in marinade, turning to coat both sides. Cover; refrigerate at least 8 hours or overnight, turning steak several times. Preheat broiler or grill. Remove steak from marinade. Broil or grill until medium-rare or medium, about 5 minutes on each side. *Do not overcook.* If cooked well-done, steak may be tough. Holding a sharp knife at a 45-degree angle, slice steak across grain as thinly as possible. **For 1000- or 1200-Calorie Menus (small serving),** place 2 ounces sliced beef on each plate. **For 1500-Calorie Menu (large serving),** place 4 ounces sliced beef on each plate. Makes about 6 small servings or 3 large servings.

---

1 small serving (2 oz. beef) = 2 meat, 1 fat, 177 calories
1 large serving (4 oz. beef) = 4 beef, 2 fat, 354 calories

1200-Calorie Dinner, clockwise from top left: Marinated-Cucumber Salad; fresh strawberries with Honey-Rum Yogurt, page 117; steamed broccoli; London Broil; baked potato.

Seafood-Citrus Salad with Lime Dressing

Shrimp and crab or imitation crab made from white fish go well with these citrus flavors.

1 medium grapefruit (2-1/2 per lb.)
1 medium orange (3 per lb.)
4 cups torn iceberg lettuce
1 medium, red or green bell pepper
   (2-1/2 per lb.), cut in strips

2 green onions with 3-inch green tops, sliced
1/4 cup canned diced green chilies
8 oz. tiny shrimp (about 35)

Lime Dressing:
2 tablespoon lime juice
2 tablespoons water
2 tablespoons vegetable oil

1/4 teaspoon salt
Dash of red (cayenne) pepper
1/8 teaspoon chili powder

Peel grapefruit and orange, removing all white membranes. Over a bowl to catch juices, section fruit by cutting on both sides of each section; remove fruit sections. Set fruit sections aside; reserve 2 tablespoons juice to use in dressing. Prepare Lime Dressing; refrigerate until served. Arrange 1 cup lettuce on each of 4 salad plates or in 4 salad bowls. Arrange 1/4 of bell-pepper strips, green onions, green chilies, shrimp, grapefruit sections and orange sections on each lettuce-lined plate or bowl. Drizzle 1 tablespoon Lime Dressing over each salad. Makes 4 servings.

To make Lime Dressing, in a small container with a tight-fitting lid, combine lime juice, water, 2 tablespoons reserved juice from grapefruit and orange, oil, salt, red pepper and chili powder. Cover tightly; shake vigorously 15 seconds. Refrigerate until served, up to 5 days. Shake before serving. Makes about 1/2 cup.

---

1 serving = 2 meat, 1 fruit, 1/2 fat, 176 calories
1 tablespoon dressing = 2/3 fat, 33 calories

Gazpacho-Yogurt Cooler

Spicy, refreshing cold soup to drink or eat with a spoon.

3/4 cup vegetable-juice cocktail
1/2 cup plain low-fat yogurt
1-1/2 cups skim milk
1/2 teaspoon red-wine vinegar
2 tablespoons shredded, peeled cucumber

2 tablespoons shredded green bell pepper
1 teaspoon finely chopped jalapeño pepper,
   if desired
Hot-pepper sauce
8 garlic-flavored croutons

In a blender, combine vegetable juice, yogurt, milk and vinegar. Process until smooth; pour into a pitcher. Stir in cucumber, bell pepper and jalapeño pepper, if desired. Season with hot-pepper sauce. Cover tightly; refrigerate 1 hour or until ready to serve, up to 12 hours. Pour cooler equally into 4 stemmed sherbet glasses or small glass bowls. Top each serving with 2 croutons. Makes 4 (3/4-cup) servings.

---

1 serving (3/4 cup) = 1/2 milk, 1/2 vegetable, 73 calories

Day 3

1000-Calorie	1200-Calorie	1500-Calorie
Breakfast		
1 serving Sombrero Muffins* 1/8 (5-inch-diameter) melon with 1 lime wedge **or** 1/2 grapefruit 1 cup (8 oz.) skim milk	1 serving Sombrero Muffins* 1/2 English muffin, toasted 1 teaspoon diet margarine 1/8 (5-inch-diameter) melon with 1 lime wedge **or** 1/2 grapefruit 1 cup (8 oz.) skim milk	1 serving Sombrero Muffins* 1/2 English muffin, toasted 2 teaspoons diet margarine 1 cup (8 oz.) skim milk
Lunch		
1 serving Cheese & Popcorn Soup* **or** 1 cup canned clam chowder prepared with undiluted evaporated skim milk 1 small serving Garden-Stuffed Pocket Sandwich* 1/2 cup unsweetened applesauce, seasoned with cinnamon **or** 1 small (2-1/2-inch) apple	1 serving Cheese & Popcorn Soup* **or** 1 cup canned clam chowder prepared with undiluted evaporated skim milk 1-1/2 cups hot-air-popped popcorn **or** 10 oyster crackers 1 small serving Garden-Stuffed Pocket Sandwich* 1/2 cup unsweetened applesauce, seasoned with cinnamon **or** 1 small (2-1/2-inch) apple	1 serving Cheese & Popcorn Soup* **or** 1 cup canned clam chowder prepared with undiluted evaporated skim milk 3 cups hot-air-popped popcorn **or** 10 oyster crackers 1 large serving Garden-Stuffed Pocket Sandwich* 1/2 cup unsweetened applesauce, seasoned with cinnamon **or** 1 small (2-1/2-inch) apple
Dinner		
1 serving Lemon-Lime Spritzer*, if desired 1 small serving Spaghetti with Italian Meat Sauce* 2 cups torn mixed salad greens 1-1/2 tablespoons Zesty Italian Dressing, page 58, **or** reduced-calorie salad dressing (25 calories/tablespoon) 1 serving Melon & Wine Mold, page 122, **or** 1/2 cup melon balls	1 serving Lemon-Lime Spritzer*, if desired 1 small serving Spaghetti with Italian Meat Sauce* 2 cups torn mixed salad greens 1-1/2 tablespoons Zesty Italian Dressing, page 58, **or** reduced-calorie salad dressing (25 calories/tablespoon) 1/2 cup sliced zucchini stir-fried in 1 teaspoon diet margarine 1 serving Melon & Wine Mold, page 122, **or** 1/2 cup melon balls	1 serving Lemon-Lime Spritzer*, if desired 1 large serving Spaghetti with Italian Meat Sauce* 2 cups torn mixed salad greens 1-1/2 tablespoons Zesty Italian Dressing, page 58, **or** reduced-calorie salad dressing (25 calories/tablespoon) 1 serving Melon & Wine Mold, page 122, **or** 1/2 cup melon balls

* Recipe follows.

Lemon-Lime Spritzer

Sparkling and refreshing with no calories!

Ice cubes
2 lemon slices

2 lime slices
2 cups club soda or mineral water, chilled

Fill 2 drinking glasses with ice cubes. Twist 1 lemon slice and 1 lime slice over each glass. Drop slices into glasses. Pour club soda equally into glasses over ice and fruit. Serve immediately. Makes 2 servings.

1 serving = 0 exchanges, 0 calories

Sombrero Muffins

Try this "Tex-Mex"-flavored egg-and-muffin sandwich to begin your day.

2 English muffins, split
1 tablespoon plus 1 teaspoon diet margarine
3 eggs
2 tablespoons skim milk
1/4 teaspoon salt

Dash of white pepper
1-1/2 teaspoons regular margarine
1/4 cup green-chili salsa
2 reduced-calorie American-cheese slices
(1-1/3 oz.)

Preheat broiler. Place muffin halves on an ungreased baking sheet. Spread each muffin half with 1 teaspoon diet margarine. Toast under broiler until lightly browned; keep warm. In a small bowl, beat eggs with a whisk until blended. Beat in milk, salt and white pepper. In a medium nonstick skillet or a skillet coated with nonstick vegetable spray, melt regular margarine. When margarine sizzles, pour egg mixture into skillet. Cook egg mixture over medium heat until softly set around edge. Lift edge so uncooked egg flows underneath. Stir egg mixture gently. Cook until eggs are set but still moist. With toasted muffin halves still on baking sheet, top each with 1/4 of cooked egg mixture. Spoon 1 tablespoon salsa over each serving. Cut each cheese slice into 4 thin strips. Crisscross 2 strips over each muffin. Broil until cheese melts. Place 1 broiled muffin on each of 4 plates. Serve immediately. Makes 4 servings.

1 serving = 1 meat, 1 bread, 1 fat, 181 calories

Spaghetti with Italian Meat Sauce

A family favorite complete with Parmesan cheese.

1 lb. extra-lean ground beef (10% to 15% fat)
1/2 cup chopped onion
2 garlic cloves, minced
1 (16-oz.) can whole tomatoes with juice
1 (8-oz.) can tomato sauce
2 tablespoons chopped fresh parsley or
    3/4 teaspoon dried leaf parsley
1 bay leaf

1 teaspoon dried leaf oregano, crushed
1/4 teaspoon dried leaf basil, crushed
1/8 teaspoon dried leaf thyme, crushed
1/4 cup red wine
1/4 cup sliced ripe olives
6 oz. uncooked spaghetti
2 tablespoons grated Parmesan cheese

In a heavy nonstick skillet or a skillet coated with nonstick vegetable spray, brown beef over medium heat. Stir with a fork to break up beef. Push browned beef to side of skillet. Tilt skillet; remove all but 1 tablespoon drippings. Add onion and garlic; sauté until onion is soft. Drain juice from tomatoes into meat mixture; chop tomatoes. Add chopped tomatoes and tomato sauce to meat mixture. Add parsley, bay leaf, oregano, basil and thyme. Stir in wine and olives. Reduce heat until mixture barely simmers. Cover; simmer 30 minutes, stirring occasionally. Remove bay leaf. Cook spaghetti according to package directions; drain. Rinse with hot water; drain again. **For 1000- or 1200-Calorie Menus (small serving),** place 1/2 cup cooked spaghetti on each plate. Ladle 2/3 cup sauce over spaghetti. Sprinkle 1 teaspoon cheese over each serving. **For 1500-Calorie Menu (large serving),** place 1 cup spaghetti on each plate. Ladle 1-1/3 cups sauce over spaghetti. Sprinkle 2 teaspoons cheese over each serving. Makes 6 small servings or 3 large servings.

Variation
Substitute 1 pound ground turkey for ground beef. Exchanges and calories will remain the same.

1 small serving (1/2 cup spaghetti, 2/3 cup sauce) = 2 meat, 1 fat, 1 vegetable, 1 bread, 276 calories
1 large serving (1 cup spaghetti, 1-1/3 cups sauce) = 4 meat, 2 fat, 2 vegetable, 2 bread, 552 calories

1000-Calorie Breakfast, clockwise from top left: cantaloupe wedge with lime slice; skim milk; Sombrero Muffin.

Garden-Stuffed Pocket Sandwich

Choose your favorite crisp fresh vegetables to complete this sandwich.

2 or 4 (6-inch) pita-bread rounds
2 cups sliced zucchini, broccoli,
    cauliflower, turnips, cucumbers,
    carrots or mushrooms, or combination
4 oz. cooked turkey or lean cooked
    ham, slivered (about 1 cup)

2 cups shredded iceberg lettuce
2 tablespoons roasted sunflower kernels
1/2 cup alfalfa sprouts (2 oz.), if desired
1/2 cup bottled low-calorie Italian
    salad dressing

Preheat oven to 200F (95C). For small servings, use 2 pita rounds; for large servings, use 4 pita rounds. Wrap pita rounds with foil or place on an ungreased baking sheet. In preheated oven, heat pita rounds 5 minutes. Meanwhile, in a medium bowl, combine vegetables and turkey or ham. Add lettuce, sunflower kernels and alfalfa sprouts, if desired. Toss again. Pour salad dressing over vegetable mixture; toss to coat with dressing. **For 1000- or 1200-Calorie Menus (small serving),** cut 2 pita rounds in half crosswise. Gently open each half pocket. Place 1 half pita round on each of 4 plates. **For 1500-Calorie Menu (large serving),** using 4 pita rounds, cut a thin strip off 1 side of each, making 4-inch openings. Gently open each whole pocket. Place 1 pita round on each plate. **For all menus,** stuff each warm pita or pita half with 1 cup vegetable mixture. Serve immediately. Makes 4 small servings or 4 large servings.

---

1 small serving (1/2 pita, 1 cup vegetable mixture) = 1 vegetable, 1 meat, 1 bread, 1/2 fat, 188 calories
1 large serving (1 whole pita, 1 cup vegetable mixture) = 1 vegetable, 1 meat, 2 bread, 1/2 fat, 258 calories

---

Cheese & Popcorn Soup

Popcorn popped in hot air—not oil—has only 25 calories per cup.

1 teaspoon regular margarine
1/4 cup chopped onion
1/4 cup chopped carrot
1/4 cup chopped celery
1/2 cup canned condensed chicken broth
2 teaspoons Dijon-style mustard

1/2 cup skim milk
1 tablespoon all-purpose flour
1 (15-oz.) can evaporated skim milk
1 cup shredded sharp Cheddar cheese (4 oz.)
1 cup hot-air-popped popcorn

In a medium nonstick skillet or a skillet coated with nonstick vegetable spray, melt margarine over medium heat. Add onion, carrot and celery; sauté until onion is soft. Pour broth over sautéed vegetables. Reduce heat until broth barely simmers. Cover; simmer 10 minutes. Pour vegetable mixture into a blender or food processor fitted with a metal blade. Puree; return puree to skillet. In a container with a tight-fitting lid, combine mustard, skim milk and flour. Cover tightly; shake vigorously until smooth. Stirring constantly, gradually pour flour mixture into vegetable mixture. Add evaporated milk and cheese. Stir soup over medium heat until cheese melts and soup thickens slightly; *do not let soup boil.* Ladle 3/4 cup soup into each of 4 soup bowls; top each with 1/4 cup popcorn. Makes 4 (3/4-cup) servings.

---

1 serving (3/4 cup soup, 1/4 cup popcorn) = 1 meat, 1 milk, 1 fat, 173 calories

---

Clockwise from center top: Piña-Colada Shake, page 80; Cranberry Blizzard, page 42; Wine Spritzer, page 104.

Day 4

1000-Calorie	1200-Calorie	1500-Calorie
	Breakfast	
1 serving Pear-Orange Shake* 1 whole-wheat-bread slice, toasted 1 tablespoon peanut butter **or** 1 table-spoon Marmalade-Cheese Spread*	1 serving Pear-Orange Shake* 2 whole-wheat-bread slices, toasted 2 teaspoons diet margarine 1 tablespoon peanut butter **or** 1 table-spoon Marmalade-Cheese Spread*	1 serving Pear-Orange Shake* 2 whole-wheat-bread slices, toasted 2 teaspoons diet margarine 1 tablespoon peanut butter **or** 1 table-spoon Marmalade-Cheese Spread*
	Lunch	
1 serving Chef's Favorite Salad* 1 (8-inch) breadstick 1 serving Sparkling Apple Cider* **or** 1/2 cup (4 oz.) apple juice	1 cup canned chicken noodle soup **or** beef noodle soup prepared as directed 1 serving Chef's Favorite Salad* 1 (8-inch) breadstick 1 serving Sparkling Apple Cider* **or** 1/2 cup (4 oz.) apple juice	1 cup canned chicken noodle soup **or** beef noodle soup prepared as directed 1 serving Chef's Favorite Salad* 2 (8-inch) breadsticks 1 serving Sparkling Apple Cider* **or** 1/2 cup (4 oz.) apple juice
	Dinner	
1 small serving Creole Gumbo* 1/3 cup white rice 1 serving Pear & Blue-Cheese Salad with Wine Dressing* 1 serving Apricot Yogurt* **or** 1-1/2 tablespoons low-sugar fruit spread stirred into 1 cup plain low-fat yogurt * Recipe follows.	1 small serving Creole Gumbo* 1/3 cup white rice 1/2 cup cooked green beans with 1/2 teaspoon crumbled cooked bacon 1 serving Pear & Blue-Cheese Salad with Wine Dressing* 1 serving Apricot Yogurt* **or** 1-1/2 tablespoons low-sugar fruit spread, stirred into 1 cup plain low-fat yogurt	1 large serving Creole Gumbo* 2/3 cup white rice 1 serving Pear & Blue-Cheese Salad with Wine Dressing* 1 serving Apricot Yogurt* **or** 1-1/2 tablespoons low-sugar fruit spread stirred into 1 cup plain low-fat yogurt

Apricot Yogurt

Evaporated skim milk makes the creamy yogurt less tangy.

1-1/2 cups plain low-fat yogurt   **1/4 cup Apricot Syrup, page 19**
1/4 cup evaporated skim milk   **1 dried apricot half**

In a medium bowl, combine yogurt, evaporated milk and Apricot Syrup. Beat with a whisk until smooth. Spoon into 2 dessert dishes. Using scissors, snip apricot half into slivers. Sprinkle equally over servings. Cover tightly; refrigerate until ready to serve, at least 1 hour. Makes 2 (1-cup) servings.

---

1 serving (1 cup) = 1 milk, 1/2 fruit, 125 calories

Pear-Orange Shake

Egg white adds protein and makes the shake light and foamy.

1/2 medium pear (3 per lb.) or
   2 small pear halves canned in water
1/4 cup orange juice
1 tablespoon lemon juice

1 pint skim milk (2 cups)
1 egg white
2 thin orange slices or lemon slices

Peel and core fresh pear. In a blender, combine cored peeled fresh or canned pear, orange juice, lemon juice, milk and egg white. Process until foamy and almost smooth. Pour into 2 drinking glasses. Serve immediately. Garnish with orange slices or lemon slices. Makes 2 servings.

1 serving = 1 fruit, 1 milk, 1/2 meat, 139 calories

Marmalade-Cheese Spread

You'll enjoy this delightful spread whether you're dieting or maintaining your weight.

2 (3-oz.) pkgs. Neufchâtel cheese,
   room temperature
2 tablespoons orange juice

1 teaspoon grated orange peel
1/4 cup low-sugar orange marmalade
1 egg white

In a small bowl, combine cheese, orange juice and orange peel. Beat with an electric mixer until blended. Stir in marmalade. In another small bowl, beat egg white with clean beater or whisk until soft peaks form. Fold beaten egg white into cheese mixture. Cover tightly; refrigerate until served, up to 5 days. Makes about 1 cup.

1 tablespoon = 1/2 meat, 35 calories

Sparkling Apple Cider   Photo on page 31.

Club soda adds sparkle without calories.

2/3 cup apple cider, chilled
1-1/2 cups club soda, chilled

2 narrow (3-inch-long) orange-peel strips

Pour 1/3 cup apple cider into each of 2 drinking glasses. Slowly pour 3/4 cup club soda into each glass. Tie each orange-peel strip in a loose knot. Drop 1 orange-peel knot into each glass. Serve immediately. Makes 2 servings.

1 serving = 1 fruit, 40 calories

Chef's Favorite Salad

Reduced-calorie salad dressings are located with regular dressings in the supermarket.

**8 cups torn spinach, iceberg lettuce, romaine
    lettuce or red-leaf lettuce or combination**
**1 cup thinly sliced red radishes
    (about 8 medium radishes)**
2 green onions, sliced
**1/3 cup bottled reduced-calorie Thousand
    Island salad dressing**
Large red-leaf-lettuce leaves

2 oz. cooked ham, diced (1/2 cup)
2 oz. cooked turkey, diced (1/2 cup)
**3 reduced-calorie American-cheese slices
    (2 oz.) cut in squares**
**1 oz. reduced-calorie Swiss cheese, diced
    (1/4 cup)**
2 small tomatoes (3 to 4 per lb.)
1 egg, hard cooked

In a large bowl, combine torn lettuce, radishes and green onions. Pour salad dressing over lettuce mixture; toss gently. Line 4 salad bowls or salad plates with large lettuce leaves. Divide tossed lettuce mixture among lettuce-lined bowls or plates. Leaving a 2-inch circle in center of salad uncovered, arrange 1/4 of ham, turkey, American cheese and Swiss cheese on top of each salad in concentric circles. Cut each tomato in half crosswise. Cut each half in 4 wedges. Place 4 tomato wedges in center of meat and cheese circles in each bowl or plate. Press hard-cooked egg through a sieve. Sprinkle sieved egg equally over tomato pieces. Serve immediately. Makes 4 servings.

---

1 serving = 2 meat, 1 vegetable, 1/2 fat, 165 calories

Pear & Blue-Cheese Salad with Wine Dressing

Blue cheese and pears are a marvelous combination.

**1 medium, ripe Bartlett pear (3 per lb.) or
    2 small pear halves canned in water**

4 cups torn romaine lettuce
2 tablespoons crumbled blue cheese

Wine Dressing:
1 tablespoon vegetable oil
2 tablespoons white wine
1 tablespoon white-wine vinegar

1 teaspoon grated onion
1/8 teaspoon salt
Dash of pepper

Prepare Wine Dressing; set aside. Quarter pear; cut out and discard core. Dice pear. In a large bowl, combine diced pear and lettuce. Pour dressing over salad; toss gently. Spoon 1/4 of salad onto each of 4 salad plates. Sprinkle cheese over top. Serve immediately. Makes 4 servings.
To make Wine Dressing, combine all ingredients in a small container with a tight-fitting lid. Cover tightly; shake vigorously 15 seconds. Refrigerate until served, up to 3 days. Shake before serving. Makes about 1/4 cup.

---

1 serving = 1/2 fruit, 1 fat, 96 calories

1000-Calorie Lunch: Chef's Favorite Salad with breadstick, Sparkling Apple Cider, page 29.

Creole Gumbo

Non-dieters in the family will want double servings of this Cajun dish.

1-1/2 cups water
1 chicken-flavored bouillon cube
3 (5-oz.) chicken-breast halves, skinned
3/4 cup chopped onion
1/4 cup chopped celery leaves
1 (16-oz.) can whole tomatoes with juice
1 bacon slice, diced
1 cup diced green bell pepper
2 tablespoons all-purpose flour

2 bay leaves
1/2 teaspoon dried leaf thyme
1/4 teaspoon red (cayenne) pepper
8 oz. fresh or frozen medium shrimp
  (about 18), shelled, deveined
1 (10-oz.) pkg. frozen cut okra or
  3/4 lb. fresh okra, chopped
1 teaspoon gumbo filé powder

In a large saucepan, combine water and bouillon cube. Bring to a boil over high heat; reduce heat until water barely simmers. Crush bouillon cube with back of a spoon. Stir until bouillon cube is completely dissolved. Trim fat from chicken. Add trimmed chicken, 1/4 cup chopped onion and celery leaves to bouillon mixture. Bring mixture back to a simmer. Cover; simmer 15 minutes. Use a slotted spoon to remove cooked chicken breasts. Pour broth mixture through a sieve into a large saucepan; discard vegetables. Set broth aside to cool. Cut cooked chicken from bones; discard bones. Cut chicken into bite-sized pieces; set aside. Drain tomatoes, reserving juice; chop tomatoes. Set aside. Fry bacon in a heavy skillet until crisp. Drain cooked bacon on paper towels. Add remaining 1/2 cup chopped onion and bell pepper to skillet. Sauté over medium heat until onion is soft. Sprinkle flour over sautéed onion mixture; stir in. Cook about 1 minute; remove from heat. Use a spoon or bulb baster to remove fat from top of cooled chicken broth. Gradually stir reserved broth into onion mixture. Return skillet to heat. Bring to a boil, stirring constantly. Pour broth mixture back into large saucepan. Add chopped tomatoes, juice from tomatoes, bay leaves, thyme and red pepper to saucepan. Cover; reduce heat to low. Simmer 15 minutes. Add chicken pieces, shrimp and okra. Simmer 10 minutes longer. Remove 1/2 cup liquid from saucepan; stir filé powder into liquid. Return filé mixture to saucepan; stir to blend. **For 1000- or 1200-Calorie Menus (small serving),** ladle 2/3 cup gumbo into each soup bowl or mug. **For 1500-Calorie Menu (large serving),** ladle 1-1/3 cups gumbo into each soup bowl or mug. **For all menus,** sprinkle reserved cooked bacon equally over servings. Serve hot. Makes 8 small servings or 4 large servings.

---

1 small serving (2/3 cup) = 2 meat, 1 vegetable, 105 calories
1 large serving (1-1/3 cups) = 4 meat, 2 vegetable, 210 calories

---

Tip *Most baby shrimp are sold precooked and shelled.*

Day 5

1000-Calorie	1200-Calorie	1500-Calorie
Breakfast		
1 small serving French Toast with Cinnamon-Apple Syrup* **or** 1 French-toast slice with 1 tablespoon reduced-calorie pancake syrup (60 calories/2 tablespoons) 1/2 oz. thinly sliced ham, cut in strips, grilled 1 serving Coffee Mocha*	1 large serving French Toast with Cinnamon-Apple Syrup* **or** 2 French-toast slices with 1-1/2 tablespoons reduced-calorie pancake syrup (60 calories/2 tablespoons) 1 serving Coffee Mocha*	1 large serving French Toast with Cinnamon-Apple Syrup* **or** 2 French-toast slices with 1-1/2 tablespoons reduced-calorie pancake syrup (60 calories/2 tablespoons) 1 serving Coffee Mocha*
Lunch		
1 small serving Fiesta Bean Soup* 2 saltine-cracker squares 1 small orange **or** tangerine (4 per lb.) 1 cup (8 oz.) skim milk	1 small serving Fiesta Bean Soup* 1 (6-inch) flour or corn tortilla, warmed, spread with 1 teaspoon diet margarine 1 small orange **or** tangerine (4 per lb.) 1 cup (8 oz.) skim milk	1 large serving Fiesta Bean Soup* 1 (6-inch) flour or corn tortilla, warmed, spread with 2 teaspoons diet margarine 1 small orange **or** tangerine (4 per lb.) 1 cup (8 oz.) skim milk
Dinner		
1 small serving Baked Fish Hawaiian* 1/2 cup Curried Rice* 1/2 cup steamed Brussels sprouts **or** other green vegetable, tossed with 1 teaspoon diet margarine and 1/4 teaspoon grated lemon peel	1 small serving Baked Fish Hawaiian* 1/2 cup Curried Rice* 3/4 cup steamed Brussels sprouts **or** other green vegetable, tossed with 1 teaspoon diet margarine and 1/4 teaspoon grated lemon peel	1 large serving Baked Fish Hawaiian* 1 cup Curried Rice* 1 cup steamed Brussels sprouts **or** other green vegetable, tossed with 1 teaspoon diet margarine and 1/2 teaspoon grated lemon peel
* Recipe follows.		

Coffee Mocha   *Photo on page 134.*

This smooth coffee is good with meals, but is also a relaxing bedtime snack.

1-1/2 teaspoons unsweetened cocoa powder
1 tablespoon sugar
1 tablespoon instant decaffeinated- or regular-coffee granules

1 pint skim milk (2 cups)
1/4 teaspoon vanilla extract

In a small saucepan, combine cocoa powder, sugar and coffee granules. Stir in milk. Stir over medium heat until tiny bubbles form around edge of pan and cocoa dissolves. Remove from heat; stir in vanilla. Pour equally into 2 cups or mugs. Makes 2 servings.

---

1 serving = 1 milk, 1/2 fruit, 1/2 fat, 130 calories

French Toast with Cinnamon-Apple Syrup

Golden French toast is accented with the sweet, spicy flavors of cinnamon and apple.

2 eggs
1/4 cup evaporated skim milk
1/4 teaspoon salt

Cinnamon-Apple Syrup:
2/3 cup unsweetened apple juice
1/3 cup water
1-1/2 teaspoons cornstarch

Dash of nutmeg, if desired
4 (3-inch-diameter, 1/2-inch-thick) French-
  or Italian-bread slices

1/4 teaspoon ground cinnamon
1 tablespoon plus 1-1/2 teaspoons
  brown sugar

In a medium bowl, beat eggs with a fork until yolk and white are just combined. Stir in evaporated milk, salt and nutmeg, if desired. Dip bread slices in egg mixture, coating both sides. Arrange coated bread in a single layer in an ungreased baking pan or casserole dish. Pour any remaining egg mixture over bread. Cover with plastic wrap or a lid. Refrigerate until ready to cook, up to 12 hours. Prepare Cinnamon-Apple Syrup. In a medium nonstick skillet or a skillet coated with nonstick vegetable spray, cook soaked bread slices over medium heat until golden brown. Turn once. Serve hot. **For 1000-Calorie Menu (small serving),** place 1 toast slice on each plate. Top each serving with 2 tablespoons syrup. **For 1200- or 1500-Calorie Menus (large serving),** place 2 toast slices on each plate. Top each serving with 1/4 cup syrup. Makes 4 small servings or 2 large servings.
To make Cinnamon-Apple Syrup, in a small saucepan, combine apple juice, water and cornstarch. Stir to dissolve cornstarch. Add cinnamon and brown sugar. Stirring constantly, bring to a boil over medium-high heat. Keep hot until ready to serve. To make ahead, cool syrup. Pour into a container with a tight-fitting lid. Cover tightly; refrigerate up to 3 days. Makes about 1 cup.

---

1 small serving (1 toast slice, 2 tablespoons syrup) = 1 bread, 1/2 meat, 1/2 fruit, 1/2 fat, 173 calories
1 large serving (2 toast slices, 1/4 cup syrup) = 2 bread, 1 meat, 1 fruit, 1 fat, 546 calories
1 slice toast without syrup = 1 bread, 1/2 meat, 1/2 fat, 152 calories
2 tablespoons syrup = 1/2 fruit, 21 calories

Fiesta Bean Soup

Soup is a natural diet food, even this hearty one.

3 cups water
3 beef-flavored bouillon cubes
8 oz. extra-lean ground beef
   (10% to 15% fat)
1 garlic clove, minced
1/2 cup chopped green bell pepper

1-1/2 cups tomato juice
1 cup rinsed, drained,
   canned red kidney beans
1 cup frozen whole-kernel corn
1/2 teaspoon dried leaf basil

In a 3-quart saucepan, combine water and bouillon cubes. Bring to a boil over high heat; reduce heat until water barely simmers. Crush bouillon cubes with back of a spoon. Stir until bouillon cubes are completely dissolved; set aside. Meanwhile, in a heavy nonstick skillet or a skillet coated with nonstick vegetable spray, brown beef. Stir with a fork to break up beef. Push browned beef to side of skillet. Tilt skillet; remove all but about 1 teaspoon drippings. Add garlic and bell pepper; sauté 30 seconds. Spoon browned beef and sautéed vegetables into bouillon mixture. Add tomato juice, beans, corn and basil. Bring to a boil over medium heat; reduce heat until mixture barely simmers. Cover; simmer 15 minutes. **For 1000- or 1200-Calorie Menus (small serving),** spoon 1-1/4 cups soup into each soup bowl or mug. **For 1500-Calorie Menu (large serving),** spoon 1-1/2 cups soup into each soup bowl or mug. Serve hot. To serve later, cool soup; pour into a container with a tight-fitting lid. Cover tightly; refrigerate up to 4 days. Reheat desired amount over medium-low heat until heated through, about 10 minutes. Makes 6 small servings or 5 large servings.

---

1 small serving (1 cup) = 1 meat, 1 bread, 1 vegetable, 1/2 fat, 160 calories
1 large serving (1-1/2 cups) = 2 meat, 1-1/2 bread, 1-1/2 vegetable, 1/2 fat, 240 calories

---

Curried Rice   *Photo on page 37.*

Refrigerate leftover rice to use in Curried Rice & Chicken Salad, Day 7, page 43.

2 cups water
2 chicken-flavored bouillon cubes
1/4 teaspoon curry powder

1 cup uncooked long-grain white rice
2 tablespoons golden raisins, chopped
3 tablespoons sliced almonds

In a medium saucepan, combine water, bouillon cubes and curry powder. Bring to a boil over high heat; reduce heat until water barely simmers. Crush bouillon cubes with back of a spoon. Stir until bouillon cubes are completely dissolved. Gradually add rice, maintaining boil. Add raisins; stir once. Reduce heat to lowest setting. Cover; simmer 25 minutes without lifting lid. Stir rice. If still moist, simmer 5 minutes longer. **For 1000- or 1200-Calorie Menus (small serving),** spoon 1/2 cup rice mixture onto each plate. **For 1500-Calorie Menu (large serving),** spoon 1 cup rice mixture onto each plate. **For all menus,** sprinkle almonds equally over servings. Makes 6 small servings or 3 large servings.

---

1 small serving (1/2 cup) = 1-1/2 bread, 1/2 fat, 143 calories
1 large serving (1 cup) = 3 bread, 1 fat, 286 calories

Baked Fish Hawaiian

Fish is so low in fat, you can afford to add a small amount of margarine for flavor.

1-1/4 lbs. fresh or frozen sole,
   snapper or pike fillets (1/2-inch thick)
1 tablespoon lemon juice
Salt
White pepper
1 tablespoon regular margarine
2 green onions, sliced
1/3 cup dry white wine

1/3 cup water
1 cup diced fresh pineapple or
   1 cup pineapple chunks canned in
   unsweetened pineapple juice, drained
1 cup drained mandarin-orange sections
   canned in water
2 tablespoons unsweetened shredded coconut

Preheat oven to 375F (190C). Partially thaw frozen fish fillets. Sprinkle fillets lightly with lemon juice, salt and white pepper. In a small saucepan, melt margarine. Add green onions, wine and water. Bring to a boil; remove from heat. Stir in pineapple and mandarin-orange sections. Arrange fresh or partially thawed fish fillets in a single layer in a large baking pan or casserole. Spoon fruit mixture over fillets. Sprinkle top with coconut. Cover with foil or a lid. Bake in preheated oven until fish is opaque and just begins to flake, about 15 minutes. Lift fish fillets and fruit onto a platter; keep warm. Pour liquid from baking pan or casserole into a small saucepan. Boil until only 1/3 cup liquid remains; pour over fish. **For 1000- or 1200-Calorie Menus (small serving),** place 2 ounces fish and 1/3 cup fruit on each plate. **For 1500-Calorie Menu (large serving),** place 4 ounces fish and 1/3 cup fruit on each plate. Spoon any leftover fruit into a container with a tight-fitting lid. Place leftover fish in another container. Cover tightly; refrigerate up to 2 days. To serve, heat leftover fish or cook more fish as directed above. Reheat fruit mixture in a skillet or a microwave. Spoon 1/3 cup fruit onto a plate. Add fish for a small or large serving as directed above. Makes 6 small servings or 3 large servings.

---

1 small serving (2 oz. fish, 1/3 cup fruit) = 2 meat, 1 fruit, 137 calories
1 large serving (4 oz. fish, 1/3 cup fruit) = 4 meat, 1 fruit, 234 calories

---

1000-Calorie Dinner, from top to bottom: Curried Rice, page 35; steamed Brussels sprouts; Baked Fish Hawaiian.

Day 6

1000-Calorie	1200-Calorie	1500-Calorie
	## Breakfast	
1 serving Fruit & Nut Granola* **or** 3/4 cup unsweetened ready-to-eat cereal 1/2 cup (4 oz.) skim milk 1/4 cup low-fat cottage cheese, topped with 1/2 cup sliced bananas and blueberries	1 serving Fruit & Nut Granola* **or** 3/4 cup unsweetened ready-to-eat cereal 1/2 cup (4 oz.) skim milk 1/4 cup low-fat cottage cheese, topped with 1/2 cup sliced bananas and blueberries 1 bread slice, toasted 1 teaspoon diet margarine	1 serving Fruit & Nut Granola* **or** 3/4 cup unsweetened ready-to-eat cereal 1/2 cup (4 oz.) skim milk 1/4 cup low-fat cottage cheese, topped with 1/2 cup sliced bananas and blueberries 1 bread slice, toasted 1 teaspoon diet margarine
	## Lunch	
1 small serving French-Dip Sandwich* 1/2 cup (4 oz.) tomato juice **or** other vegetable juice, with celery-stick stirrer 1/2 fresh peach **or** 1/2 peach canned in juice, filled with 1/4 cup fresh or frozen unsweetened raspberries 1 cup (8 oz.) skim milk	1 small serving French-Dip Sandwich* 5 potato chips 1/2 cup (4 oz.) tomato juice **or** other vegetable juice, with celery-stick stirrer 1/2 fresh peach **or** 1/2 peach canned in juice, filled with 1/4 cup fresh or frozen unsweetened raspberries 1 cup (8 oz.) skim milk	1 large serving French-Dip Sandwich* 10 potato chips 1/2 cup (4 oz.) tomato juice **or** other vegetable juice, with celery-stick stirrer 1/2 fresh peach **or** 1/2 peach canned in juice, filled with 1/4 cup fresh or frozen, unsweetened raspberries 1 cup (8 oz.) skim milk
	## Dinner	
1 small serving Teriyaki Kabobs* 1/3 cup cooked rice tossed with 1 teaspoon diet margarine and 1 teaspoon chopped parsley 1-1/2 cups torn Bibb lettuce **or** other salad greens 2 tablespoons Cool Cucumber Dressing* **or** 1 tablespoon reduced-calorie salad dressing (25 calories/tablespoon) 1/2 cup mandarin-orange sections and pineapple chunks with 1 serving Lemon Yogurt, page 118	1 small serving Teriyaki Kabobs* 1/3 cup cooked rice tossed with 1 teaspoon diet margarine and 1 teaspoon chopped parsley 1/2 cup steamed green beans 1-1/2 cups torn Bibb lettuce **or** other salad greens 2 tablespoons Cool Cucumber Dressing* **or** 1 tablespoon reduced-calorie salad dressing (25calories/tablespoon) 1/2 cup mandarin-orange sections and pineapple chunks with 1 serving Lemon Yogurt, page 118	1 large serving Teriyaki Kabobs* 2/3 cup cooked rice tossed with 1 teaspoon diet margarine and 1 teaspoon chopped parsley 1-1/2 cups torn Bibb lettuce **or** other salad greens 2 tablespoons Cool Cucumber Dressing* **or** 1 tablespoon reduced-calorie salad dressing (25 calories/tablespoon) 1/2 cup mandarin-orange sections and pineapple chunks with 1 serving Lemon Yogurt, page 118

* Recipe follows.

Teriyaki Kabobs

Perfect for entertaining because no one will guess this is diet food.

1 (6-oz.) beef loin tenderloin steak
2 (3-oz.) boned, skinned chicken-breast
   halves
6 oz. uncooked medium shrimp (about 12),
   shelled, deveined

1/2 medium onion (4 per lb.)
1 medium, green bell pepper (2-1/2 per lb.)
6 cherry tomatoes

Soy Marinade:
3 tablespoons soy sauce
1/2 cup water
1 tablespoon honey

1 green onion, chopped
1 teaspoon lime juice
1 tablespoon dry sherry or white wine

Prepare Soy Marinade; set aside. Cut beef in 3/4-inch cubes. Cut chicken in 3/4-inch cubes. Place beef cubes, chicken cubes and shrimp in a shallow casserole. Pour marinade over top; toss gently to coat. Cover tightly; refrigerate 1 to 8 hours. Preheat a broiler or grill. Cut onion and bell pepper into 1-inch-square pieces. Drain marinade from beef, chicken and shrimp, reserving marinade. Using 6 skewers, alternately skewer beef and chicken cubes, shrimp and vegetable squares. Broil or grill 4 inches from heat to desired doneness, about 10 minutes, turning frequently. Baste with marinade once during cooking. Before serving, add a cherry tomato to end of each skewer. **For 1000- or 1200-Calorie Menus (small serving),** place 1 kabob on each plate. **For 1500-Calorie Menu (large serving),** place 2 kabobs on each plate. Makes 6 small servings or 3 large servings.
To make Soy Marinade, in a small bowl, combine all ingredients. Makes about 3/4 cup.

---

1 small serving (1 kabob) = 2 meat, 1 vegetable, 140 calories
1 large serving (2 kabobs) = 4 meat, 2 vegetable, 280 calories

---

Cool Cucumber Dressing

Use as a dressing for coleslaw or on a wedge of iceberg lettuce.

1/2 medium cucumber (2 per lb.), peeled
1/2 teaspoon salt
1/2 cup plain low-fat yogurt
1/4 cup bottled reduced-calorie mayonnaise

1/2 teaspoon lemon juice
1 tablespoon chopped fresh parsley
1/4 teaspoon dried dill weed
1 green onion, chopped

Shred cucumber. Spread on a clean towel. Sprinkle with salt. Let stand 30 minutes. Bring ends of towel together; squeeze moisture from cucumber. In a small bowl, combine yogurt, mayonnaise and lemon juice. Stir in drained cucumber shreds, parsley, dill weed and green onion. Cover tightly; refrigerate until served, up to 2 days. Stir before serving. Makes about 1 cup.

---

2 tablespoons = 1/2 fat, 30 calories

Fruit & Nut Granola   *Photo on page 134.*

Serve over low-fat yogurt to add crunch and fruity sweetness.

3 tablespoons vegetable oil
1/4 cup lightly packed brown sugar
1/4 cup water
1/2 teaspoon vanilla extract
1/4 teaspoon salt
3 cups quick-cooking or regular rolled oats

1/4 cup wheat germ
4 cups ready-to-eat oat cereal
1/2 cup sliced almonds
1/2 cup diced dried raisins, dates,
    apricots, prunes or mixed fruit

Preheat oven to 275F (135C). In a small saucepan, combine oil, brown sugar, water, vanilla and salt. Stir over medium heat until sugar dissolves; set aside. In a large bowl, combine rolled oats, wheat germ, ready-to-eat cereal and almonds. Pour brown sugar mixture over top; toss to coat cereal. Spread cereal mixture in a nonstick 15'' x 10'' jelly-roll pan or a jelly-roll pan coated with nonstick vegetable spray. Bake in preheated oven 45 minutes, stirring every 15 minutes. Stir in dried fruit. Cool to room temperature. Store in a container with a tight-fitting lid. Store at room temperature up to 3 weeks. Makes about 24 (1/3-cup) servings.

---

1 serving (1/3 cup) = 1 bread, 1 fat, 110 calories

French-Dip Sandwich

Ask for lean roast beef at the deli and trim off any fat.

1/3 cup canned condensed beef broth
2 tablespoons red wine
1/2 cup water
1 teaspoon Worcestershire sauce
1 small garlic clove, minced

1/4 teaspoon dry mustard
8 oz. cooked boneless lean roast beef,
    thinly sliced
2 or 4 (5-inch) French rolls, split

In a small saucepan, combine broth, wine, water, Worcestershire sauce, garlic and mustard. Bring to a boil. Add roast beef. Reduce heat until mixture barely simmers. Cover; simmer until beef is heated through, about 5 minutes. Preheat broiler. For small servings, use 2 French rolls; for large servings, use 4 French rolls. Arrange rolls, cut-side up, on an ungreased baking sheet. Toast under broiler until lightly browned. **For 1000- or 1200-Calorie Menus (small serving),** place 1 toasted half roll on each plate. Lift beef from broth, letting excess broth drip into saucepan. Arrange 1/4 of beef on each toasted half roll. Serve sandwich open-faced. **For 1500-Calorie Menu (large serving),** place 1 toasted half roll on each plate. Arrange 1/4 of beef on each toasted half roll. Top each with another toasted half roll. **For all menus,** pour 1/4 cup broth into each of 4 small bowls for dipping. Serve sandwiches and dipping broth immediately. Makes 4 small servings or 4 large servings.

---

1 small serving (1 open-faced sandwich on 1/2 roll) = 1 bread, 2 meat, 1/2 fat, 199 calories
1 large serving (1 sandwich on 1 whole roll) = 2 bread, 2 meat, 1 fat, 265 calories

---

1000-Calorie Breakfast, from top left: skim milk; coffee; Fruit & Nut Granola; low-fat cottage cheese with bananas and blueberries.

Day 7

1000-Calorie	1200-Calorie	1500-Calorie
Breakfast		
1 serving Tropical Parfait* 1 whole-wheat-bread slice, toasted 1 teaspoon diet margarine	1 serving Tropical Parfait* 2 whole-wheat-bread slices, toasted 2 teaspoons diet margarine	1 serving Tropical Parfait* 2 whole-wheat-bread slices, toasted 2 teaspoons diet margarine
Lunch		

1 serving Curried-Rice & Chicken Salad*
Vegetable kabob on a skewer:
  1 cherry tomato
  3 pieces mixed pickled vegetables
  1 fresh mushroom
1 serving Cranberry Blizzard*
	1 serving Curried-Rice & Chicken Salad*
	2 puffed-rice cakes **or** 1/2 (6-inch) pita-bread round, cut in wedges
	Vegetable kabob on a skewer:
	  1 cherry tomato,
	  3 pieces mixed pickled vegetables
	  1 fresh mushroom
	1 serving Cranberry Blizzard*
		1 serving Curried-Rice & Chicken Salad*
		1 (6-inch) pita-bread round, cut in wedges, spread with 1 tablespoon Chutney Dressing* from Curried-Rice & Chicken Salad **or** 1 tablespoon diet margarine
		Vegetable kabob on a skewer:
		  1 cherry tomato
		  3 pieces mixed pickled vegetables
		  1 fresh mushroom
		1 serving Cranberry Blizzard*

Dinner		
1 serving Seafood Chowder* 1/2 carrot, shredded, and 1/2 cup cauliflowerets on 1 large lettuce leaf 1 tablespoon Lemon-Paprika Dressing* **or** reduced-calorie salad dressing (25 calories/tablespoon) 1 serving Honey-Broiled Pineapple, page 117	1 serving Seafood Chowder* 1 carrot, shredded, and 3/4 cup cauliflowerets on 1 large lettuce leaf 1 tablespoon Lemon-Paprika Dressing* **or** reduced-calorie salad dressing (25 calories/tablespoon) 1 serving Honey-Broiled Pineapple, page 117	1 serving Seafood Chowder* 1 (3-oz.) piece halibut or cod, brushed with teriyaki sauce, grilled 20 oyster crackers 1 carrot, shredded, and 1 cup cauliflowerets on 1 large lettuce leaf 1 tablespoon Lemon-Paprika Dressing* **or** reduced-calorie salad dressing (25 calories/tablespoon) 1 serving Honey-Broiled Pineapple, page 117

* Recipe follows.

Cranberry Blizzard *Photo on page 27.*

A rosy drink that looks like an old-fashioned soda.

1/3 cup unsweetened cranberry juice
3 ice cubes

1 cup skim milk
1/2 cup club soda

In a blender, combine cranberry juice and ice cubes. Process until frothy and ice is finely chopped. Add milk; process until foamy. Pour into 2 drinking glasses. Pour 1/4 cup club soda into each glass; stir. Serve immediately. Makes 2 servings.

1 serving = 1/2 fruit, 1/2 milk, 72 calories

Tropical Parfait

Flavor abounds in this special tropical breakfast dish.

1/4 cup ricotta cheese
8 oz. plain low-fat yogurt (1 cup)
1/2 teaspoon vanilla extract
1 teaspoon rum extract or vanilla extract
1 egg white
1 tablespoon orange juice
1/2 cup diced, peeled, fresh papaya,
   mango or peach

1/4 cup drained crushed pineapple
   canned in unsweetened pineapple juice
1 maraschino cherry, cut in half
1 teaspoon shredded fresh coconut or
   packaged unsweetened shredded coconut

In a medium bowl, combine cheese, yogurt, vanilla and rum extract or vanilla. In a small bowl, combine egg white and orange juice; beat until soft peaks form. Fold egg-white mixture into cheese mixture. Spoon about 1/3 cup cheese mixture into each of 2 parfait glasses or other stemmed glasses. Sprinkle 2 tablespoons papaya, mango or peach and 1 tablespoon pineapple over each serving. Repeat layering, ending with cheese mixture. Top each with 1/2 cherry and 1/2 teaspoon coconut. Cover tightly; refrigerate until served, up to 24 hours. Makes 2 servings.

---

1 serving = 1 meat, 1/2 milk , 1 fruit, 152 calories

Curried-Rice & Chicken Salad

Chutney Dressing can be used with other rice or pasta salads.

1-1/2 cups Curried Rice, page 35
8 oz. cooked chicken, diced (2 cups)

4 large Bibb-lettuce or other lettuce leaves
1/4 cup sliced almonds

Chutney Dressing:
1/4 cup plain low-fat yogurt
2 tablespoons reduced-calorie mayonnaise
1/4 cup buttermilk

1/8 teaspoon curry powder
2 tablespoons chopped mango chutney or
   other fruit chutney

Prepare Curried Rice as directed; refrigerate at least 2 hours. Prepare Chutney Dressing; refrigerate until served. In a medium bowl, combine chilled Curried Rice and chicken. Pour 1/3 cup dressing over salad; toss to distribute. Arrange lettuce leaves on each of 4 salad plates. Spoon 1/4 of salad on each lettuce-lined plate. Sprinkle 1/4 of almonds over each serving. Makes 4 servings.
To make Chutney Dressing, in a small bowl, combine all ingredients. Cover tightly; refrigerate until served. Stir before serving. Pour unused dressing into a container with a tight-fitting lid. Cover tightly; refrigerate up to 3 days. Makes about 3/4 cup.

Variations
Substitute 8 ounces cooked tiny shrimp or 2 cups (8 ounces) diced cooked ham for chicken. Exchanges and calories will remain the same.

---

1 serving (salad with dressing) = 2 meat, 1 bread, 3/4 fruit, 208 calories
1 tablespoon plus 1-1/2 teaspoons dressing = 1/2 fat, 25 calories
1 tablespoon dressing = 1/3 fat, 17 calories

Seafood Chowder

Rich with fish, shrimp and vegetables.

2 small (2-inch-diameter) boiling potatoes
  (4 to 5 per lb.)
6 oz. fresh or frozen halibut,
  snapper, sole or cod
1 teaspoon vegetable oil
1/2 cup chopped onion
1 celery stalk, sliced
6 oz. uncooked small shrimp
  (about 18), shelled, deveined

1/2 cup water
2 tablespoons plus 1-1/2 teaspoons
  all-purpose flour
1 qt. skim milk (4 cups)
1/3 cup instant mashed-potato flakes
1/2 teaspoon salt
1/8 teaspoon pepper
1/4 teaspoon paprika

In a small saucepan, simmer whole, unpeeled potatoes in lightly salted boiling water until tender, about 30 minutes. Drain potatoes; set aside until cool enough to handle. Partially thaw frozen fish fillets. Cut fresh or partially thawed fish into bite-sized pieces; set aside. In a medium nonstick skillet or a skillet coated with a nonstick vegetable spray, heat oil. Add onion and celery; sauté until onion is soft. Stir in fish pieces and shrimp. Add 1/2 cup water; bring to a simmer. Cover. Simmer until fish just begins to flake when pierced with a fork, about 5 minutes; set aside. Peel and dice cooled potatoes; set aside. Combine flour and 1/2 cup milk in a small container with a tight-fitting lid. Cover tightly; shake until smooth. In a large saucepan, heat remaining milk until small bubbles form around edge of pan. Gradually add flour mixture, stirring constantly with a whisk. Continue stirring until mixture comes to a boil and thickens slightly. Sprinkle instant potatoes over soup; stir in with a whisk. Add diced potatoes and shrimp mixture. Season with salt, pepper and paprika. Cook over low heat until heated through or until potato cubes are hot, stirring frequently. *Do not let chowder boil.* To serve, ladle 1-1/2 cups chowder into each of 4 soup bowls. Serve hot. Makes 4 servings.

---

1 serving (1-1/2 cups) = 2 meat, 1 bread, 1 milk, 1 fat, 310 calories

---

Lemon-Paprika Dressing

Tart, spicy and especially good on vegetable salads.

1 teaspoon grated lemon peel
2 tablespoons lemon juice
1 tablespoon white-wine vinegar
3 tablespoons water
2 tablespoons vegetable oil

1 teaspoon Dijon-style mustard
2 teaspoons dry pectin
1/4 teaspoon paprika
1/8 teaspoon salt
2 or 3 drops hot-pepper sauce

In a small container with a tight-fitting lid or in a blender, combine lemon peel, lemon juice, vinegar, water, oil, mustard, pectin, paprika and salt. Cover tightly; shake vigorously or process 15 seconds. Season with hot-pepper sauce. If processed in blender, pour into a container with a tight-fitting lid. Cover tightly; refrigerate until served, up to 5 days. Shake before serving. Makes about 1/2 cup.

---

1 tablespoon = 1/2 fat, 30 calories

1200-Calorie Dinner, from top left: carrot and cauliflower salad with Lemon-Paprika Dressing; Honey-Broiled Pineapple, page 117; Seafood Chowder.

Day 8

1000-Calorie	1200-Calorie	1500-Calorie
	Breakfast	
1 serving Choco-Banana Smoothie* 1 small serving Cinnamon Toast* **or** 1 whole-wheat-bread slice, toasted, spread with 1 teaspoon diet margarine	1 serving Choco-Banana Smoothie* 1 small serving Cinnamon Toast* **or** 1 whole-wheat-bread slice, toasted, spread with 1 teaspoon diet margarine	1 serving Choco-Banana Smoothie* 1 large serving Cinnamon Toast* **or** 2 whole-wheat-bread slices, toasted, spread with 2 teaspoons diet margarine
	Lunch	
1 small serving Chili-Bean Tostada* 1/4 cup Chunky Salsa, page 68 1/2 cup orange sections **or** grapefruit sections sprinkled with 1 tablespoon pomegranate seeds, if desired 1 serving Citrus Spritzer*	1 large serving Chili-Bean Tostada* 1/4 cup Chunky Salsa, page 68 1/2 cup orange sections **or** grapefruit sections sprinkled with 1 tablespoon pomegranate seeds, if desired 1 serving Citrus Spritzer*	1 large serving Chili-Bean Tostada* 1/4 cup Chunky Salsa, page 68 1 cup canned beef noodle soup prepared with water 1/2 cup orange sections **or** grapefruit sections sprinkled with 1 tablespoon pomegranate seeds, if desired 1 serving Citrus Spritzer*
	Dinner	

1 small serving Ginger-Beef Sauté*
1/3 cup steamed white or brown rice
Salad:
  1 cup torn red-leaf lettuce
  1 teaspoon chopped green onion
  1/4 small fresh pear, sliced
1 tablespoon Lemon-Ginger Dressing* **or** reduced-calorie salad dressing (25 calories/tablespoon)
1 serving Snow Pudding, page 124, **or** 1 teaspoon low-sugar strawberry spread stirred into 1/2 cup plain low-fat yogurt
	1 small serving Ginger-Beef Sauté*
	1/3 cup steamed white or brown rice
	6 edible pea pods and 1/2 carrot, cut in sticks, steamed in 1 tablespoon dry sherry
	Salad:
	  1 cup torn red-leaf lettuce
	  1 teaspoon chopped green onion
	  1/4 small fresh pear, sliced
	1 tablespoon Lemon-Ginger Dressing* **or** reduced-calorie salad dressing (25 calories/tablespoon)
	1 serving Snow Pudding, page 124, **or** 1 teaspoon low-sugar strawberry spread stirred into 1/2 cup plain low-fat yogurt
		1 large serving Ginger-Beef Sauté
		2/3 cup steamed white or brown rice
		Salad:
		  1 cup torn red-leaf lettuce
		  1 tablespoon chopped green onion
		  1/4 small pear, sliced
		1 tablespoon Lemon-Ginger Dressing* **or** reduced-calorie salad dressing (25 calories/tablespoon)
		1 serving Snow Pudding, page 124, **or** 1 teaspoon low-sugar strawberry spread stirred into 1/2 cup plain low-fat yogurt

* Recipe follows.

Choco-Banana Smoothie

Prepare just before serving so the bananas won't darken.

1 pint skim milk (2 cups)
1 teaspoon unsweetened cocoa powder

1 egg white
1 small banana (4 per lb.), sliced

In a blender, combine all ingredients. Process until foamy and almost smooth. Pour into 2 drinking glasses. Serve immediately. Makes 2 servings.

---

1 serving = 1 milk, 1/2 meat, 1/2 fruit, 150 calories

Cinnamon Toast

Crispy toast with a hint of spicy sweetness.

1 (1-lb.) loaf unsliced white bread
  or whole-wheat bread
2 tablespoons diet margarine, melted

1 tablespoon sugar
1/2 teaspoon ground cinnamon

Preheat oven to 400F (205C). Cut crust from one end of bread loaf. Cut 2 (1-inch-thick) slices. Reserve end slice and remaining loaf for another purpose. Remove crusts from bread slices; use crusts for another purpose. Cut each trimmed bread slice lengthwise into 4 strips. Lightly brush margarine on all sides of bread strips. In a small bowl, combine sugar and cinnamon. Holding bread strips over bowl, spoon sugar mixture over all sides. Arrange coated bread strips on an ungreased baking sheet. Bake in preheated oven 7 minutes, turning strips over after 3 minutes. **For 1000- or 1200-Calorie Menus (small serving),** place 2 toast strips on each plate. **For 1500-Calorie Menu (large serving),** place 4 toast strips on each plate. Serve warm. Makes 8 strips, 4 small servings or 2 large servings.

---

1 small serving (2 strips) = 1 bread, 3/4 fat, 1/4 fruit, 118 calories
1 large serving (4 strips) = 2 bread, 1-1/2 fat, 1/2 fruit, 236 calories

---

Citrus Spritzer   *Photo on page 49.*

Relax and enjoy this no-calorie sipper before dinner or as a mid-afternoon refresher.

1 teaspoon partially thawed frozen
  lemonade concentrate
1 cup club soda, chilled

Ice cubes
1 lemon slice
1 lime slice

Spoon lemonade concentrate into a drinking glass. Pour about 1/4 cup club soda into glass. Stir to dissolve lemonade concentrate. Stir in remaining club soda. Add ice cubes, lemon slice and lime slice. Serve cold. Makes 1 serving.

---

1 serving = 0 exchanges, 0 calories

Chili-Bean Tostada

Beans are good diet food because they provide good-quality protein and are so filling.

2 or 6 (6-inch) corn tortillas
1 tablespoon diet margarine, melted
1 cup cooked or canned pinto beans with
   2 tablespoons cooking liquid or
   liquid from can
Dash of salt
Dash of pepper
6 oz. extra-lean ground beef
   (10% to 15% fat)
1 tablespoon chopped onion

1 small garlic clove, minced
1 teaspoon all-purpose flour
1 tablespoon chili powder
1/4 teaspoon ground cumin
1/4 cup canned or homemade beef broth
3 cups shredded iceberg lettuce
1 medium tomato (3 per lb.), diced
1/2 cup shredded Cheddar cheese (2 oz.)
4 ripe olives
1 cup Chunky Salsa, page 68

Preheat oven to 400F (205C). For small servings, use 2 tortillas; for large servings, use 6 tortillas. Brush 1 side of each tortilla with margarine. Cut each tortilla into 4 wedges. Arrange wedges on an ungreased baking sheet, buttered-sides up. Bake in preheated oven until crisp, about 5 minutes. Cool on a wire rack. In a blender or food processor fitted with a metal blade, puree beans and cooking liquid. In a small saucepan, heat bean puree over low heat. Season with salt and pepper. In a heavy medium nonstick skillet or a skillet coated with a nonstick vegetable spray, brown beef. Stir with a fork to break up beef. Push browned beef to side of skillet. Tilt skillet; remove all but 1 tablespoon drippings. Add onion and garlic; sauté until onion is soft, about 3 minutes. In a small bowl, combine flour, chili powder and cumin. Sprinkle flour mixture over browned meat; stir in. Stirring constantly, cook about 1 minute. Add broth; bring to a boil, stirring constantly. Continue to stir until mixture thickens slightly. **For 1000-Calorie Menu (small serving),** arrange 2 tortilla wedges on each plate, with points in center of plate. **For 1200- and 1500-Calorie Menus (large serving),** arrange 6 tortillas wedges on each plate, with points in center of plate. **For all menus,** spread 1/4 cup bean mixture over tortillas on each plate . Spoon 2 generous tablespoons meat mixture over beans on each plate. Divide lettuce equally among plates. Sprinkle tomato and cheese equally over each serving. Slice 1 olive over each serving. Serve Chunky Salsa separately or spoon 1/4 cup salsa over each serving. Makes 4 small servings or 4 large servings.

---

1 small serving (2 tortilla wedges) = 2 meat, 1 bread, 1 vegetable, 1 fat, 266 calories
1 large serving (6 tortilla wedges) = 2 meat, 2 bread, 1 vegetable, 1 fat, 284 calories
Chunky Salsa (1/4 cup) = 1/2 vegetable, 14 calories

1200-Calorie Lunch, from top left: orange sections sprinkled with pomegranate seeds; Citrus Spritzer, page 47; Chili-Bean Tostada.

Ginger-Beef Sauté

Flank steak and round steak are lean cuts of beef made tender by thin slicing.

1 (12-oz.) beef flank steak or
  boneless beef round steak, fat removed
1 garlic clove, minced
1 tablespoon soy sauce
1 teaspoon shredded fresh gingerroot
1 teaspoon rice vinegar
1 teaspoon cornstarch
1/3 cup canned or homemade beef broth

1 teaspoon dry sherry or white wine
4 green onions
1 cup broccoli flowerets
4 teaspoons vegetable oil
1-1/2 oz. fresh mushrooms, sliced (1/2 cup)
1/2 cup sliced bok choy or celery
2 tablespoons sliced water chestnuts
2 tablespoons white wine or water

Place steak in freezer until firm but not frozen solid, about 30 minutes. Slice partially frozen steak across the grain in strips as thin as possible. In a medium bowl, combine garlic, soy sauce, gingerroot, vinegar, cornstarch, broth and 1 teaspoon sherry or wine; stir until cornstarch dissolves. Add beef strips; stir to coat beef completely. Refrigerate; let marinate at least 30 minutes or up to 2 hours. Cut green onions into 1-1/2-inch pieces. Cut each piece lengthwise into thin strips. Cut broccoli into bite-sized pieces. In a well-seasoned wok, a medium nonstick skillet or a skillet coated with nonstick vegetable spray, heat 2 teaspoons oil. Drain beef strips, reserving marinade. Brown marinated beef in hot oil until no longer pink. Remove from wok or skillet; keep warm. Heat remaining 2 teaspoons oil in wok or skillet. Add broccoli pieces, onion strips, mushrooms and bok choy or celery. Stir-fry until vegetables are crisp-tender. Add cooked beef strips and water chestnuts; stir gently to distribute. Stir 2 tablespoons wine or water into reserved marinade. Add to beef mixture; stir until sauce thickens. **For 1000- or 1200-Calorie Menus (small serving),** spoon 3/4 cup beef-and-vegetable mixture onto each plate. **For 1500-Calorie Menu (large serving),** spoon 1-1/2 cups beef-and-vegetable mixture onto each plate. Serve hot. Makes 4 small servings or 2 large servings.

---

1 small serving (3/4 cup) = 2 meat, 1 vegetable, 1 fat, 236 calories
1 large serving (1-1/2 cups) = 4 meat, 2 vegetable, 2 fat, 472 calories

---

Lemon-Ginger Dressing

Look for crystallized ginger with the spices and seasonings in your local supermarket.

3 tablespoons lemon juice
3 tablespoons water
2 tablespoons vegetable oil
2 teaspoons dry pectin
1/8 teaspoon ground ginger

1/2 small garlic clove, minced
1/8 teaspoon ground cumin
Dash of salt
Dash of pepper
1/4 teaspoon minced crystallized ginger

In a small container with a tight-fitting lid or in a blender, combine lemon juice, water, oil, pectin, ground ginger, garlic and cumin. Cover tightly; shake vigorously, or process 15 seconds. Season with salt and pepper. Stir in crystallized ginger. If processed in blender, pour into a container with a tight-fitting lid. Cover tightly; refrigerate until served, up to 5 days. Stir before serving. Makes about 1/2 cup.

---

1 tablespoon = 1/2 fat, 30 calories

Day 9

1000-Calorie	1200-Calorie	1500-Calorie
Breakfast		
1 serving Puffy Strawberry Omelet* 1/2 raisin English muffin **or** plain English muffin, toasted 1 teaspoon diet margarine 1 cup (8 oz.) skim milk	1 serving Puffy Strawberry Omelet* 1 raisin English muffin **or** plain English muffin, toasted 2 teaspoons diet margarine 1 cup (8 oz.) skim milk	1 serving Puffy Strawberry Omelet* 1 raisin English muffin **or** plain English muffin, toasted 2 teaspoons diet margarine 1 cup (8 oz.) skim milk
Lunch		
1 serving Turkey-Cabbage Salad* 1 small dinner roll, warmed 1 teaspoon diet margarine 1 serving Fruit & Rum Yogurt, page 117	1 serving Turkey-Cabbage Salad* 2 small dinner rolls, warmed 2 teaspoons diet margarine 1 serving Fruit & Rum Yogurt, page 117	1 serving Turkey-Cabbage Salad* tossed with 1/3 cup chow mein noodles 2 small dinner rolls, warmed 2 teaspoons diet margarine 1 serving Fruit & Rum Yogurt, page 117
Dinner		
1 small serving Stuffed Potato Jackets* 1/2 cup steamed mixed vegetables, such as broccoli, carrot and cauliflower, tossed with 1 teaspoon chopped cilantro or dash ground cumin 1 (2-inch) iceberg-lettuce wedge 2 tablespoons Ranch Yogurt Dressing* **or** 1 tablespoon reduced-calorie salad dressing (25 calories/tablespoon) 1 serving Honey-Lemon Poached Pears*	1 small serving Stuffed Potato Jackets* 1 cup steamed mixed vegetables, such as broccoli, carrot and cauliflower, tossed with 1 teaspoon chopped cilantro or dash ground cumin 1 (2-inch) iceberg-lettuce wedge 2 tablespoons Ranch Yogurt Dressing* **or** 1 tablespoon reduced-calorie salad dressing (25 calories/tablespoon) 1 serving Honey-Lemon Poached Pears*	1 large serving Stuffed Potato Jackets* 1 cup steamed mixed vegetables, such as broccoli, carrot and cauliflower, tossed with 1 teaspoon chopped cilantro or dash ground cumin 1 (2-inch) iceberg-lettuce wedge 2 tablespoons Ranch Yogurt Dressing* **or** 1 tablespoon reduced-calorie salad dressing (25 calories/tablespoon) 1 serving Honey-Lemon Poached Pears*
* Recipe follows.		

Ranch Yogurt Dressing

Serve this delicious combination as a dressing or as a dip for raw-vegetable snacks.

1/4 cup plain low-fat yogurt
1/2 cup buttermilk
1/4 cup reduced-calorie mayonnaise

1 tablespoon dry ranch-style
salad-dressing mix

In a small bowl, combine yogurt, buttermilk and mayonnaise. Add dressing mix; stir until blended. Cover tightly; refrigerate until served, up to 5 days. Stir before serving. Makes about 1 cup.

2 tablespoons = 1/2 fat, 30 calories

Puffy Strawberry Omelet

No one will ever guess this delicious omelet has so few calories.

4 eggs, separated
1 tablespoon lemon juice
2 tablespoons water
1/4 teaspoon salt
1 tablespoon white wine or
   white-grape juice

1-1/2 cups sliced fresh or partially thawed,
   frozen unsweetened strawberries
1/4 cup plain low-fat yogurt
2 tablespoons low-sugar strawberry spread

Preheat oven to 300F (150C). In a medium bowl, beat egg yolks, lemon juice, water and salt with an electric mixer or a whisk until thick and lemon-colored. Using clean beaters or a whisk, in another medium bowl, beat egg whites until soft peaks form. Fold beaten egg whites into egg-yolk mixture. Pour omelet mixture into a medium, ovenproof, nonstick skillet or an ovenproof skillet coated with nonstick vegetable spray. While cooking over very low heat, use back of a spoon to push omelet mixture up side of skillet forming an edge. Cook until edge is lightly browned, about 5 minutes. Bake omelet in preheated oven until a knife inserted in center comes out clean, about 15 minutes. In a small bowl, sprinkle wine or grape juice over strawberries; toss gently. In another small bowl, combine yogurt and strawberry spread; set aside. Using a serrated knife, carefully cut omelet into 4 wedges. Using a spatula, place 1 omelet wedge on each of 4 plates. Top each serving with 1/4 of yogurt mixture and about 1/3 cup sliced strawberries. Makes 4 servings.

---

1 serving = 1 meat, 1 fruit, 1/2 fat, 125 calories

Turkey-Cabbage Salad

Cabbage is a good source of vitamin C and fiber and is also low in calories.

1/2 small red bell pepper (3 per lb.)
   or 1 whole canned pimento
6 cups shredded cabbage (1-1/2 lbs.)
2 green onions, sliced

8 oz. cooked turkey, diced (2 cups)
1/3 cup chow-mein noodles
6 small red-cabbage leaves

Rice-Vinegar Dressing:
2 tablespoons vegetable oil
1 teaspoon sugar
1/2 teaspoon salt

1/8 teaspoon pepper
3 tablespoons rice vinegar
2 tablespoons water

Prepare Rice-Vinegar Dressing; refrigerate until served. Cut bell pepper or pimento in thin strips. In a large bowl, combine bell-pepper or pimento strips, cabbage, green onions, turkey and noodles. Pour dressing over salad; toss gently. Place 1 red-cabbage leaf on each of 6 salad plates. Spoon 1 heaping cup cabbage mixture on each cabbage-lined plate. Makes 6 (1-cup) servings.
To make Rice-Vinegar Dressing, in a small jar with a tight-fitting lid, combine all ingredients. Cover tightly; shake vigorously. Refrigerate up to 5 days; stir before serving. Makes about 1/2 cup.

---

1 serving (1 cup) = 2 meat, 1 vegetable, 1/2 fat, 162 calories
2 tablespoons dressing = 1-1/3 fat, 64 calories

1200-Calorie Breakfast, left to right: raisin English muffin; Puffy Strawberry Omelet.

Stuffed Potato Jackets

Potatoes supply vitamin C and potassium and are filling without having a lot of calories.

4 medium baking potatoes (3 per lb.)
1-1/2 teaspoons regular margarine, melted
Salt
2 teaspoons regular margarine
1 tablespoon all-purpose flour
1 cup skim milk
3 reduced-calorie American-cheese slices
  (2 oz.), cut in strips

6 oz. cooked lean ham, cut in thin strips
About 1 tablespoon chopped pickled
  jalapeño pepper
2 or 4 pickled cherry peppers or
  4 cherry tomatoes

Preheat oven to 350F (175C). Scrub potatoes with a brush under running water. Remove any blemishes. Pierce potatoes several times with a fork or point of a knife. Bake in preheated oven until tender and potatoes give when squeezed, about 1 hour. Remove potatoes from oven. Turn oven to broil. Cut potatoes in half lengthwise. Scoop out potato pulp, leaving a 1/2-inch shell. Reserve removed potato pulp for another purpose. Lightly brush insides of potato jackets with 1-1/2 teaspoons melted margarine. Sprinkle each with salt. Place buttered potato jackets on an ungreased baking sheet, cut-side up. Broil about 6 inches from heat until potatoes are crisp and lightly browned, about 10 minutes, turning potatoes once during cooking. In a small saucepan, melt 2 teaspoons margarine over medium-high heat. Stir in flour, making a smooth paste. Gradually stir in milk. Stirring constantly, cook until mixture thickens and comes to a boil. Add cheese; stir until cheese melts. Stir in ham strips and jalapeño pepper. **For 1000- or 1200-Calorie Menus (small serving),** place 2 baked potato jackets on each plate. **For 1500-Calorie Menu (large serving),** place 4 baked potato jackets on each plate. **For all menus,** spoon 1/4 cup ham-and-cheese sauce into each potato jacket. Garnish each serving with a cherry pepper or cherry tomato. Makes 4 small servings or 2 large servings.

---

1 small serving (2 potato jackets) = 1 bread, 2 meat, 1 fat, 241 calories
1 large serving (4 potato jackets) = 2 bread, 4 meat, 2 fat, 482 calories

---

Honey-Lemon Poached Pears

A delicate and elegant dessert even if you're not on a diet!

1/2 small lemon (4 per lb.)
1/2 small lime (5 per lb.)
1/2 cup water

1 tablespoon honey
1 medium, fresh Bartlett pear (2-1/2 per lb.)
  or 2 medium pear halves canned in water

Use a vegetable peeler to peel lemon and lime, removing only colored part of peel. Cut colored peel into very thin strips. Juice lemon and lime. Reserve 1 tablespoon lemon juice and 1-1/2 teaspoons lime juice. Refrigerate remaining juice for another purpose. In a medium saucepan, combine lemon-peel and lime-peel strips, reserved lemon and lime juices, water and honey. Bring to a boil; reduce heat until mixture barely simmers. Cover; simmer 5 minutes. Peel pear. Cut in half lengthwise. Remove and discard core; slice pear. Place in honey syrup; stir gently to coat pear slices. Cover; simmer until tender, 10 to 15 minutes. Use a slotted spoon to lift poached pear slices from syrup. Divide equally among 4 dessert dishes. Spoon 2 tablespoons syrup over each serving. Serve warm. To serve chilled, cover tightly; refrigerate at least 2 hours. Makes 4 servings.

---

1 serving = 1 fruit, 44 calories

Day 10

1000-Calorie	1200-Calorie	1500-Calorie
Breakfast		
1 Raisin-Bran Muffin* 1 teaspoon diet margarine 1/4 small cantaloupe, topped with 1/4 cup low-fat cottage cheese 1 cup (8 oz.) skim milk	2 Raisin-Bran Muffins* 2 teaspoons diet margarine 1/4 small cantaloupe, topped with 1/4 cup low-fat cottage cheese 1 cup (8 oz.) skim milk	2 Raisin-Bran Muffins* 2 teaspoons diet margarine 1/4 small cantaloupe, topped with 1/4 cup low-fat cottage cheese 1 cup (8 oz.) skim milk
Lunch		
1 serving Quick Vegetable Soup* **or** 1/2 cup (4 oz.) tomato juice **or** other vegetable juice 1 serving Crispy Chicken Rolls* 1 Frozen-Yogurt Pop*	1 serving Quick Vegetable Soup* **or** 1/2 cup (4 oz.) tomato juice **or** other vegetable juice 6 saltine crackers 1 serving Crispy Chicken Rolls* 1 Frozen-Yogurt Pop*	1 serving Quick Vegetable Soup* with 1/4 cup dry noodles, cooked in soup 6 saltine crackers 1 serving Crispy Chicken Rolls* 1 Frozen-Yogurt Pop*
Dinner		

1 small serving Spinach Fettuccine with Salmon*
1/2 cup steamed sliced zucchini and yellow squash with a pinch of dill weed
Salad:
  1-1/2 cups torn romaine lettuce
  1 teaspoon freshly grated Parmesan cheese
1-1/2 tablespoons Zesty Italian Dressing* **or** reduced-calorie Italian salad dressing (25 calories/tablespoon)
1 serving Cappuccino Mousse, page 122, **or** 1/2 cup fresh or frozen, unsweetened berries stirred into 1/2 cup plain low-fat yogurt
	1 small serving Spinach Fettuccine with Salmon*
	1/2 cup steamed cooked zucchini and yellow squash with a pinch of dill weed
	Salad:
	  1-1/2 cups torn romaine lettuce
	  1 teaspoon freshly grated Parmesan cheese
	1-1/2 tablespoons Zesty Italian Dressing* **or** reduced-calorie Italian salad dressing (25 calories/tablespoon)
	1 serving Cappuccino Mousse, page 122, **or** 1/2 cup fresh or frozen, unsweetened berries stirred into 1/2 cup plain low-fat yogurt
		1 large serving Spinach Fettuccine with Salmon*
		1/2 cup steamed cooked zucchini and yellow squash with a pinch of dill weed
		Salad:
		  1-1/2 cups torn romaine lettuce
		  1 teaspoon freshly grated Parmesan cheese
		1-1/2 tablespoons Zesty Italian Dressing* **or** reduced-calorie Italian salad dressing (25 calories/tablespoon)
		1 serving Cappuccino Mousse, page 122, **or** 1/2 cup fresh or frozen, unsweetened berries stirred into 1/2 cup plain low-fat yogurt

* Recipe follows.

Tip *Reduced-calorie mayonnaise has less than half the fat and calories of regular mayonnaise.*

Raisin-Bran Muffins

Refrigerate the batter and bake as needed for fresh, hot muffins.

1-1/3 cups all-purpose flour
2 teaspoons baking powder
1/4 teaspoon salt
1/4 teaspoon ground cinnamon
1 cup ready-to-eat unsweetened bran cereal

1/4 cup raisins, chopped
1 egg
1 tablespoon molasses
1 cup buttermilk
1 tablespoon regular margarine, melted

Preheat oven to 350F (175C). Line a 12-cup muffin pan with paper liners, use a nonstick muffin pan or spray a muffin pan with nonstick vegetable spray. Muffins will stick to paper liners. Set pan aside. In a sifter, combine flour, baking powder, salt and cinnamon; sift into a medium bowl. Stir in bran cereal and raisins. In a small bowl, beat egg; stir in molasses, buttermilk and margarine. Stir into bran mixture only until flour is moistened. Spoon about 2 tablespoons batter into each muffin cup. Bake in preheated oven until muffins are lightly browned, about 20 minutes. Serve muffins hot. Batter may be stored in refrigerator in a container with a tight-fitting lid, up to 3 days. Bake refrigerated batter 22 to 25 minutes. To reheat leftover muffins, wrap muffins in foil; place in preheated 350F (175C) oven 10 minutes. Makes 12 muffins.

1 muffin = 1 bread, 1/4 fat, 96 calories

Frozen Yogurt Pops

Save for a mid-afternoon or bedtime snack, if you like.

3 small ripe Bartlett pears (4 per lb.)
   or 6 small pear halves canned in water
1 tablespoon lemon juice

1/2 cup partially thawed frozen
   grape-juice concentrate
16 oz. plain low-fat yogurt (2 cups)

Peel, core and slice pears. In a medium saucepan, bring 1/2 cup water and lemon juice to a boil. Add sliced pears. Reduce heat until mixture barely simmers. Cover; simmer until pears are tender, about 15 minutes. Drain, discarding liquid. In a blender or food processor fitted with a metal blade, combine cooked pears and grape-juice concentrate. Process until smooth. Add yogurt; process until blended. Pour yogurt mixture into 12 (4-ounce) paper cups, using 1/3 cup puree in each paper cup. Insert a popsicle stick or plastic spoon in center of each pop. Freeze until firm, about 3 hours. To serve, peel paper cups from frozen pops. Makes 12 frozen pops.

Variations
Substitute 6 fresh apricots or 3 medium, fresh or unsweetened frozen peaches for pears. Cook as directed above. Substitute frozen lemonade concentrate for grape-juice concentrate. Complete as directed above. Exchanges and calories will remain the same.

Substitute 1-1/2 cups strawberries, raspberries, blueberries, or blackberries for pears. Omit water and lemon juice. Substitute frozen lemonade concentrate for grape-juice concentrate. Puree berries with lemonade concentrate. Add yogurt; process only until blended. Freeze as directed above.

1 pop = 1 fruit, 1/4 milk, 70 calories

Crispy Chicken Rolls

These savory chicken rolls are an excellent dish to serve to company.

4 (6-inch) flour tortillas
2/3 (3-oz.) pkg. Neufchâtel cheese,
   room temperature
2 tablespoons plain low-fat yogurt
1/4 cup skim milk
1/4 teaspoon garlic salt
1/4 teaspoon curry powder

Curry-Chutney Dressing:
1/4 cup plain low-fat yogurt
2 teaspoons mango chutney or
   other fruit chutney

1/2 cup cooked fresh or frozen spinach
4 ripe olives, thinly sliced
4 oz. cooked chicken, diced (1 cup)
1 to 2 tablespoons skim milk, if needed
1 tablespoon diet margarine, melted
2 cups shredded iceberg lettuce
4 radishes with green tops

Curry powder

Prepare Curry-Chutney Dressing; refrigerate until ready to serve. Preheat oven to 300F (150C). Wrap flour tortillas with foil; warm in preheated oven. Meanwhile, in a small saucepan, combine cheese, yogurt, milk, garlic salt and curry powder. Stir over medium heat until cheese melts and sauce is smooth; *do not boil*. Reduce heat to low. Squeeze spinach to remove as much liquid as possible. Add drained spinach, olives and chicken to sauce; stir. Heat until mixture almost comes to a simmer. Cover; keep over very low heat until chicken is warmed through, about 5 minutes. If mixture becomes too thick, stir in 1 to 2 tablespoons milk. Remove tortillas from oven. Preheat broiler. Lay 1 tortilla on a flat surface. Spoon 1/4 of chicken mixture in a strip across center of tortilla. Fold sides of tortilla over chicken filling. Roll up tortilla. Repeat with remaining tortillas and chicken mixture. Place filled tortillas, seam-side down, on an ungreased baking sheet. Lightly brush tops with margarine. Broil until lightly browned, about 2 minutes. Divide shredded lettuce among 4 plates. Place 1 browned chicken roll on each lettuce-lined plate. Place a radish next to each chicken roll. Spoon 1 tablespoon dressing over each serving. Makes 4 servings.
To make Curry-Chutney Dressing, in a small bowl, combine yogurt and chutney. Season with curry powder. Refrigerate until ready to serve. Makes about 1/4 cup.

---

1 serving = 2 meat, 1 bread, 1/4 vegetable, 2 fat, 300 calories

---

Quick Vegetable Soup   Photo on page 87.

Quick and satisfying for very few calories!

3 cups water
1 beef-flavored bouillon cube
2 chicken-flavored bouillon cubes
1 bay leaf
1/8 teaspoon dried leaf thyme

1/4 teaspoon paprika
1 cup frozen broccoli, cauliflower and
   carrot mixture
1 large romaine-lettuce, Swiss-chard or
   spinach leaf

In a medium saucepan, combine water, bouillon cubes, bay leaf, thyme and paprika. Bring to a boil over high heat; reduce heat until water barely simmers. Crush bouillon cubes with back of a spoon. Stir until bouillon cubes are completely dissolved. Cover; simmer 5 minutes. Add vegetables. Cover; simmer 5 minutes longer. Cut romaine lettuce, chard or spinach into shreds; add to soup. Simmer 1 minute; serve hot in soup bowls. Makes 4 (1-cup) servings.

---

1 serving (1 cup) = 1 vegetable, 32 calories

Spinach Fettuccine with Salmon

You'll find sour half and half in the dairy case at your supermarket.

6 oz. uncooked spinach fettuccine
 (about 2-1/2 cups)
1 tablespoon regular margarine
1 garlic clove, minced
1/2 cup sliced fresh mushrooms (1-1/2 oz.)
1/4 cup diced red bell pepper or pimento

1/4 cup dairy sour half and half
2 tablespoons white wine or canned or
 homemade chicken broth
1 (16-oz.) can salmon, drained, cartilage and
 skin removed, crumbled slightly
3 tablespoons grated Parmesan cheese

Cook fettuccine in lightly salted boiling water until al dente or just tender to the bite, 5 to 7 minutes. While fettuccine cooks, in a medium skillet, melt margarine. Add garlic, mushrooms and bell pepper or pimento. Sauté until mushrooms begin to soften, about 1 minute. Stir in sour half and half and wine or broth; set aside. Pour salmon into a small saucepan or stovetop casserole dish. Place over low heat until warmed through; keep hot. Drain cooked fettuccine; rinse with hot water. Add to mushroom mixture. Toss to coat noodles. Sprinkle cheese over noodles; toss again. **For 1000- or 1200-Calorie Menus (small serving),** spoon 1/2 cup fettuccine mixture onto each plate. Top each serving with about 1/4 cup salmon chunks. **For 1500-Calorie Menu (large serving),** spoon 1 cup fettuccine mixture onto each plate. Top each serving with about 1/2 cup salmon chunks. Makes 4 small servings or 2 large servings.

---

1 small serving (1/2 cup fettuccine mixture, 1/4 cup salmon) = 1 bread, 2 meat, 1 fat, 247 calories
1 large serving (1 cup fettuccine mixture, 1/2 cup salmon) = 2 bread, 4 meat, 2 fat, 494 calories

---

Zesty Italian Dressing

The zesty garlic flavor becomes stronger with storage.

2 tablespoons white-wine vinegar
1 tablespoon olive oil
3 tablespoons water
1 teaspoon dry pectin
1/8 teaspoon salt

Dash of pepper
1 tablespoon chopped fresh parsley
Pinch of Italian seasoning
2 teaspoons grated Parmesan cheese
1 garlic clove

In a small container with a tight-fitting lid or in a blender, combine vinegar, olive oil, water, pectin, salt, pepper, parsley and Italian seasoning. Cover tightly; shake vigorously, or process 15 seconds. Add cheese. Shake again or process with quick on/off motions. If processed in blender, pour into a container with a tight-fitting lid. Press a wooden pick through garlic clove; add to dressing. Cover tightly; refrigerate until served, up to 2 days. Remove garlic; shake before using. Makes about 1/3 cup.

---

1 tablespoon = 1/2 fat, 30 calories

1000-Calorie Dinner, from top right: Cappuccino Mousse, page 122; romaine-lettuce salad with fresh Parmesan cheese and Zesty Italian Dressing; steamed sliced zucchini and yellow squash with a pinch of dill; Spinach Fettuccine with Salmon.

Day 11

1000-Calorie	1200-Calorie	1500-Calorie
	Breakfast	
1 serving Alpine Toast* 1 serving Orange-Blossom Wake-Up, page 116	1 serving Alpine Toast* 1 serving Fruit & Nut Granola, page 40, **or** 3/4 cup unsweetened ready-to-eat cereal 1/4 cup (2 oz.) skim milk 1 serving Orange-Blossom Wake-up, page 116	1 serving Alpine Toast* 1 serving Fruit & Nut Granola, page 40, **or** 3/4 cup unsweetened ready-to-eat cereal 1/4 cup (2 oz.) skim milk 1 serving Orange-Blossom Wake-Up, page 116
	Lunch	
1 serving Tuna-Broccoli Pie* 2 (1/2-inch-thick) fresh pineapple rings **or** 1 pineapple ring canned in juice, sprinkled with cinnamon, broiled 1 cup (8 oz.) skim milk **or** 1 cup plain low-fat yogurt	1 serving Tuna-Broccoli Pie* 1 Raisin-Bran Muffin, page 56, **or** 1/2 cinnamon-raisin bagel 1 teaspoon diet margarine 2 (1/2-inch-thick) fresh pineapple rings **or** 1 pineapple ring canned in juice, sprinkled with cinnamon, broiled 1 cup (8 oz.) skim milk **or** 1 cup plain low-fat yogurt	1 serving Tuna-Broccoli Pie* 2 Raisin-Bran Muffins, page 56, **or** 1 cinnamon-raisin bagel 1 tablespoon diet margarine 2 (1/2-inch-thick) fresh pineapple rings **or** 1 pineapple ring, canned in juice, sprinkled with cinnamon, broiled 1 cup (8 oz.) skim milk **or** 1 cup plain low-fat yogurt
	Dinner	

1 small serving Chicken Mediterranean*
1/2 cup cooked noodles with 1 teaspoon diet margarine and 1/2 teaspoon poppy seeds
Salad:
  1-1/2 cups torn fresh spinach or red-leaf lettuce
  2 orange slices
1 tablespoon Citrus-Vinaigrettete Dressing* **or** reduced-calorie salad dressing (25 calories/tablespoon)
1 serving Raspberry Sherbet, page 118
	1 small serving Chicken Mediterranean*
	4 fresh asparagus spears, cooked, **or** 1/2 cup other cooked green vegetable, page 136
	1/2 cup cooked noodles with 1 teaspoon diet margarine and 1/2 teaspoon poppy seeds
	Salad:
	  1-1/2 cups torn fresh spinach or red-leaf lettuce
	  2 orange slices
	1-1/2 tablespoons Citrus-Vinaigrette Dressing* **or** reduced-calorie salad dressing (25 calories/tablespoon)
	1 serving Raspberry Sherbet, page 118
		1 large serving Chicken Mediterranean*
		1/2 cup cooked noodles with 1 teaspoon diet margarine and 1/2 teaspoon poppy seeds
		Salad:
		  1-1/2 cups torn fresh spinach or red-leaf lettuce
		  2 orange slices
		1-1/2 tablespoons Citrus-Vinaigrette Dressing* **or** reduced-calorie salad dressing (25 calories/tablespoon)
		1 serving Raspberry Sherbet, page 118

* Recipe follows.

Alpine Toast

This dish is reminiscent of a delicious Swiss breakfast.

1 bacon slice
1/4 cup ricotta cheese
1/2 cup shredded Swiss cheese (2 oz.)
4 whole-wheat-bread or
   pumpernickel-bread slices

2 small fresh Bartlett pears (4 per lb.)
   or 4 small pear halves canned in water
Ground nutmeg or ground cardamom,
   if desired

In a small skillet, fry bacon until crisp; drain on paper towels. Crumble when cool. In a small bowl, combine cheeses and crumbled bacon. Toast bread. Spread 1/4 of cheese mixture on each toast slice; set aside. Peel and core fresh pears; slice peeled, cored fresh or canned pears. Arrange pear slices on cheese-covered toast. Sprinkle with nutmeg or cardamom, if desired. Preheat broiler. Place toast on a rack on a broiler pan. Broil 4 inches from heat until cheese bubbles. Place 1 broiled toast on each of 4 plates. Serve warm. Makes 4 servings.

---

1 serving = 1 meat, 1 bread, 1 fat, 1/2 fruit, 199 calories

Tuna-Broccoli Pie

Reheat the leftover pie for another lunch.

3/4 cup all-purpose flour
1 teaspoon baking powder
1/4 teaspoon salt
1 tablespoon plus 1-1/2 teaspoons
   vegetable shortening
1/4 cup buttermilk
2 eggs, beaten
1-1/2 teaspoons diet margarine

1/4 cup chopped onion
1/3 cup chopped red or green bell pepper
2 cups broccoli flowerets, cut in
   bite-sized pieces
1 (6-3/4-oz.) can tuna packed in water,
   drained
1/2 cup evaporated skim milk

Preheat oven to 400F (205C). In a sifter, combine flour, baking powder and salt; sift into a medium bowl. With a pastry blender or 2 knives, cut in shortening until mixture resembles coarse crumbs. Add buttermilk; stir only until flour mixture is moistened. Turn out on a lightly floured surface. Gently knead dough 10 strokes. Roll dough into an 11-inch circle. Fit dough into a 9-inch pie pan. Trim and flute edge; prick crust. Bake crust in preheated oven 9 minutes or until lightly browned. Brush crust lightly with beaten eggs; reserve remaining beaten eggs for filling. Bake crust 1 minute longer; remove to a wire rack. Reduce oven temperature to 350F (175C). In a medium nonstick skillet or a skillet coated with nonstick vegetable spray, melt margarine. Add onion, bell pepper and broccoli; sauté until onion is soft. Gently stir in tuna. Spoon tuna mixture into baked crust. Stir evaporated milk into reserved beaten eggs. Pour egg mixture over tuna. Bake in preheated oven until a wooden pick inserted in center comes out clean, about 30 minutes. Cool 5 minutes before cutting into 6 wedges. Place 1 wedge on each of 6 plates. Makes 6 servings.

---

1 serving = 2 meat, 1 bread, 1 vegetable, 198 calories

Tip   *Water-packed tuna has only 75 calories for a two-ounce serving.*

Chicken Mediterranean

Feta cheese is a very salty, yet mild-flavored Greek cheese.

4 (3-oz.) boned, skinned chicken-breast
   halves or 4 (4-oz.) chicken thighs
1/2 teaspoon dried leaf tarragon
1 tablespoon diet margarine
2 garlic cloves, minced
1/2 cup canned or homemade chicken broth
1/3 cup white wine or canned or
   homemade chicken broth

1 medium tomato, peeled, diced
1 cup sliced fresh mushrooms (3 oz.)
1 cup diced green bell pepper
1 teaspoon cornstarch
1 tablespoon water
2 tablespoons crumbled feta cheese

Cut chicken breasts in half lengthwise. Sprinkle skinned chicken with tarragon. In a medium nonstick skillet or a skillet coated with nonstick vegetable spray, melt margarine over medium heat. Add garlic; sauté 15 seconds. Add chicken pieces; sauté until browned. Pour chicken broth and wine or broth into skillet. Reduce heat until mixture barely simmers. Cover; simmer 15 minutes. Remove cooked chicken; keep warm. Add tomato, mushrooms and bell pepper to skillet; stir. Cover; simmer 5 minutes. In a small bowl, combine cornstarch and water. Stirring constantly, slowly pour cornstarch mixture into skillet. Continue to stir over medium heat until mixture thickens and comes to a boil. Return cooked chicken to skillet. Sprinkle cheese over chicken and vegetables. Cover; cook until cheese melts, about 3 minutes. **For 1000- or 1200-Calorie Menus (small serving),** spoon 1/3 cup vegetables onto each plate. Top each serving with 1 chicken piece. **For 1500-Calorie Menu (large serving),** spoon 2/3 cup vegetables onto each plate. Top each serving with 2 chicken pieces. **For all menus,** spoon sauce equally over servings. Makes 4 small servings or 2 large servings.

---

1 small serving (1/3 cup vegetables, 1 chicken piece) = 2 meat, 1 vegetable, 169 calories
1 large serving (2/3 cup vegetables, 2 chicken pieces) = 4 meat, 2 vegetable, 338 calories

---

Citrus-Vinaigrette Dressing

A perfect complement for a spinach salad.

1/4 cup orange juice
1 tablespoon lemon juice
1 tablespoon water
2 tablespoons vegetable oil

1 teaspoon Dijon-style mustard
2 teaspoons dry pectin
1/8 teaspoon salt
Dash of white pepper

In a small container with a tight-fitting lid or in a blender, combine all ingredients. Cover tightly; shake vigorously or process 30 seconds. If processed in blender, pour into a container with a tight-fitting lid. Cover tightly; refrigerate until served, up to 5 days. Makes about 1/2 cup.

---

1 tablespoon = 1/2 fat, 30 calories
1-1/2 tablespoons = 3/4 fat, 45 calories

1500-Calorie Dinner, clockwise from top of plate: spinach and orange salad with Citrus-Vinaigrette Dressing; noodles with margarine and poppy seeds; Chicken Mediterranean; Raspberry Sherbet, page 118.

Day 12

1000-Calorie	1200-Calorie	1500-Calorie
Breakfast		
1 Apple-Spice Muffin* 1 teaspoon diet margarine 1 large egg, scrambled with 1 teaspoon diet margarine 1/4 cup sliced banana marinated in 2 tablespoons orange juice 1 cup (8 oz.) skim milk	2 Apple-Spice Muffins* 2 teaspoons diet margarine 1 large egg, scrambled with 1 teaspoon diet margarine 1/4 cup sliced banana marinated in 2 tablespoons orange juice 1 cup (8 oz.) skim milk	2 Apple-Spice Muffins* 2 teaspoons diet margarine 1 large egg, scrambled with 1 teaspoon diet margarine 1/4 cup sliced banana marinated in 2 tablespoons orange juice 1 cup (8 oz.) skim milk
Lunch		
1 serving Cheese & Noodles Florentine* 1 serving Apple-Walnut Salad* 1 serving Cherry-Cloud Pudding, page 120, **or** 1/4 cup (2 oz.) fruit juice blended with 3/4 cup (6 oz.) club soda	1 serving Cheese & Noodles Florentine* 1 (1/2-inch-thick) French-bread or Italian-bread slice 1 teaspoon diet margarine 1 serving Apple-Walnut Salad* 1 serving Cherry-Cloud Pudding, page 120, **or** 1/4 cup (2 oz.) fruit juice blended with 3/4 cup (6 oz.) club soda	1 serving Cheese & Noodles Florentine* 2 (1/2-inch-thick) French-bread or Italian-bread slices 2 teaspoons diet margarine 1 serving Apple-Walnut Salad* 1 serving Cherry-Cloud Pudding, page 120, **or** 1/4 cup (2 oz.) fruit juice blended with 3/4 cup (6 oz.) club soda
Dinner		

1 small serving Fried Rice & Green Chilies*
Cucumber-radish salad:
  1/4 cucumber, sliced
  3 radishes, sliced,
  1 lettuce leaf
1 tablespoon French Dressing* **or** reduced-calorie French salad dressing (25 calories/tablespoon)
1 serving Orange Sherbet, page 121, **or** 1 small orange and 1/2 cup (4 oz.) skim milk
	1 small serving Fried Rice & Green Chilies*
	1/2 cup cut green beans, simmered in 1 tablespoon Chunky Salsa*
	Cucumber-radish salad:
	  1/4 cucumber, sliced
	  3 radishes, sliced
	  1 lettuce leaf
	1 tablespoon French Dressing* **or** reduced-calorie French salad dressing (25 calories/tablespoon)
	1 serving Orange Sherbet, page 121, **or** 1 small orange and 1/2 cup (4 oz.) skim milk
		1 large serving Fried Rice & Green Chilies*
		1/2 cup cut green beans, simmered in 1 tablespoon Chunky Salsa*
		Cucumber-radish salad:
		  1/4 cucumber, sliced
		  3 radishes, sliced
		  1 lettuce leaf
		1 tablespoon French Dressing* **or** reduced-calorie French salad dressing (25 calories/tablespoon)
		1 serving Orange Sherbet, page 121, **or** 1 small orange and 1/2 cup (4 oz.) skim milk

* Recipe follows.

Cheese & Noodles Florentine

Delicious and rich tasting!

3 oz. uncooked extra-wide noodles
4 cups packed, shredded,
   fresh spinach leaves or
   1 (10-oz.) pkg. thawed frozen
   chopped spinach
1 tablespoon diet margarine

2 tablespoons finely chopped onion
1/2 teaspoon seasoned salt
1-1/4 cups low-fat cottage cheese
3/4 cup diced part-skim-milk mozzarella
   cheese (3 oz.)

Spicy Tomato Sauce:
1/2 cup tomato sauce
1 small garlic clove, minced
Pinch of dried leaf basil

Pinch of dried leaf oregano
Dash of salt

Cook noodles in lightly salted boiling water until al dente or just tender to the bite, 5 to 7 minutes. Drain; rinse with hot water. Keep hot. Prepare Spicy Tomato Sauce; keep hot. Steam fresh or frozen spinach until tender, about 5 minutes. Drain in a sieve; press with back of a spoon to remove excess moisture. In a 10-inch nonstick skillet or a skillet coated with nonstick vegetable spray, melt margarine. Add onion; sauté until onion is soft. Stir in cooked spinach; sprinkle with seasoned salt. Stir over medium heat until excess moisture evaporates, 2 to 3 minutes. Stir in cottage cheese and mozzarella cheese. Remove from heat. Preheat oven to 350F (175C). Spread 1/2 of cooked noodles in an ungreased 8-inch-square baking dish or 2-quart casserole dish with a lid. Spoon spinach-cheese filling over noodles. Arrange remaining noodles over filling. Pour hot Spicy Tomato Sauce over top. Cover dish or casserole with foil or lid. Bake in preheated oven 20 minutes or until sauce is bubbly and cheese melts. Cut into 4 squares or wedges. Place 1 square or wedge on each of 4 plates. Makes 4 servings.
To make Spicy Tomato Sauce, combine all ingredients in a small saucepan. Bring to a boil, stirring frequently. Reduce heat until mixture barely simmers. Cover; simmer 5 minutes. Keep hot until served. Makes about 1/2 cup.

---

1 serving = 2 meat, 1 bread, 1 vegetable, 250 calories

French Dressing

Reduced-calorie ketchup has half the calories of regular ketchup.

2 tablespoons red-wine vinegar
2 tablespoons vegetable oil
1/4 cup water
1 tablespoon bottled reduced-calorie
   ketchup

2 teaspoons dry pectin
1/4 teaspoon paprika
4 drops Worcestershire sauce
1/8 teaspoon salt
Dash of pepper

In a small container with a tight-fitting lid or in a blender, combine all ingredients. Cover tightly; shake vigorously, or process 15 seconds. If processed in blender, pour into a container with a tight-fitting lid. Cover tightly; refrigerate until served, up to 4 days. Shake before using. Makes about 1/2 cup.

---

1 tablespoon = 1/2 fat, 30 calories

Apple-Spice Muffins

Using egg white instead of the whole egg eliminates 65 calories and six grams of fat.

1-1/4 cups sifted all-purpose flour	1/2 cup whole-wheat flour
1 tablespoon baking powder	1 egg white, lightly beaten
1/2 teaspoon salt	3/4 cup skim milk
1/2 teaspoon ground cinnamon	1 tablespoon regular margarine, melted
1/4 teaspoon ground ginger	1/2 cup unsweetened applesauce
1 tablespoon brown sugar	1 tablespoon wheat germ

Preheat oven to 400F (205C). Line a 12-cup muffin pan with paper liners or spray a 12-cup muffin pan with nonstick vegetable spray; set aside. Muffins will stick to paper liners. In a sifter, combine all-purpose flour, baking powder, salt, cinnamon and ginger; sift into a medium bowl. Stir in brown sugar and whole-wheat flour. In another medium bowl, combine egg white, milk, margarine and applesauce. Stir into flour mixture only until flour is moistened. Spoon about 2 tablespoons batter into each prepared muffin cup. Sprinkle wheat germ equally over batter. Bake in preheated oven until tops are lightly browned, 20 to 25 minutes. Immediately remove muffins from muffin cups. Serve warm. Muffins may also be baked in small batches. Refrigerate extra batter in a container with a tight-fitting lid up to 2 days. Bake refrigerated batter 25 to 27 minutes. To reheat leftover muffins, wrap muffins in foil; place in preheated 350F(175C) oven 10 minutes. Makes 12 muffins.

1 muffin = 1 bread, 1/4 fat, 83 calories

Apple-Walnut Salad

The fresh fruit adds refreshing flavor to a tossed salad.

1 small Red Delicious or other eating apple (4 per lb.)	2 cups shredded iceberg lettuce
1 celery stalk, sliced	4 large red-leaf-lettuce leaves

Walnut Dressing:

3 tablespoons unsweetened apple juice	1/8 teaspoon salt
1 tablespoon apple-cider vinegar	1/8 teaspoon paprika
1 tablespoon vegetable oil	6 small walnut halves, chopped

Prepare Walnut Dressing; refrigerate until served. Cut apple into quarters, top to bottom; core each piece. Cut each quarter in crosswise slices. In a large bowl, combine apple slices, celery and shredded lettuce. Shake Walnut Dressing; pour over apple mixture. Toss to distribute. Arrange 1 lettuce leaf on each of 4 salad plates. Spoon 1/4 of salad onto each lettuce-lined plate. Serve immediately. Makes 4 servings.
To make Walnut Dressing, combine apple juice, vinegar, oil, salt and paprika in a small container with a tight-fitting lid. Cover tightly; shake vigorously 15 seconds. Add walnuts; cover and shake again. Shake again before adding to salad. Makes about 1/3 cup.

1 serving = 3/4 fruit, 3/4 fat, 62 calories

1000-Calorie Breakfast, clockwise from top: skim milk, banana slices marinated in orange juice; scrambled egg; Apple-Spice Muffin.

Fried Rice & Green Chilies

Prepare the rice early in the day for an extra-quick meal.

3/4 cup uncooked long-grain white rice
1 tablespoon plus 1 teaspoon vegetable oil
1/2 cup chopped green bell pepper
1 (4-oz.) can diced green chilies

1/4 cup chopped red bell pepper or pimento
2 green onions, sliced
2 (6-3/4-oz.) cans tuna packed in water,
   drained

Cooling Cream Sauce:
1/3 cup sour half and half
2 tablespoons skim milk or buttermilk
1 tablespoon chopped cilantro or parsley

1 tablespoon Chunky Salsa, below,
   or canned salsa
Dash of ground cumin

In a medium saucepan, cook rice according to package directions. Stir cooked rice; let stand until cool. Prepare Cooling Cream Sauce. Refrigerate until served. In a large nonstick skillet or a skillet coated with nonstick vegetable spray, heat 1 teaspoon oil. Add green bell pepper, chilies, red bell pepper or pimento and green onions. Sauté until onions are soft. Remove vegetables to a small bowl; set aside. Heat remaining 1 tablespoon oil in same skillet. Add cooled rice; sauté until lightly browned. Add tuna and sautéed vegetables. Stir-fry 3 to 5 minutes until heated through. **For 1000- or 1200-Calorie Menus (small serving),** place 1 cup rice mixture on each plate. Spoon 1 tablespoon sauce over each serving. **For 1500-Calorie Menu (large serving),** place 2 cups rice mixture on each plate. Spoon 2 tablespoons sauce over each serving. Makes 6 small servings or 3 large servings.
To make Cooling Cream Sauce, in a small bowl, combine all sauce ingredients. Cover tightly; refrigerate until served, up to 5 days. Makes about 1/2 cup.

---

1 small serving (1 cup salad, 1 tablespoon sauce) = 2 meat, 1 bread, 1/2 vegetable, 215 calories
1 large serving (2 cups salad, 2 tablespoons sauce) = 4 meat, 2 bread, 1 vegetable, 430 calories
1 tablespoon sauce = 1/4 milk, 17 calories

Chunky Salsa

Delicious with any Mexican-style dish.

4 canned tomatoes, in a 1-cup measure,
   with juice from can to cover
2 tablespoons canned diced green chilies
1/2 cup chopped green bell pepper

1 green onion, chopped
1 teaspoon chili powder
1/8 teaspoon ground cumin
Salt

Pour juice from tomatoes into a medium bowl. Dice tomatoes; add to juice. Stir in chilies, bell pepper, green onion, chili powder and cumin. Season with salt. Cover; refrigerate at least 2 hours or up to 5 days. Makes 1-1/2 cups.

1/4 cup = 1/2 vegetable, 14 calories

Day 13

1000-Calorie	1200-Calorie	1500-Calorie
Breakfast		
1 small serving Lemon-Blueberry Pancakes* 1 oz. sliced Canadian bacon **or** lean ham, grilled 1/2 cup (4 oz.) skim milk	1 large serving Lemon-Blueberry Pancakes* 1 oz. sliced Canadian bacon **or** lean ham, grilled 1 cup (8 oz.) skim milk	1 large serving Lemon-Blueberry Pancakes* 1 oz. sliced Canadian bacon **or** lean ham, grilled 1 cup (8 oz.) skim milk
Lunch		
1 serving Crispy Egg-Topper Sandwich* 1/2 cup cold, cooked asparagus, sprinkled with lemon juice 2 small plums **or** prunes 1 cup (8 oz.) skim milk	1 cup canned minestrone soup prepared as directed 1 serving Crispy Egg-Topper Sandwich* 1/2 cup cold cooked asparagus, sprinkled with lemon juice 2 small plums **or** prunes 1 cup (8 oz.) skim milk	1 cup canned minestrone soup prepared as directed 6 saltine crackers 1 serving Crispy Egg-Topper Sandwich* 1/2 cup cold cooked asparagus, sprinkled with lemon juice 2 small plums **or** prunes
Dinner		
1 small serving Scalloped Potatoes & Ham* 1/2 cup cooked sliced beets **or** cooked Brussels sprouts 1-1/2 cups torn romaine lettuce 2 tablespoons Ranch Yogurt Dressing, page 51, **or** 1 tablespoon reduced-calorie salad dressing (25 calories/tablespoon), sprinkled with 1 tablespoon sunflower kernels 1 serving Minty Pears* **or** 1/2 medium, fresh pear * Recipe follows.	1 small serving Scalloped Potatoes & Ham* 3/4 cup cooked sliced beets **or** cooked Brussels sprouts 1-1/2 cups torn romaine lettuce 2 tablespoons Ranch Yogurt Dressing, page 51, **or** 1 tablespoon reduced-calorie salad dressing (25 calories/tablespoon), sprinkled with 1 tablespoon sunflower kernels 1 serving Minty Pears* **or** 1/2 medium, fresh pear	1 large serving Scalloped Potatoes & Ham* 3/4 cup cooked sliced beets **or** cooked Brussels sprouts 1-1/2 cups torn romaine lettuce 2 tablespoons Ranch Yogurt Dressing, page 51, **or** 1 tablespoon reduced-calorie salad dressing (25 calories/tablespoon), sprinkled with 1 tablespoon sunflower kernels 1 serving Minty Pears* **or** 1/2 medium, fresh pear

Lemon-Blueberry Pancakes

Buttermilk sounds rich, but is made from skim milk and has the same calories as skim milk.

1 cup sifted all-purpose flour	1 tablespoon lemon juice
2 teaspoons baking powder	1 teaspoon lemon peel
1/4 teaspoon salt	1 tablespoon regular margarine, melted
2 teaspoons sugar	1 cup fresh blueberries or drained, thawed,
1 egg, lightly beaten	frozen blueberries
1 cup buttermilk	8 oz. lemon-flavored low-fat yogurt (1 cup)

In a sifter, combine flour, baking powder, salt and sugar; sift into a small bowl. In a medium bowl, combine egg, buttermilk, lemon juice, lemon peel and margarine. Add flour mixture; stir only until flour is moistened. Batter will be lumpy. Using a nonstick griddle or large nonstick skillet, or a griddle or skillet coated with nonstick vegetable spray, place over medium heat until a drop of water sizzles and bounces across surface. For each pancake, pour 1/4 cup batter on griddle or skillet. Sprinkle a generous tablespoon blueberries over each pancake, or reserve blueberries for topping. Bake until bubbles on uncooked side begin to pop and underside is golden brown. Turn; brown other side. **For 1000-Calorie Menu (small serving),** place 1 pancake on each plate. Top each serving with 2 tablespoons yogurt. **For 1200- or 1500-Calorie Menus (large serving),** place 2 pancakes on each plate. Top each serving with 1/4 cup yogurt. Serve immediately. Cool leftover pancakes; wrap in plastic wrap or foil. Refrigerate up to 4 days. To serve, reheat on a griddle or in a toaster. Serve as directed above. Makes 8 small servings or 4 large servings.

---

1 small serving (1 pancake, 2 tablespoons yogurt) = 1/4 milk, 1/2 fruit, 1/2 fat, 135 calories
1 large serving (2 pancakes, 1/4 cup yogurt) = 1/2 milk, 1 fruit, 1 fat, 270 calories
1 pancake = 1 bread, 1/4 fruit, 1/2 fat, 105 calories
2 tablespoons yogurt = 1/4 milk, 1/4 fruit, 30 calories

Crispy Egg-Topper Sandwich

Rice cakes are a crisp alternative to bread at only 35 calories per cake.

2 eggs, hard cooked	1/4 teaspoon salt
1/2 cup low-fat cottage cheese	Dash of white pepper
1 green onion, chopped	2 puffed-rice cakes
1 teaspoon prepared mustard	2/3 cup shredded iceberg lettuce
2 teaspoons reduced-calorie mayonnaise	2 small ripe olives, finely chopped
2 tablespoons buttermilk	

Cut eggs in half crosswise. Cut 2 thin slices of egg; set aside. Remove yolks from remaining eggs. Chop egg whites. In a small bowl, combine chopped egg whites, cottage cheese and green onion; set aside. In another small bowl, mash egg yolks with a fork. Stir in mustard, mayonnaise and buttermilk until blended. Stir egg-yolk mixture into egg-white mixture. Season with salt and white pepper. Place 1 rice cake on each of 2 plates. Spread 1/2 of egg mixture on each rice cake. Arrange 1/3 cup shredded lettuce over top of each serving. Place 1 reserved egg slice on top of each serving. Sprinkle each egg slice with 1/2 of chopped olives. Makes 2 servings.

---

1 serving = 2 meat, 1 bread, 1/2 fat, 180 calories

1200-Calorie Breakfast, clockwise from top right: skim milk; grilled Canadian bacon; Lemon-Blueberry Pancakes.

Scalloped Potatoes & Ham

Evaporated skim milk makes a rich-tasting sauce without many calories.

4 medium boiling potatoes (3 per lb.)
1 tablespoon regular margarine
2 tablespoons all-purpose flour
3/4 cup evaporated skim milk

1-1/2 cups skim milk
1/2 teaspoon salt
2 teaspoons Dijon-style mustard
12 oz. cooked lean ham, cubed (3 cups)

Cook potatoes in 3/4 cup lightly salted boiling water until almost tender, about 20 minutes; drain. Set cooked potatoes aside until cool enough to handle. Peel cooked potatoes; cut in 1/4-inch slices. In a medium saucepan, melt margarine. Add flour; stir until smooth. Gradually add evaporated milk, stirring constantly to prevent lumps. Stir in skim milk, salt and mustard. Stir constantly over medium heat until thickened. Preheat oven to 375F (190C). Layer about 1/3 of potato slices in an ungreased 2-quart casserole dish with a lid. Sprinkle 1/2 of ham over potatoes. Pour 1/3 of thickened sauce over top. Add another layer of potatoes, remaining ham and another 1/3 of sauce. Add remaining potatoes and sauce. Cover; bake in preheated oven until potatoes are tender, about 45 minutes. For a crisp top, remove lid for final 15 minutes of baking. **For 1000- or 1200-Calorie Menus (small serving),** spoon 1 cup scalloped-potato mixture onto each plate. **For 1500-Calorie Menu (large serving),** spoon 1-1/2 cups scalloped-potato mixture onto each plate. Makes 6 small servings or 4 large servings.

---

1 small serving (1 cup) = 2 meat, 1-1/2 bread, 1/2 milk, 1/2 fat, 275 calories
1 large serving (1-1/2 cups) = 3 meat, 2 bread, 3/4 milk, 3/4 fat, 413 calories

---

Minty Pears

The pear slices pick up a light-green color from the minty syrup.

2 tablespoons lemon juice
2 medium, ripe Bartlett, D'Anjou or
    Bosc pears (2-1/2 per lb.)
1/3 cup white-grape juice

1/3 cup water
2 tablespoons green crème de menthe
3 drops green food coloring
6 fresh mint sprigs, if desired

In a medium bowl, combine 1-1/2 cups water and lemon juice; set aside. Peel and core pears; cut in thin lengthwise slices. Immerse pear slices in lemon-water to prevent darkening. In a medium saucepan, combine grape juice and 1/3 cup water. Bring to a boil over medium heat. Using a slotted spoon, lift pears from lemon-water; place in grape-juice mixture. Reduce heat until mixture barely simmers. Cover saucepan; simmer until pears are tender yet still firm, about 10 minutes. Use slotted spoon to remove pears to a medium bowl. Stir crème de menthe and green food coloring into cooking liquid. To remove any small particles of pear, pour mint syrup through a sieve over pears. Let pears and cooking liquid cool to room temperature, stirring gently several times. Serve at room temperature or refrigerate until served, 2 to 3 days. For each serving, spoon 4 or 5 pear slices into a dessert bowl; top with 1/4 cup mint syrup. Garnish each serving with a mint sprig, if desired. Makes 6 servings.

---

1 serving = 1-1/2 fruit, 60 calories

Day 14

1000-Calorie	1200-Calorie	1500-Calorie
	Breakfast	
1/2 cup cooked oatmeal **or** other cooked cereal topped with 2 table-spoons raisins and ground cinnamon to taste 1 serving Breakfast Sausage* 1 cup (8 oz.) skim milk	1/2 cup cooked oatmeal **or** other cooked cereal topped with 2 tablespoons raisins and ground cinnamon to taste 1 serving Breakfast Sausage* 1 whole-wheat-bread slice, toasted 1 teaspoon diet margarine 1 cup (8 oz.) skim milk	1/2 cup cooked oatmeal **or** other cooked cereal topped with 2 tablespoons raisins and ground cinnamon to taste 1 serving Breakfast Sausage* 1 whole-wheat-bread slice, toasted 1 teaspoon diet margarine 1 cup (8 oz.) skim milk
	Lunch	

1 serving Easy Vegetable Chowder* **or** 1 cup canned tomato soup pre-pared with skim milk
Ham and cheese roll:
  1 oz. thinly sliced ham spread with mustard
  1 oz. sliced Swiss cheese
3 saltine crackers
1 small apple **or** 1/2 cup unsweetened applesauce
	1 serving Easy Vegetable Chowder* **or** 1 cup canned tomato soup prepared with skim milk
	1 serving Ham & Cheese Sticks*
	1 small apple **or** 1/2 cup unsweetened applesauce
		1 serving Easy Vegetable Chowder* **or** 1 cup canned tomato soup prepared with skim milk
		6 saltine crackers
		1 serving Ham & Cheese Sticks*
		1 small apple **or** 1/2 cup unsweetened applesauce

	Dinner	

1 serving Ginger-Chicken Soup*, if desired
1 small serving Oriental-Noodles & Meatballs*
Edible-pea-pod salad:
  2 large lettuce leaves
  6 cooked edible pea pods
  4 fresh mushrooms, sliced
  1 tablespoon Sesame-Seed Dressing*
1 serving Peachy Frozen Yogurt* **or** 1/3 cup sliced peaches canned in extra-light syrup and 1/2 cup (4 oz.) skim milk
	1 serving Ginger-Chicken Soup*, if desired
	1 small serving Oriental Noodles & Meatballs*
	12 edible pea pods and 4 fresh mush-rooms, sliced, steamed in 2 table-spoons chicken broth, sprinkled with 1/2 teaspoon sesame seeds **or** 3/4 cup cut green beans
	1 serving Peachy Frozen Yogurt* **or** 1/3 cup sliced peaches canned in extra-light syrup and 1/2 cup (4 oz.) skim milk
		1 serving Ginger-Chicken Soup*, if desired
		1 large serving Oriental Noodles & Meatballs*
		16 edible pea pods and 4 fresh mush-rooms, sliced, steamed in 2 table-spoons chicken broth, sprinkled with 1/2 teaspoon sesame seeds **or** 1 cup cut green beans
		1 serving Peachy Frozen Yogurt* **or** 1/3 cup sliced peaches canned in extra-light syrup and 1/2 cup (4 oz.) skim milk

* Recipe follows.

T̄ip *Peaches canned in extra-light syrup have better color and flavor than water-packed peaches.*

Breakfast Sausage

Look for pork steak with little or no marbling or fat distributed through the meat.

1 lb. boneless lean pork
1/2 whole-wheat-bread slice
1/2 cup skim milk

1 teaspoon salt
1/4 teaspoon dried sage, rubbed
1 tablespoon water

Sausage Seasoning:
2 tablespoons plus 1 teaspoon pepper
1 teaspoon ground cloves

1 teaspoon ground ginger
1 teaspoon ground nutmeg

Prepare Sausage Seasoning; set aside until needed. Trim all fat from pork. Grind pork in a meat grinder or chop in a food processor fitted with a metal blade. Grind or chop several times until meat looks uniform and holds together; set aside. Tear bread into small pieces. In a blender, process bread pieces to fine crumbs. Pour crumbs into a medium bowl. Pour milk over crumbs; let stand 5 minutes. Add ground pork; stir until blended. In a small bowl, combine 3/4 teaspoon Sausage Seasoning, salt and sage. Sprinkle seasoning mixture over meat mixture; stir until blended. Divide sausage mixture into 16 equal portions of about 1 heaping tablespoon each. Shape each portion into a 1/2-inch-thick patty. In a large nonstick skillet or a skillet coated with nonstick vegetable spray, cook sausage patties over medium heat until browned on both sides. Add water to skillet. Reduce heat until water barely simmers. Cover; simmer 5 minutes. Serve sausage hot. To serve later, cool sausage patties; wrap in foil or plastic wrap. Store in refrigerator up to 2 days. For longer storage, wrap cooked or uncooked patties in freezer paper or heavy foil; freeze up to 3 months. Thaw frozen patties in refrigerator overnight. Cook as directed above. Makes 16 patties.
To make Sausage Seasoning, combine all ingredients in a small container with a tight-fitting lid. Cover tightly; shake 10 seconds. Label container with contents and date. Use immediately or store seasoning in a cool dark place 9 to 12 months. Makes about 3 tablespoons.

1 patty = 1 meat, 55 calories

Easy Vegetable Chowder

Instant mashed potatoes thicken the chowder.

1 (14-1/2-oz.) can regular-strength
  chicken broth
Pinch of dried leaf thyme
2 cups frozen mixed vegetables,
  such as green beans, corn and
  green or red bell peppers

2/3 cup instant mashed-potato flakes
1 cup evaporated skim milk, warmed
Salt
Black pepper
1 tablespoon crushed corn chips

In a medium saucepan, combine broth and thyme; bring to a boil. Add vegetables; reduce heat until mixture barely simmers. Cover; simmer 5 minutes. Stirring constantly, slowly sprinkle potato flakes over vegetable mixture. Stir in evaporated milk; season with salt and black pepper. Continue to simmer only until heated through. *Do not let chowder boil.* Ladle into soup bowls. Top each serving with 1/4 of corn chips. Serve hot. Makes 4 (1-cup) servings.

1 serving (1 cup) = 1/2 milk, 3/4 bread, 1 vegetable, 112 calories

How to Make Ham & Cheese Sticks

1/Lay 1 strip of cheese across 1 ham slice. Lay breadstick on ham and cheese, letting extend 1/2 inch beyond both ends of cheese.

2/Roll ham and cheese around breadstick. Place 1/2 teaspoon mustard-cheese mixture at ham point. Roll to point; press to seal.

Ham & Cheese Sticks

These tasty main-dish sticks are fun to make and fun to eat.

2/3 (3-oz.) pkg. Neufchâtel cheese,   room temperature
2 teaspoons reduced-calorie mayonnaise
2 teaspoons Dijon-style mustard

4 (1-oz.) cooked lean ham slices
2 (1-oz.) reduced-calorie Swiss-cheese   or American-cheese slices
8 (4-inch) or 4 (8-inch) breadsticks

In a small bowl, combine Neufchâtel cheese, mayonnaise and mustard. Cut ham slices in half diagonally. Cut each Swiss cheese or American cheese slice into 4 strips. Lay 1 strip of cheese across 1 ham slice from point to diagonally cut edge, letting cheese extend about 1/2 inch beyond diagonally cut edge of ham. Cut 8-inch breadsticks in half. Spread about 1 teaspoon mustard mixture lengthwise on each breadstick, starting and ending about 1/2 inch from both ends. Lay 1 breadstick on ham and cheese so breadstick extends about 1/2 inch beyond both ends of cheese as shown. Roll up to within 1 inch of point of ham. Place 1/2 teaspoon mustard-cheese mixture in a dollop at ham point. Roll breadstick to point; press to seal. Repeat with remaining ingredients. Spoon leftover mustard-cheese mixture into a container with a tight-fitting lid; refrigerate up to 3 days. Makes 8 sticks or 4 servings.

---

1 serving (2 sticks) = 2 meat, 1 bread, 1/2 fat, 200 calories

---

Oriental Noodles & Meatballs

Oriental food stores and some supermarkets have fresh Chinese noodles.

6 oz. fresh Chinese noodles or
   4 oz. dry vermicelli
1/2 cup canned condensed beef broth
1/3 cup water

Oriental Meatballs:
12 oz. extra-lean ground beef
   (10% to 15% fat)
4 oz. lean ground pork (15% fat)
1/4 cup chopped fresh mushrooms (3/4 oz.)

1 tablespoon soy sauce
1 teaspoon cornstarch
1 or 2 green onions with 2-inch green tops

1 teaspoon shredded fresh gingerroot
2 tablespoons chopped green onion
2 tablespoons soy sauce
1 teaspoon sesame oil

Prepare Oriental Meatballs; keep hot. While meatballs bake, cook noodles in lightly salted boiling water until al dente or just tender to the bite. Cook fresh noodles 3 to 5 minutes; cook dry noodles 5 to 7 minutes. Drain cooked noodles; rinse with hot water. Pour noodles into a medium bowl; keep warm. In saucepan used to cook noodles, combine broth, 1/3 cup water, soy sauce and cornstarch. Bring to a boil, stirring constantly. Add drained noodles; stir gently until coated. Cut green onions into brushes or into 2-inch pieces. Cut each piece lengthwise into thin strips. **For 1000- or 1200-Calorie Menus (small serving),** spoon 1/2 cup noodles onto each plate. Top each serving with 5 meatballs. **For 1500-Calorie Menu (large serving),** spoon 1 cup noodles onto each plate. Top each serving with 10 meatballs. **For all menus,** garnish with onion brushes or sprinkle green-onion strips equally over meatballs. Makes 6 small servings or 3 large servings.
To make Oriental Meatballs, preheat oven to 375F (190C). In a medium bowl, combine all ingredients. Roll heaping teaspoons of meat mixture into 30 balls about 1/2-inch in diameter. Place on a nonstick 15'' x 10'' jelly-roll pan or a jelly-roll pan coated with nonstick vegetable spray. Bake in preheated oven until lightly browned, 10 to 15 minutes. Drain off any drippings before serving. Makes 30 meatballs.

---

1 small serving (1/2 cup noodles, 5 meatballs) = 2 meat, 1 bread, 2 fat, 305 calories
1 large serving (1 cup noodles, 10 meatballs) = 4 meat, 2 bread, 4 fat, 610 calories

---

1000-Calorie Dinner, clockwise from top left: Peachy Frozen Yogurt, page 78; Ginger-Chicken Soup, page 79; edible-pea-pod and mushroom salad with Sesame-Seed Dressing, page 78; Oriental Noodles & Meatballs.

Peachy Frozen Yogurt   *Photo on page 77.*

This has the fruity flavor of a sherbet plus the creaminess of ice cream.

1/4 cup water
2 teaspoons lemon juice
2 tablespoons sugar
1-1/3 cups peach nectar

1/2 cup evaporated skim milk
16 oz. plain low-fat yogurt (2 cups)
3 drops yellow food coloring
1 drop red food coloring

In a small saucepan, combine water, lemon juice and sugar. Stir over medium heat until sugar dissolves. Stir in peach nectar. In a medium bowl, combine nectar mixture, evaporated milk and yogurt. Stir in food colorings. Freeze in an ice-cream freezer according to manufacturer's directions or pour into an 8-inch-square baking pan. Cover; still-freeze in freezer compartment of your refrigerator until almost firm, about 1 hour. Spoon partially frozen mixture into a food processor fitted with a metal blade. Process until almost smooth. Or, spoon into a large bowl; beat with an electric mixer until almost smooth. Return mixture to pan. Cover; freeze until firm, about 2 hours. To serve, let sherbet stand at room temperature 10 minutes. Process or beat sherbet again. Serve in sherbet glasses or small glass dessert dishes. Spoon unused portion into a container with a tight-fitting lid; store in freezer up to 3 weeks. Makes 8 (1/2-cup) servings.

Variation
Substitute apricot nectar or strawberry nectar for peach nectar. Delete food coloring. Exchanges and calories will remain the same.

---

1 serving (1/2 cup) = 1 fruit, 1/2 milk, 85 calories

Sesame-Seed Dressing   *Photo on page 77.*

Toasting the sesame seeds brings out the nutty flavor.

1 teaspoon sesame seeds
2 tablespoons vegetable oil
1/4 cup water
2 tablespoons rice vinegar

1 teaspoon soy sauce
2 teaspoons dry pectin
1/4 teaspoon salt
Dash of paprika

In a small heavy skillet, stir sesame seeds over medium-high heat until golden. Watch carefully so seeds don't burn. Set toasted seeds aside. In a small container with a tight-fitting lid, combine oil, water, vinegar, soy sauce, pectin and salt. Cover tightly; shake vigorously 15 seconds. Add toasted sesame seeds and paprika; shake again. Refrigerate until served, up to 24 hours. Shake before using. Makes about 1/2 cup.

---

1 tablespoon = 1/2 fat, 30 calories

Tip   *You'll find rice vinegar in the Oriental-food section of your supermarket.*

How to Make Ginger-Chicken Soup

1/Peel and thinly slice 1-inch-gingerroot piece. Add to broth; simmer 15 minutes. Discard sliced gingerroot.

2/Marinate tofu slices 15 minutes. Add 1 marinated tofu slice to each bowl of soup.

Ginger-Chicken Soup   Photo on page 77.

The spicy tofu gets its flavor from the soy-ginger marinade.

1 (14-1/2-oz.) can regular-strength
  chicken broth
2 teaspoons soy sauce
1 small garlic clove, minced
1 teaspoon minced fresh gingerroot
1 cup water

1 chicken-flavored bouillon cube
1 (1-inch) fresh gingerroot piece
1 oz. tofu, cut in 4 slices
2 large spinach leaves, shredded or chopped
1 tablespoon dry sherry, if desired

In a small bowl, combine 1/4 cup broth, soy sauce, garlic and minced gingerroot; set aside. In a medium saucepan, combine remaining broth, water and bouillon cube. Bring to a boil over high heat; reduce heat until mixture barely simmers. Crush bouillon cube with back of a spoon. Stir until bouillon cube is completely dissolved. Cover; simmer 5 minutes. Meanwhile, peel and thinly slice gingerroot piece; add to hot broth mixture. Cover; simmer over low heat 15 minutes. Add tofu to soy-ginger marinade, turning to coat all sides. Let marinate 15 minutes. Using a slotted spoon, remove and discard sliced gingerroot from bouillon mixture. Add spinach to simmering broth; add sherry, if desired. Simmer 1 minute longer. Remove tofu from marinade. Place 1 marinated tofu slice into each of 4 soup bowls. Ladle 3/4 cup hot broth mixture into each bowl. Makes 4 servings.

---

1 serving (3/4 cup soup, 1 tofu slice) = 1/2 vegetable, 1/4 meat, 35 calories

---

Day 15

1000-Calorie	1200-Calorie	1500-Calorie
Breakfast		
1 small serving French Jelly Rolls* 1/4 cup fresh or frozen unsweetened raspberries with 2 tablespoons low-fat cottage cheese 1 cup (8 oz.) skim milk	1 large serving French Jelly Rolls* 1 tablespoon fresh or frozen un-sweetened raspberries 1 cup (8 oz.) skim milk	1 large serving French Jelly Rolls* 1 tablespoon fresh or frozen un-sweetened raspberries 1 cup (8 oz.) skim milk
Lunch		
1 small serving Pepper-Beef Pocket* 1 serving Piña-Colada Shake* **or** 1 cup (8 oz.) skim milk and 1/2 medium orange 1 Lemon Wafer, page 125	1 small serving Pepper-Beef Pocket* 1 serving Piña-Colada Shake* **or** 1 cup (8 oz.) skim milk and 1/2 medium orange 2 Lemon Wafers, page 125	1 large serving Pepper-Beef Pocket* 1 serving Piña-Colada Shake* **or** 1 cup (8 oz.) skim milk and 1/2 medium orange 2 Lemon Wafers, page 125
Dinner		

1 small serving Fruit & Lamb Kabobs*
2 (1-inch-diameter) new potatoes, cooked, sprinkled with 1 teaspoon chopped green onion
1 serving Artichokes & Lemon-Butter Sauce* **or** 1/2 cup cut green beans
Salad:
  1 cup torn lettuce
  Several watercress sprigs
  Several radish slices
1 tablespoon Thousand Island Dress-ing* **or** reduced-calorie salad dress-ing (25 calories/tablespoon)
 	
* Recipe follows.
	1 small serving Fruit & Lamb Kabobs*
	2 (1-inch-diameter) new potatoes, cooked, sprinkled with 1 teaspoon chopped green onion
	1 serving Artichokes & Lemon-Butter Sauce* **or** 1 cup cut green beans
	Salad:
	  1 cup torn lettuce
	  Several watercress sprigs
	  Several radish slices
	1 tablespoon Thousand Island Dressing* **or** reduced-calorie salad dressing (25 calories/tablespoon)
		1 large serving Fruit & Lamb Kabobs*
		2 (1-inch-diameter) new potatoes, cooked, sprinkled with 1 teaspoon chopped green onion
		1 serving Artichokes & Lemon-Butter Sauce* **or** 1 cup cut green beans
		Salad:
		  1 cup torn lettuce
		  Several watercress sprigs
		  Several radish slices
		1 tablespoon Thousand Island Dressing* **or** reduced-calorie salad dressing (25 calories/tablespoon)

Piña Colada Shake   **Photo on page 27.**

Serve this refreshing drink with a meal or as a snack.

1/2 cup crushed pineapple canned in juice
1-1/2 cups skim milk
2 tablespoons instant nonfat milk powder
1/4 teaspoon coconut extract

1 teaspoon rum extract
2 ice cubes
1 teaspoon unsweetened shredded coconut

In a blender, process pineapple and juice until smooth. Add skim milk, milk powder, coconut extract, rum extract and ice cubes. Process until frothy. Pour shake into 2 drinking glasses. Sprinkle 1/2 teaspoon coconut over each shake. Makes 2 servings.

---

1 serving = 1 milk, 1 fruit, 130 calories

Pepper-Beef Pockets

Like a hamburger in a pocket, only better!

1 or 2 (6-inch) plain or
  whole-wheat pita-bread rounds
1/3 cup canned condensed beef broth
1/3 cup water
1/8 teaspoon ground ginger
1/2 teaspoon soy sauce
6 oz. extra-lean ground beef
  (10% to 15% fat)
2 tablespoons fresh bread crumbs

Black pepper
1/2 medium onion (4 per lb.),
  thinly sliced
1/2 medium, green bell pepper
  (2-1/2 per lb.), cut in strips
1/2 teaspoon cornstarch
2 large romaine-lettuce leaves,
  cut in shreds

Use 1 pita round for small servings and 2 pita rounds for large servings. Wrap pita rounds with foil; place on an ungreased baking sheet. Set aside. In a small bowl, combine broth, water, ginger and soy sauce. In a medium bowl, combine beef, bread crumbs and 2 tablespoons broth mixture. Reserve remaining broth mixture. Shape beef mixture into 2 patties; season with black pepper. Preheat oven to 200F (95C). In a medium nonstick skillet or a skillet coated with nonstick vegetable spray, cook beef patties to desired doneness. Remove beef patties; keep warm. Placed wrapped pita rounds in preheated oven; warm 5 minutes. Meanwhile, add onion and bell pepper to skillet. Sauté until onion is soft. Stir cornstarch into reserved broth mixture until dissolved. Add to skillet; stirring constantly, cook over medium heat until sauce thickens and comes to a boil. Remove from heat. **For 1000- or 1200-Calorie Menus (small serving),** cut 1 warmed pita round in half crosswise. Gently open each half pita. **For 1500-Calorie Menu (large serving),** using 2 warmed pita rounds, cut a thin strip off 1 side of each, making 4-inch openings. Gently open pita pockets. **For all menus,** place 1 pita half or whole pita on each of 2 plates. Insert 1 cooked beef patty in each. Spoon 1/2 of onion mixture into each pocket. Add 1/2 of shredded lettuce to each pocket. Makes 2 small servings or 2 large servings.

---

1 small serving (1 beef patty in half pita) = 2 meat, 1-1/2 bread, 1 vegetable, 1-1/2 fat, 310 calories
1 large serving (1 beef patty in whole pita) = 2 meat, 3 bread, 1 vegetable, 1-1/2 fat, 380 calories

---

Thousand Island Dressing   *Photo on page 83.*

A favorite for salads and sandwiches.

1/4 cup plain low-fat yogurt
1/4 cup reduced-calorie mayonnaise
1/4 cup buttermilk
1 tablespoon chopped dill pickle

1 tablespoon reduced-calorie ketchup
1 teaspoon chopped fresh parsley
Seasoned salt

In a small bowl, combine yogurt, mayonnaise and buttermilk. Stir in pickle, ketchup and parsley. Season with seasoned salt. Cover tightly; refrigerate until served, up to 3 days. Makes about 3/4 cup.

---

2 tablespoons = 3/4 fat, 35 calories

Fruit & Lamb Kabobs

Two kinds of kabobs—each deliciously flavored.

1/4 cup soy sauce
1 garlic clove, crushed
1 teaspoon grated fresh gingerroot
1 tablespoon water
1 tablespoon dry sherry or white wine
1 tablespoon lime juice or lemon juice

1 teaspoon brown sugar
1 teaspoon Dijon-style mustard
1 lb. well-trimmed boneless leg of lamb
1 (16-oz.) can chunky salad fruit
  in extra-light syrup, drained, rinsed
6 large cilantro sprigs, if desired

In a medium bowl, combine soy sauce, garlic, gingerroot, water, sherry or wine, lime juice or lemon juice, brown sugar and mustard. Stir until sugar dissolves. Trim any fat from lamb; discard fat. Cut trimmed lamb into 1-inch cubes. Add lamb cubes to soy-sauce mixture. Cover; marinate 1 to 3 hours in refrigerator, turning occasionally. Drain lamb cubes, reserving marinade. Preheat broiler. Put 4 or 5 lamb cubes on each of 6 skewers. Brush skewered lamb with reserved marinade. Place lamb kabobs on a rack in a broiler pan. Broil lamb kabobs 4 inches from heat, 5 to 7 minutes. Turn kabobs once, brushing with marinade before and after turning. Meanwhile, put 4 or 5 fruit chunks on each of 3 skewers for large servings or 6 skewers for small servings. Brush skewered fruit with reserved marinade. Broil fruit kabobs during last 2 minutes lamb kabobs are broiled, turning and brushing with marinade once. **For 1000- or 1200-Calorie Menus (small serving),** place 1 lamb kabob and 1 fruit kabob on each plate. **For 1500-Calorie Menu (large serving),** place 2 lamb kabobs and 1 fruit kabob on each plate. **For all menus,** garnish with 1 or 2 cilantro sprigs, if desired. Makes 6 small servings or 3 large servings.

---

1 small serving (1 lamb kabob, 1 fruit kabob) = 2-1/2 meat, 1 fruit, 195 calories
1 large serving (2 lamb kabobs, 1 fruit kabob) = 5 meat, 1 fruit, 350 calories

---

French Jelly Rolls

Use soft bread because a firm-textured bread will not roll up.

1/3 (3-oz.) pkg. Neufchâtel cheese,
  room temperature
3 tablespoons skim milk
4 soft bread slices

2 tablespoons plus 2 teaspoons
  reduced-calorie raspberry spread
1 egg, lightly beaten
1 tablespoon regular margarine

In a small bowl, stir cheese and 1 tablespoon milk until smooth. Trim crusts from bread. Use crusts for another purpose. Using a rolling pin, roll over each trimmed bread slice to flatten slightly. Spread about 1 tablespoon cheese mixture and 2 teaspoons raspberry spread on each flattened bread slice. Roll up each slice, jelly-roll style. Wrap separately in waxed paper or plastic wrap. Refrigerate until ready to serve, up to 24 hours. In a pie plate, combine egg and remaining 2 tablespoons milk. In a medium nonstick skillet or a skillet coated with nonstick vegetable spray, melt margarine. Remove waxed paper or plastic wrap from jelly rolls. Working quickly, dip jelly rolls into egg mixture, turning to coat all sides. Cook coated jelly rolls in skillet until lightly browned. **For 1000-Calorie Menu (small serving),** serve 1 browned jelly roll on each plate. **For 1200- or 1500-Calorie Menus (large serving),** serve 2 browned jelly rolls on each plate. Serve warm. Makes 4 small servings or 2 large servings.

---

1 small serving (1 roll) = 1 bread, 1/2 meat, 1/2 fruit, 1 fat, 165 calories
1 large serving (2 rolls) = 2 bread, 1 meat, 1 fruit, 2 fat, 330 calories

---

1200-Calorie Dinner, clockwise from center top: Artichokes & Lemon-Butter Sauce, page 84; salad with Thousand Island Dressing, page 81; Fruit & Lamb Kabobs; new potatoes.

Artichokes & Lemon-Butter Sauce   *Photo on page 83.*

This butter sauce is excellent on cooked vegetables.

4 medium artichokes (1-1/2 per lb.)   **1 lemon (5 per lb.), sliced**

Lemon-Butter Sauce:
1 tablespoon regular margarine   **1/4 cup fresh lemon juice**
1 small garlic clove, minced   **2 tablespoons tarragon-flavored vinegar or**
2 tablespoons chopped fresh parsley   **wine vinegar**
1/4 teaspoon seasoned salt

Using kitchen shears, cut sharp tips from outer leaves of artichokes. Cut off stem ends so artichokes stand level. Cut off top 1 inch of tightly closed inner leaves. Separate inner leaves enough to insert a spoon; use spoon to remove choke from center of artichokes. Pour water into a 4-quart pot until half full. Bring water to a boil over high heat. Add lemon and trimmed artichokes; cover. When water comes back to a boil, reduce heat until water barely simmers. Simmer 20 to 30 minutes until artichokes are tender when pierced with a fork at stem ends. While artichokes cook, prepare Lemon-Butter Sauce. Drain artichokes, discarding water and lemon. Invert artichokes on paper towels to drain 1 minute. To serve, place 1 cooked artichoke on each of 4 plates. Spoon 2 tablespoons sauce onto each plate for dipping leaves. Serve hot. Makes 4 servings.
To make Lemon-Butter Sauce, in a small saucepan, melt margarine. Add garlic and parsley; sauté 1 minute. Add seasoned salt, lemon juice and vinegar. Stir over medium heat 1 minute. Serve warm. Makes about 1/2 cup.

---

1 serving (1 artichoke, 2 tablespoons sauce) = 1 vegetable, 1 fat, 65 calories
2 tablespoons sauce = 1 fat, 30 calories

 Tip   *Reduced-calorie cheese has half the calories of regular-process cheese.*

Day 16

1000-Calorie	1200-Calorie	1500-Calorie
## Breakfast		
2 small prunes, cooked in water, no sugar added 1 serving Cottage Breakfast Pudding*	2 small prunes, cooked in water, no added sugar 1 serving Cottage Breakfast Pudding* 1 whole-wheat-bread slice, toasted 1 teaspoon diet margarine	2 small prunes, cooked in water, no sugar added 1 serving Cottage Breakfast Pudding* 1 whole-wheat-bread slice, toasted 1 teaspoon diet margarine
## Lunch		
1 serving Quick Vegetable Soup, page 57, **or** 1/2 cup (4 oz.) tomato juice **or** vegetable-juice cocktail 1 serving Asparagus-Pasta Salad* 10 fresh or frozen unsweetened dark sweet cherries 1 cup (8 oz.) skim milk	1 serving Quick Vegetable Soup, page 57, **or** 1/2 cup (4 oz.) tomato juice **or** vegetable-juice cocktail 1 serving Asparagus-Pasta Salad* 1 small crusty hard roll 1 teaspoon diet margarine 10 fresh or frozen, unsweetened dark sweet cherries 1 cup (8 oz.) skim milk	1 cup canned Manhattan-style clam chowder prepared as directed 1 serving Asparagus-Pasta Salad* 1 small crusty hard roll 1 teaspoon diet margarine 10 fresh or frozen, unsweetened dark sweet cherries 1 cup (8 oz.) skim milk
## Dinner		
1 serving Orange Chicken Breasts* 1/3 cup cooked brown rice tossed with 1 teaspoon diet margarine and pinch each of parsley and rosemary 1/3 cup French-style green beans cooked with 2 tablespoons julienned carrot and 1 teaspoon diet margarine 1 serving Hawaiian Soufflé, page 120, **or** 1/3 cup low-fat pineapple-flavored yogurt * Recipe follows.	1 serving Orange Chicken Breasts* 1/3 cup cooked brown rice tossed with 1 teaspoon diet margarine and pinch each of parsley and rosemary 1/2 cup French-style green beans cooked with 1/4 cup julienned carrot and 1 teaspoon diet margarine 1 serving Hawaiian Soufflé, page 120, **or** 1/3 cup low-fat pineapple-flavored yogurt	1 serving Orange Chicken Breasts* 1 cup cooked brown rice, tossed with 1 teaspoon diet margarine and pinch each of parsley and rosemary 2/3 cup French-style green beans, cooked with 1/4 cup julienned carrot and 1 teaspoon diet margarine 1 serving Hawaiian Soufflé, page 120, **or** 1/3 cup low-fat pineapple-flavored yogurt

Asparagus-Pasta Salad

An easy salad to pack for a brown-bag lunch.

4 oz. uncooked spiral pasta (1 cup)
6 fresh asparagus stalks or
   3/4 cup thawed frozen cut asparagus
1/4 cup coarsely chopped red onion

7 oz. cooked lean ham, diced (1-3/4 cups)
2 tablespoons crumbled blue cheese
4 red-leaf-lettuce leaves
4 lemon slices

Lemon-Tarragon Dressing:
1 tablespoon vegetable oil
1 tablespoon plus 1 teaspoon
   tarragon-flavored vinegar or
   wine vinegar

1 tablespoon plus 2 teaspoons water
1/4 teaspoon grated lemon peel
1/8 teaspoon dried leaf tarragon, crushed
1 teaspoon beaten egg

Prepare Lemon-Tarragon Dressing; refrigerate until served. Cook pasta in lightly salted boiling water until al dente or just tender to the bite, 5 to 7 minutes. Drain; rinse with cold water. Pour into a large bowl or container with a tight-fitting lid; cover. Cut fresh asparagus in 1-inch pieces. Steam fresh asparagus pieces until crisp-tender, about 3 minutes. Cool quickly in cold water to prevent overcooking. Drain cooked fresh asparagus or thawed frozen asparagus on paper towels. Add drained asparagus pieces, onion, ham and cheese to pasta; toss gently to distribute. Pour dressing over pasta mixture; toss again. Cover and refrigerate until ready to serve, up to 3 days. Arrange 1 lettuce leaf on each of 4 plates. Spoon salad equally onto lettuce-lined plates. Cut each lemon slice from center through peel. Twist cut edges of peel in opposite directions, making lemon twists. Garnish each salad with a lemon twist. Makes 4 servings.
To make Lemon-Tarragon Dressing, in a small bowl, combine all dressing ingredients. Beat with a whisk until blended. Combine with salad. Makes about 1/4 cup dressing.

Variations
Substitute 1 cup steamed cut fresh green beans, steamed cut fresh broccoli flowerets or thawed frozen chopped broccoli for asparagus. Prepare salad and dressing as directed above. Exchanges and calories will remain the same.

---

1 serving = 2 meat, 1 bread, 1/2 vegetable, 1 fat, 225 calories

---

Tip   *Spiral pasta is also called "fusilli" or "rotelle."*

1000-Calorie Lunch, clockwise from top left: Asparagus-Pasta Salad; fresh or frozen dark sweet cherries; Quick Vegetable Soup, page 57.

Cottage Breakfast Pudding

You can prepare this the night before and bake it in the morning for a quick hot breakfast.

1 small Rome Beauty or other cooking apple (4 per lb.)	1 cup skim milk
2 tablespoons water	1 cup evaporated skim milk
1 teaspoon diet margarine	1/4 teaspoon salt
3/4 teaspoon ground cinnamon	2-1/2 teaspoons sugar
2 eggs	4 whole-wheat-bread or white-bread slices
	1/3 cup low-fat cottage cheese

Peel, core and slice apple. In a small saucepan, combine sliced apple, water, margarine and 1/2 teaspoon cinnamon. Cover; simmer until apple is tender, about 15 minutes. In a medium bowl, beat eggs; stir in skim milk, evaporated milk, salt and 2 teaspoons sugar until blended. Set aside. Cut crusts from bread; use crusts for another purpose. Place 2 trimmed bread slices in a single layer in a shallow casserole dish. Spread cottage cheese over bread slices. Use a slotted spoon to lift cooked apple slices from cooking liquid. Arrange over cottage cheese. Stir any cooking liquid from apples into egg mixture. Top apple slices with remaining 2 bread slices. Pour egg mixture over bread stacks. Refrigerate at least 1 hour or overnight. Preheat oven to 350F (175C). In a small bowl, combine remaining 1/2 teaspoon sugar and 1/4 teaspoon cinnamon. Sprinkle over pudding. Bake in preheated oven until puffy and lightly browned, about 1 hour. Cut each bread stack in half diagonally. Place 1/2 of each stack on each of 4 plates. Makes 4 servings.

1 serving = 1 bread, 1 meat, 1/2 fruit, 1/2 milk, 1/2 fat, 205 calories

Orange Chicken Breasts

Special enough for company, but quick to prepare.

1 medium orange (2 per lb.)	1 chicken-flavored bouillon cube
4 (3-oz.) boned, skinned chicken-breast halves or 4 (4-oz.) skinned chicken thighs	1/8 teaspoon dried leaf tarragon
2 teaspoons vegetable oil	1 tablespoon cornstarch
1/2 cup water	1 tablespoon cold water

Using a vegetable peeler, remove only colored part of orange peel. Cut peel into thin strips. Juice orange; reserve 1/2 cup orange juice and orange-peel strips. Remove and discard fat from chicken breasts or thighs; set aside. In a large nonstick skillet or a skillet coated with nonstick vegetable spray, heat oil. Add trimmed chicken; brown on all sides. Add 1/2 cup water and bouillon cube. Bring to a boil over high heat; reduce heat until water barely simmers. Crush bouillon cube with back of a spoon. Stir until bouillon cube is completely dissolved. Sprinkle tarragon and 1/2 of orange-peel strips over chicken. Cover; simmer 15 minutes. Remove cooked chicken from skillet; keep warm. Strain cooking liquid through a sieve into a small saucepan; discard strained out orange peel. Add reserved orange juice to strained cooking liquid. In a small bowl, combine cornstarch and 1 tablespoon water. Stir into orange-juice mixture. Bring to a boil, stirring constantly. Continue stirring until slightly thickened. If using chicken breasts, make crosswise parallel cuts in thickest parts, 1 inch apart, almost all the way through. Return scored chicken breasts or thighs to skillet. Pour orange sauce over chicken. Sprinkle with remaining orange peel. Simmer 5 minutes. To serve, place 1 cooked chicken breast or thigh on each of 4 plates. Pour 1/4 of orange sauce over each serving. Makes 4 servings.

1 serving = 3 meat, 1/2 fruit, 170 calories

Day 17

1000-Calorie	1200-Calorie	1500-Calorie
Breakfast		
1 serving Egg 'n Ham Muffins* 1/2 grapefruit **or** 1/2 cup (4 oz.) orange juice 1 cup (8 oz.) skim milk	1 serving Egg 'n Ham Muffins* 1/2 English muffin, toasted 1-1/2 teaspoons diet margarine 1/2 grapefruit **or** 1/2 cup (4 oz.) orange juice 1 cup (8 oz.) skim milk	1 serving Egg 'n Ham Muffins* 1/2 English muffin, toasted 1-1/2 teaspoons diet margarine 1/2 grapefruit **or** 1/2 cup (4 oz.) orange juice 1 cup (8 oz.) skim milk
Lunch		
1 serving Reuben Sandwich* 1 dill-pickle spear 1 serving Spicy Date Shake* **or** 1 cup (8 oz.) skim milk and 4 dried apricot halves	1 serving Reuben Sandwich* 1 small serving Oven-Fried Potatoes* 1 dill-pickle spear 1 serving Spicy Date Shake* **or** 1 cup (8 oz.) skim milk and 4 dried apricot halves	1 serving Reuben Sandwich* 1 large serving Oven-Fried Potatoes* 1 dill-pickle spear 1 serving Spicy Date Shake* **or** 1 cup (8 oz.) skim milk and 4 dried apricot halves
Dinner		
1 small serving Turkey in Lacy Corn Crepes* Salad: 1-1/2 cups torn romaine lettuce 1 tablespoon coarsely shredded carrot 1-1/2 tablespoons Blue-Cheese Dressing* **or** reduced-calorie salad dressing (25 calories/tablespoon) 1 serving Caramel Baked Apple, page 124, **or** 1/2 cup warm unsweetened applesauce with ground cinnamon to taste	1 small serving Turkey in Lacy Corn Crepes* 2 tomato slices, sprinkled with dill weed, broiled Salad: 1 cup torn romaine lettuce 1 tablespoon coarsely shredded carrot 1-1/2 tablespoons Blue-Cheese Dressing* **or** reduced-calorie salad dressing (25 calories/tablespoon) 1 serving Caramel Baked Apple, page 124, **or** 1/2 cup warm unsweetened applesauce with ground cinnamon to taste	1 large serving Turkey in Lacy Corn Crepes* 2 tomato slices sprinkled with dill weed, broiled Salad: 1 cup torn romaine lettuce, 1 tablespoon coarsely shredded carrot 1 tablespoon seasoned croutons 1-1/2 tablespoons Blue-Cheese Dressing* **or** reduced-calorie salad dressing (25 calories/tablespoon) 1 serving Caramel Baked Apple, page 124, **or** 1/2 cup warm unsweetened applesauce, with ground cinnamon to taste

* Recipe follows.

Blue-Cheese Dressing   *Photo on page 93.*

A small amount of blue cheese makes a flavorful dressing.

1/4 cup plain low-fat yogurt
1/4 cup reduced-calorie mayonnaise
1/4 cup buttermilk
1/4 teaspoon prepared mustard

1/8 teaspoon garlic salt
1 tablespoon crumbled blue cheese
Beau Monde seasoning or
Bon Appetit seasoning

In a small bowl, combine yogurt, mayonnaise and buttermilk. Stir in mustard and garlic salt. Stir in cheese. Season with Beau Monde seasoning or Bon Appetit seasoning. Cover tightly; refrigerate until served, up to 3 days. Makes about 3/4 cup.

1-1/2 tablespoons = 3/4 fat, 35 calories

Egg 'n Ham Muffins

For nondieters, add another muffin half for an easy-to-eat breakfast sandwich.

4 cherry tomatoes
2 whole-wheat or plain English muffins,
  split
2 tablespoons plus 1 teaspoon diet margarine
3 large eggs
1 tablespoon skim milk
1/8 teaspoon salt

1 tablespoon finely chopped onion
1 tablespoon finely chopped
  green bell pepper
1 oz. cooked lean ham, diced (1/4 cup)
1 tablespoon plus 1 teaspoon chopped
  ripe olives

Cut each cherry tomato in half from top to bottom; set aside. Toast English muffins. Spread each half with 1 teaspoon margarine. Keep muffins warm. In a medium bowl, beat eggs; stir in milk and salt. In a 10-inch skillet, melt remaining 1 tablespoon margarine. Add onion, bell pepper and ham; sauté until onion is soft. Pour egg mixture over ham mixture. Cook over medium heat, stirring frequently, until eggs are set but still moist. To serve, place 1 toasted muffin half on each of 4 plates. Spoon 1/4 of egg mixture onto each toasted muffin half. Top each with 1 teaspoon olives and 1/2 cherry tomato. Serve immediately. Makes 4 servings.

1 serving = 1 meat, 1 bread, 1 fat, 185 calories

Reuben Sandwich

Be sure to ask for corned bottom round of beef because corned brisket has too much fat.

1 (15-oz.) can sauerkraut, drained
4 dark-rye-bread or
  pumpernickel-bread slices
4 oz. very thinly sliced lean corned
  bottom round of beef

4 reduced-calorie Swiss-cheese slices
  (2-2/3 oz.)
1 teaspoon regular margarine

Special Dressing:
1 tablespoon plus 1-1/2 teaspoons
  plain low-fat yogurt
1 tablespoon plus 1-1/2 teaspoons
  reduced-calorie mayonnaise

1/2 teaspoon prepared mustard
1/2 teaspoon regular ketchup
1 tablespoon chopped dill pickle
Dash of paprika

Prepare Special Dressing; refrigerate until served. Rinse and drain sauerkraut. In a small saucepan, heat sauerkraut over medium-low heat. Arrange bread slices on a flat surface. Top each bread slice with 1 ounce corned beef and 1 cheese slice. Spread 1/4 of dressing over each sandwich. Spoon 1/3 cup hot sauerkraut onto each serving. In a large nonstick skillet or griddle or a skillet or griddle coated with nonstick vegetable spray, melt margarine. Place open-faced sandwiches in skillet or on griddle, bread-side down. Cook until bread is toasted and cheese begins to melt. Place 1 toasted sandwich on each of 4 plates. Serve warm. Makes 4 servings.
To make Special Dressing, in a small bowl, blend yogurt and mayonnaise. Stir in mustard, ketchup and pickle. Season with paprika. Cover tightly; refrigerate until served, up to 3 days. Makes about 1/4 cup.

1 serving = 1 bread, 2 meat, 1 vegetable, 1/2 fat, 228 calories

Oven-Fried Potatoes

These crisp potato rounds are tender on the inside, crispy on the outside.

3 tablespoons fine dried bread crumbs
1/4 teaspoon salt
1/4 teaspoon paprika

1/2 teaspoon dried parsley
2 medium baking potatoes (3 per lb.)
2 tablespoons diet margarine, melted

Preheat oven to 400F (205C). In a pie pan, combine crumbs, salt, paprika and parsley; set aside. Scrub potatoes lightly with a brush; rinse. Cut scrubbed potatoes in 1/4-inch crosswise slices. Brush both sides of potato slices with margarine. Dip in crumb mixture, turning to coat both sides. Place coated potato slices in a 13'' x 9'' nonstick baking pan or in a baking pan coated with nonstick vegetable spray. Sprinkle with any remaining margarine. Bake in preheated oven until potatoes are tender and lightly browned, about 30 minutes. Turn once during baking. **For 1000- or 1200-Calorie Menus (small serving),** serve 3 potato slices on each plate. **For 1500-Calorie Menu (large serving),** serve 6 potato slices on each plate. Makes 4 small servings or 2 large servings.

1 small serving (3 potato slices) = 1 bread, 1 fat, 115 calories
1 large serving (6 potato slices) = 2 bread, 2 fat, 230 calories

Spicy Date Shake

Serve immediately for an icy, foamy drink.

1/3 cup chopped dried dates
3/4 cup water
1/4 teaspoon pumpkin-pie spice
3 cups skim milk

1/3 cup instant nonfat milk powder
1 teaspoon vanilla extract
6 ice cubes

In a small saucepan, combine dates, water and pumpkin-pie spice. Bring to a boil. Cook over medium-low heat until dates soften and form a paste, about 10 minutes, stirring occasionally. In a blender, combine skim milk, milk powder and vanilla. Process until smooth. Add date paste; process 30 seconds. Add ice cubes; process until ice cubes are finely chopped. Serve in drinking glasses. Makes 4 servings.

1 serving = 1 fruit, 1 milk, 130 calories

Turkey in Lacy Corn Crepes

Freeze the extra crepes and serve for a breakfast with fruit and yogurt.

2 tablespoons diet margarine
1/4 cup chopped onion
2 cups fresh broccoli flowerets or
    partially thawed frozen cut broccoli
1 cup sliced fresh mushrooms (3 oz.)
8 oz. cooked turkey or chicken,
    diced (2 cups)

3/4 cup canned or homemade chicken broth
2 tablespoons all-purpose flour
1 tablespoon cornstarch
1 cup skim milk
1/4 teaspoon dried leaf thyme
Dash of salt
Dash of pepper

Lacy Corn Crepes:
1 cup cornmeal
1/3 cup all-purpose flour
1/2 teaspoon salt

2 eggs, lightly beaten
2 cups buttermilk
2 tablespoons diet margarine, melted

In a large nonstick skillet or a skillet coated with nonstick vegetable spray, melt margarine. Add onion, broccoli and mushrooms. Cook 1 minute, stirring gently to coat vegetables. Reserve 4 or 6 mushroom slices and 4 or 6 broccoli flowerets or broccoli pieces for garnish. Add turkey or chicken and 2 tablespoons broth to skillet; toss again. Reduce heat until mixture barely simmers. Cover; simmer 10 minutes. Meanwhile, in a medium saucepan, combine flour and cornstarch. Stir in remaining broth until mixture is smooth. Stir in milk. Cook over medium-high heat, stirring constantly, until sauce comes to a boil and thickens slightly. Season with thyme, salt and pepper. Keep sauce warm. Prepare Lacy Corn Crepes. Stir turkey-and-vegetable mixture into warm sauce. Place 1 crepe on a flat surface. Spoon about 1/3 cup sauce mixture across center of crepe. Fold crepe over filling; roll up. Repeat with remaining crepes and filling. **For 1000- or 1200-Calorie Menus (small serving),** place 2 rolled crepes on each plate. **For 1500-Calorie Menu (large serving),** place 3 rolled crepes on each plate. **For all menus,** garnish servings equally with reserved mushroom slices and broccoli flowerets or broccoli pieces. Makes 6 small servings or 4 large servings. **To make Lacy Corn Crepes,** in a medium bowl, blend cornmeal, flour and salt. In another medium bowl, combine egg, buttermilk and margarine. Stir into flour mixture. Place a 7-inch nonstick skillet or a skillet coated with nonstick vegetable spray over medium heat. When hot, pour 1/4 cup crepe batter into skillet. Rotate pan to cover bottom with batter. Cook until lightly browned. Turn crepe; cook 30 seconds longer. Remove from pan, cover and keep warm. Repeat with remaining batter, making 12 crepes. Serve as directed above. Wrap unused cooled crepes in foil or place in a plastic bag; refrigerate up to 2 days. For longer storage, place in a freezer bag; freeze up to 3 weeks. Thaw in refrigerator overnight or at room temperature about 20 minutes. Makes 12 crepes.

---

1 small serving (2 filled crepes with garnish) = 2 meat, 1/2 milk, 1 vegetable, 1-1/2 bread, 1 fat, 340 calories

1 large serving (3 filled crepes with garnish) = 3 meat, 3/4 milk, 1-1/2 vegetables, 2-1/4 bread, 1-1/2 fat, 511 calories

1 crepe without sauce = 3/4 bread, 1/2 fat, 70 calories

1200-Calorie Dinner, clockwise from top left: Caramel Baked Apple, page 124; romaine lettuce and shredded carrot salad with Blue-Cheese Dressing, page 89; broiled tomato slices with dill; Turkey in Lacy Corn Crepes.

Day 18

1000-Calorie	1200-Calorie	1500-Calorie
Breakfast		
1 serving Whole-Wheat-Banana Toast* 1/2 cup plain low-fat yogurt, flavored with almond or vanilla extract **or** 1/2 cup (4 oz.) skim milk	1 serving Whole-Wheat-Banana Toast* 3/4 cup unsweetened ready-to-eat cereal 1/2 cup (4 oz.) skim milk	1 serving Whole-Wheat-Banana Toast* 3/4 cup unsweetened ready-to-eat cereal 1/2 cup (4 oz.) skim milk
Lunch		
1 serving Fruited Chicken Salad* 1 serving Cool Chlodnick Soup* 2 rye wafers	1 serving Fruited Chicken Salad* 1 serving Cool Chlodnick Soup* 1/2 pumpernickel bagel **or** whole-wheat bagel 1-1/2 teaspoons diet margarine	1 serving Fruited Chicken Salad* 1 serving Cool Chlodnick Soup* 1 pumpernickel bagel **or** whole-wheat bagel 1 tablespoon diet margarine
Dinner		

1 small serving South-of-the-Border Shrimp Cocktail*
1 small serving Green-Chili Enchiladas*
Salad:
  1 cup shredded iceberg lettuce
  1 tomato slice
  1 pickled mild pepper
  2 tablespoons Chunky Salsa, page 68
1 serving Marinated-Melon Kabobs* **or** 1/3 cup fruit cocktail in extra-light syrup
	1 small serving South of the Border Shrimp Cocktail*
	1 small serving Green-Chili Enchiladas*
	Salad:
	  1 cup shredded iceberg lettuce
	  1 tomato slice
	  1 pickled mild pepper
	  2 tablespoons Chunky Salsa, page 68
	1/2 cup sliced zucchini cooked with 3 small red onion rings and 1 teaspoon diet margarine
	1 serving Marinated-Melon Kabobs* **or** 1/3 cup fruit cocktail in extra-light syrup
		1 large serving South-of-the-Border Shrimp Cocktail*
		1 large serving Green-Chili Enchiladas*
		Salad:
		  1 cup shredded iceberg lettuce
		  1 tomato slice
		  1 pickled mild pepper
		  2 tablespoons Chunky Salsa, page 68
		1/2 cup sliced zucchini cooked with 3 small red onion rings and 1 teaspoon diet margarine
		1 serving Marinated-Melon Kabobs* **or** 1/3 cup fruit cocktail in extra-light syrup

* Recipe follows.

Whole-Wheat-Banana Toast

Good for a quick breakfast.

4 whole-wheat-bread slices, toasted
1/4 cup peanut butter
2 small bananas (4 per lb.)

1/4 cup granola or other unsweetened ready-to-eat cereal

Spread each toast slice with 1 tablespoon peanut butter. For each slice, cut 1/2 banana into thin slices. Arrange slices in rows diagonally across toast. Sprinkle 1 tablespoon granola or other cereal over banana slices. Place 1 banana-and-granola-topped toast slice on each of 4 plates. Serve immediately. Makes 4 servings.

1 serving = 1 bread, 1/2 meat, 1 fruit, 1-1/2 fat, 215 calories

Fruited Chicken Salad

Peaches, grapes, avocado and a tart honey dressing make this chicken salad special.

1/2 cup uncooked small pasta shells
6 oz. cooked chicken, diced (1-1/2 cups)
1/4 medium avocado (3 per lb.), diced
1 green onion, sliced
2 tablespoons chopped fresh parsley

Mustard-Poppy-Seed Dressing:
3 tablespoons rice vinegar
1 tablespoon honey
2 teaspoons vegetable oil
1/8 teaspoon dry mustard

2 medium peaches (3 per lb.), peeled,
 sliced, or 2/3 cup peach slices canned
 in extra-light syrup, drained
5 red seedless grapes, cut in half
1/2 head iceberg lettuce, shredded

1/8 teaspoon salt
1 teaspoon grated onion
1 teaspoon poppy seeds

Prepare Mustard-Poppy-Seed Dressing; refrigerate until served. Cook pasta shells in lightly salted boiling water according to package directions until al dente or just tender to the bite, 5 to 7 minutes. Drain pasta; rinse with cold water to cool and stop cooking. Pour cooked pasta shells into a large bowl. Add chicken, avocado, green onion, parsley, peaches and grapes. Pour dressing over salad; stir gently. Refrigerate until ready to serve, up to 1 hour. Arrange 1/4 of lettuce on each of 4 plates. Top each with about 1 cup salad mixture. Serve immediately. Makes 4 servings.
To make Mustard-Poppy-Seed Dressing, in a small container with a tight-fitting lid, combine all ingredients except poppy seeds. Cover tightly; shake vigorously 15 seconds. Add poppy seeds; cover and shake again. Refrigerate until served, up to 3 days. Shake before using. Makes about 1/4 cup.

---

1 serving = 2 meat, 1/2 bread, 1 fruit, 190 calories
1 tablespoon dressing = 1/4 fruit, 1/2 fat, 35 calories

Cool Chlodnick Soup

This delicate, pink, Russian beet soup is cool and refreshing.

1 qt. buttermilk (4 cups)
1 tablespoon lemon juice
1 (16-oz.) can small whole beets,
 drained, thinly sliced
1/2 medium cucumber (2 per lb.),
 peeled, shredded

1/2 teaspoon salt
1/8 teaspoon white pepper
1 teaspoon dried dill weed
4 fresh dill sprigs or fresh parsley sprigs

Pour buttermilk into a large container with a tight-fitting lid. Stir in lemon juice. Add beets, cucumber, salt, white pepper and dill weed. Stir gently. Refrigerate soup at least 4 hours. Serve cold soup in glass bowls or other soup bowls. Garnish each with a dill sprig or parsley sprig. Makes 6 (1-cup) servings.

---

1 serving (1 cup) = 3/4 milk, 1 vegetable, 80 calories

South-of-the-Border Shrimp Cocktail

Delightfully flavored with lime and cilantro.

8 oz. medium shrimp (about 20)
1 teaspoon vegetable oil
1 garlic clove, minced
2 tablespoons chopped onion

Lime Marinade:
1/4 cup dry white wine
2 tablespoons lime juice
1 tablespoon chopped cilantro or
   fresh parsley

2 or 4 Bibb-lettuce leaves
4 pimento-stuffed green olives,
   each cut in 3 slices
4 cilantro sprigs or parsley sprigs

1/4 teaspoon salt
1 canned jalapeño pepper, if desired, diced

Prepare Lime Marinade; set aside. Peel and devein shrimp. Rinse under running cold water. Drain shrimp on paper towels. Place a small nonstick skillet or a skillet coated with nonstick vegetable spray over medium heat. Brush oil over bottom of skillet. Add cleaned shrimp, garlic and onion. Cook, stirring constantly, until shrimp turn pink. Let cool to room temperature. Place cooled shrimp mixture in a container with a tight-fitting lid. Pour marinade over shrimp mixture; stir to coat shrimp. Cover; refrigerate shrimp mixture at least 4 hours or overnight. Drain off and discard marinade. To serve, arrange lettuce leaves on individual plates. **For 1000- or 1200-Calorie Menus (small serving),** arrange 5 shrimp and 3 olive slices on each plate. **For 1500-Calorie Menu (large serving),** arrange 10 shrimp and 6 olive slices on each plate. **For all menus,** garnish each plate with a cilantro sprig or parsley sprig. Makes 4 small servings or 2 large servings. **To make Lime Marinade,** in a small bowl, combine wine, lime juice, chopped cilantro or parsley, salt and jalapeño pepper, if desired. Makes about 1/2 cup.

---

1 small serving (5 shrimp) = 1-1/2 meat, 1/2 fat, 82 calories
1 large serving (10 shrimp) = 3 meat, 1 fat, 165 calories

1000-Calorie Dinner, clockwise from right: Marinated-Melon Kabobs, page 98; South-of-the-Border Shrimp Cocktail; Green-Chili Enchiladas, page 98; lettuce and tomato salad with pickled pepper.

Green-Chili Enchiladas   *Photo on page 97.*

This Mexican-American dish is a favorite in the American Southwest.

4 oz. Monterey Jack cheese
1 (4-oz.) can whole green chilies, drained

6 (6-inch) corn tortillas
1/2 cup shredded sharp Cheddar cheese (2 oz.)

Enchilada Sauce:
1 cup water
1 chicken-flavored bouillon cube
1 cup tomato juice
2 tablespoons all-purpose flour

1 tablespoon chili powder
1/2 teaspoon ground cumin
1/4 cup cold water

Prepare Enchilada Sauce; keep warm. Cut Monterey Jack cheese into 6 sticks. Cut each green chili in half lengthwise; discard seeds. Cut each half into 2 lengthwise strips. Preheat oven to 350F (175C). Heat 1 tortilla at a time on an ungreased griddle until tortilla softens, turning several times. Dip 1 hot tortilla at a time into warm Enchilada Sauce, coating both sides. Place coated tortilla in an ungreased 11'' x 7'' casserole dish. Lay 1 cheese stick across center of tortilla; add 2 chili strips. Fold tortilla in half over cheese and chili strips; roll up. Turn seam-side down; leave in dish. Repeat with remaining tortillas. Pour remaining Enchilada Sauce over rolled tortillas. Bake in preheated oven 15 minutes. Sprinkle Cheddar cheese over top; bake 5 minutes longer. Serve hot. **For 1000- or 1200-Calorie Menus (small serving),** serve 1 enchilada on each plate. **For 1500-Calorie Menu (large serving),** serve 2 enchiladas on each plate. Makes 6 small servings or 3 large servings.
To make Enchilada Sauce, in a medium saucepan, combine 1 cup water and bouillon cube. Bring to a boil over high heat; reduce heat until water barely simmers. Crush bouillon cube with back of a spoon. Stir until bouillon cube is completely dissolved. Stir in tomato juice. In a small container with a tight-fitting lid, blend flour, chili powder and cumin. Add 1/4 cup cold water. Cover tightly; shake vigorously until no lumps remain. Stirring constantly, slowly pour flour mixture into bouillon mixture. Stirring constantly, cook until slightly thickened. Keep sauce warm until served. Or cool sauce; pour into a container with a tight-fitting lid. Cover tightly; refrigerate up to 5 days. Reheat before serving. Makes about 2 cups.

---

1 small serving (1 enchilada) = 1 meat, 1 bread, 1 vegetable, 1 fat, 190 calories
1 large serving (2 enchiladas) = 2 meat, 2 bread, 2 vegetable, 2 fat, 380 calories

---

Marinated-Melon Kabobs   *Photo on page 97.*

Three kinds of melon make colorful kabobs.

2 cups cantaloupe balls or 1-inch cubes
2 cups honeydew-melon balls or 1-inch cubes
2 cups watermelon balls or 1-inch cubes
1 tablespoon lime juice

2 tablespoons dry white wine
1 teaspoon poppy seeds
6 mint sprigs

In a large bowl, combine melon balls or cubes. In a small bowl, combine lime juice, wine and poppy seeds. Pour over melon balls or cubes; toss gently. Cover; refrigerate at least 2 hours or up to 2 days. Skewer melon balls on wooden picks or bamboo skewers, alternating colors. Garnish with a mint sprig. Makes 6 servings.

---

1 serving (1 kabob) = 1 fruit, 50 calories

Day 19

1000-Calorie	1200-Calorie	1500-Calorie
Breakfast		
1 serving Orange Breakfast Crepes* 1 cup (8 oz.) skim milk **or** 1 cup plain low-fat yogurt	1 serving Orange Breakfast Crepes* 1 cup plain low-fat yogurt, with 2 tablespoons Fruit & Nut Granola, page 40, **or** 2 tablespoons unsweetened ready-to-eat cereal	1 serving Orange Breakfast Crepes* 1 cup plain low-fat yogurt, with 2 tablespoons Fruit & Nut Granola, page 40, **or** 2 tablespoons unsweetened ready-to-eat cereal
Lunch		

French Peasant Lunch:
  1/2 (5-inch-long) French roll
  1 serving Cold Chicken Mousse* **or** 1 oz. sliced turkey with 1 oz. low-calorie cheese
  1 red-leaf-lettuce leaf
  2 small French cornichons **or** small sour pickles
  1 tablespoon Dijon-style mustard
  1 serving Marinated Bean Salad*
1 serving Wine Spritzer* **or** 1/4 cup (2 oz.) fruit juice in 3/4 cup (6 oz.) club soda over ice
	French Peasant Lunch:
	  1 (5-inch-long) French roll
	  1 serving Cold Chicken Mousse* **or** 1 oz. sliced turkey with 1 oz. low-calorie cheese
	  1 red-leaf-lettuce leaf
	  2 small French cornichons **or** small sour pickles
	  1 tablespoon Dijon-style mustard
	  1 serving Marinated Bean Salad*
	1 serving Wine Spritzer* **or** 1/4 cup (2 oz.) fruit juice in 3/4 cup (6 oz.) club soda over ice
		French Peasant Lunch:
		  1 (5-inch-long) French roll
		  1 serving Cold Chicken Mousse* **or** 1 oz. sliced turkey with 1 oz. low-calorie cheese
		  1 red-leaf-lettuce leaf
		  2 small French cornichons **or** small sour pickles
		  1 tablespoon Dijon-style mustard
		  1 serving Marinated Bean Salad*
		  1 cup canned chicken noodle soup or beef-noodle soup prepared as directed
		1 serving Wine Spritzer* **or** 1/4 cup (2 oz.) fruit juice in 3/4 cup (6 oz.) club soda over ice

Dinner		

1 small serving Hearthside Beef Stew*
Salad:
  2 Bibb-lettuce leaves
  1/4 small apple, cubed
  6 green grapes, cut in half
1 tablespoon Poppy-Seed Dressing*
1 cup (8 oz.) skim milk
	1 small serving Hearthside Beef Stew*
	1/2 cup steamed carrots with dill weed to taste, tossed with 1 teaspoon diet margarine
	Salad:
	  2 Bibb-lettuce leaves
	  1/4 small apple, cubed
	  6 green grapes, cut in half
	1 tablespoon Poppy-Seed Dressing*
	1 cup (8 oz.) skim milk
		1 large serving Hearthside Beef Stew*
		Salad:
		  2 Bibb-lettuce leaves
		  1/4 small apple, cubed
		  6 green grapes, cut in half
		1 tablespoon Poppy-Seed Dressing*
		1 cup (8 oz.) skim milk

* Recipe follows.

Orange Breakfast Crepes

These crepes make breakfast a special occasion.

1 teaspoon cornstarch
1 teaspoon sugar
1/2 cup orange juice
1 (3-oz.) pkg. Neufchâtel cheese,
   room temperature

1/2 teaspoon orange extract
1 egg white
1 tablespoon low-sugar orange marmalade
1/2 small banana (4 per lb.), thinly sliced

Orange Crepes:
3/4 cup skim milk
2 teaspoons stirred egg yolk
1 teaspoon grated orange peel
1/4 teaspoon orange extract

1/2 cup all-purpose flour
Dash of salt
1/2 teaspoon regular margarine

Prepare Orange Crepes; keep warm. In a small saucepan, blend cornstarch and sugar. Gradually stir in orange juice. Stirring constantly, cook over medium heat until slightly thickened. Cover; keep warm until served. In a small bowl, combine cheese and orange extract. In another small bowl, beat egg white with an electric mixer or whisk until foamy. Beat in marmalade, 1 teaspoon at a time; beat until soft peaks form. Fold beaten egg-white mixture into cheese mixture. Place 1 warm crepe on a flat surface. Spoon 1 heaping tablespoon cheese filling in a strip across center of crepe. Place 3 or 4 thin banana slices on top of cheese filling. Fold crepe over filling; roll up. Repeat with remaining crepes and filling. Place 2 crepes on each of 4 plates. Spoon 1 tablespoon warm orange syrup over top of each rolled crepe. Makes 4 servings.

To make Orange Crepes, preheat oven to 200F (95C). In a blender, combine milk, egg yolk, orange peel and orange extract. Process 10 seconds. Add flour and salt; process 10 seconds longer. Scrape down side of container; process another 5 seconds. Place a 5-inch nonstick skillet or a skillet coated with nonstick vegetable spray over medium heat. When hot, lightly brush with margarine. Pour 2 tablespoons crepe batter into hot skillet. Rotate skillet until batter covers bottom. Cook until top of crepe looks dry, about 30 seconds. Turn; cook 10 seconds longer. Place crepe on an ovenproof plate. Cover with foil. Keep warm in preheated oven while cooking remaining crepes. Brush skillet with margarine as needed, using no more than 1/2 teaspoon total. Serve as directed above. Wrap unused crepes in foil or place in a plastic bag; refrigerate up to 2 days. For longer storage, place in a freezer bag; freeze up to 3 weeks. Thaw in refrigerator overnight or at room temperature about 20 minutes. Makes 8 crepes.

---

1 serving (2 crepes with sauce) = 1 bread, 1 meat, 1 fruit, 1/2 fat, 190 calories
1 crepe without sauce = 1/2 bread, 40 calories

How to Make Poppy-Seed Dressing

1/In a small container with a tight-fitting lid, combine all ingredients. Shake vigorously.

2/Serve over fruit salads or tossed salads containing fruit.

Poppy-Seed Dressing

Complements fruit salads or tossed salads containing fruit.

2 tablespoons white-wine vinegar
1/4 cup water
2 teaspoons dry pectin
2 tablespoons vegetable oil
1 teaspoon sugar

1/4 teaspoon dry mustard
1/8 teaspoon salt
1/2 teaspoon grated onion
1 teaspoon poppy seeds

In a small container with a tight-fitting lid or in a blender, combine all ingredients. Cover tightly; shake vigorously, or process 15 seconds. If processed in blender, pour into a container with a tight-fitting lid. Cover tightly; refrigerate until served, up to 2 days. Shake before using. Makes about 1/2 cup.

1 tablespoon = 1/2 fat, 30 calories

Cold Chicken Mousse

Serve this versatile mousse as a salad or as a sandwich filling with a spicy mustard.

1 (1/4-oz.) envelope unflavored gelatin
 (1 tablespoon)
1/4 cup cold water
1/2 cup low-fat cottage cheese
1/3 cup sour half & half
1 green onion, white part only, chopped
2 tablespoons Dijon-style mustard
1/4 teaspoon salt

1/4 teaspoon white pepper
1/2 teaspoon dried dill weed
1 cup canned or homemade chicken broth
4 oz. cooked chicken, diced (1 cup)
5 pimento-stuffed olives, sliced
1 tablespoon chopped chives or
 green-onion tops
6 French cornichons, if desired

In a small bowl, stir gelatin into water; let stand 3 minutes to soften. Meanwhile, in a blender or food processor fitted with a metal blade, combine cottage cheese, half & half, white part of green onion, mustard, salt, white pepper and dill weed. Process until blended and fluffy; set aside. In a small saucepan, bring broth to a boil. Pour several spoonfuls of hot broth into softened gelatin; stir until gelatin dissolves. Pour gelatin mixture into remaining hot broth. Stir in cottage-cheese mixture; pour into a medium bowl. Cover and refrigerate until mixture has consistency of unbeaten egg whites, 20 to 45 minutes. Beat partially set gelatin mixture with an electric mixer until fluffy. Stir in chicken, olives and chives or green-onion tops. Pour into 2 clean, empty 16-ounce food cans, completely filling 1 can. Refrigerate until firm, at least 4 hours. Invert can onto a flat surface. Using a can opener, cut around can bottom; do not remove bottom. Turn can on its side. Push 1/2 or 1 inch of chicken mousse from can by pushing against can bottom. Cut off mousse slice; continue with remaining mousse. Serve 1 (1-inch) or 2 (1/2-inch) slices for each serving. Top with cornichons, if desired. Refrigerate any unused mousse up to 3 days. Makes 6 (1-inch) servings.

1 serving = 1 meat, 50 calories

Marinated Bean Salad

The flavor of this all-time favorite improves as it marinates.

1 (15-oz.) can cut green beans, drained
1 (15-oz.) can cut wax or yellow beans,
 drained
1 (8-3/4-oz.) can kidney beans or
 garbanzo beans, drained
1/2 cup chopped green bell pepper
1/2 cup diced celery

1/4 cup chopped onion
3 tablespoons white-wine vinegar
1 tablespoon lemon juice
3 tablespoons olive oil or
 other vegetable oil
1/8 teaspoon garlic salt
1/4 teaspoon celery salt

In a large container with a tight-fitting lid, combine beans, bell pepper, celery and onion. In a small container with tight-fitting lid, combine remaining ingredients. Cover tightly; shake until blended. Pour over bean mixture. Stir to coat vegetables. Cover; refrigerate at least 4 hours or up to 5 days. Makes 12 (1/2-cup) servings.

1 serving (1/2 cup) = 1 vegetable, 1/2 fat, 60 calories

1200-Calorie French Peasant Lunch, clockwise from top left: Marinated Bean Salad; Wine Spritzer, page 104; small French roll; Dijon-style mustard; Cold Chicken Mousse with curly leaf lettuce and French cornichons.

Hearthside Beef Stew

Hearty, delicious and filling!

1 (1-lb.) boneless beef round steak
1-1/2 teaspoons vegetable oil
1 garlic clove, minced
3 cups hot water
2 beef-flavored bouillon cubes
1 teaspoon Worcestershire sauce
1/2 teaspoon dried leaf basil
1 large bay leaf

4 small boiling potatoes (10 per lb.),
  peeled, cubed
1 medium carrot (6 per lb.), peeled, sliced
1 celery stalk, sliced
1 (9-oz.) pkg. frozen cut green beans
1 tablespoon all-purpose flour
1 tablespoon cornstarch
1/2 cup water

Trim fat from beef; cut trimmed beef into 1-inch cubes. In a large nonstick skillet or a skillet coated with nonstick vegetable spray, heat oil; add beef cubes. Sauté until browned on all sides. Add garlic; sauté 30 seconds longer. Meanwhile, in a 4-quart pot, combine 3 cups hot water and bouillon cubes. Bring to a boil over high heat; reduce heat until water barely simmers. Crush bouillon cubes with back of a spoon. Stir until bouillon cubes are completely dissolved. Add browned beef mixture, Worcestershire sauce, basil and bay leaf. Cover; simmer until meat is tender when pierced with a fork, about 1 hour. Remove and discard bay leaf. Add potatoes, carrot, celery and green beans. Cover; simmer until vegetables are tender, about 20 minutes. In a small bowl, combine flour and cornstarch. Stir in 1/2 cup cold water until smooth. Stir flour mixture into hot stew. Stirring constantly, cook until cooking liquid is slightly thickened. **For 1000- and 1200-Calorie Menus (small serving),** ladle 1 cup stew into each soup bowl. **For 1500-Calorie Menu (large serving),** ladle 1-1/2 cups stew into each soup bowl. Makes 6 small servings or 4 large servings.

1 small serving (1 cup) = 2 meat, 1-1/2 bread, 1 vegetable, 1/2 fat, 280 calories
1 large serving (1-1/2 cups) = 3 meat, 2 bread, 1-1/2 vegetable, 1 fat, 425 calories

Wine Spritzer   Photos on pages 27 and 103.

You'll enjoy this spicy, bubbly wine drink.

1 apple-spice herb-tea bag
1 cup boiling water
1 teaspoon honey
1/3 cup red wine

Ice cubes
1 cup club soda, chilled
1 thin orange slice, cut in half

Place tea bag in a small pitcher or 2-cup heatproof measuring cup. Pour boiling water over tea bag; let steep 5 minutes. Remove and discard tea bag. Add honey; stir until dissolved. Refrigerate at least 30 minutes. Stir wine into tea. Fill 2 drinking glasses with ice cubes. Pour 1/2 of tea mixture over ice in each glass. Add 1/2 cup club soda to each glass. Garnish each serving with an orange-slice half. Makes 2 servings.

Variation
Substitute another flavored herb tea for apple-spice herb tea. Exchanges and calories will remain the same.

1 serving = 3/4 bread, 50 calories

Day 20

1000-Calorie	1200-Calorie	1500-Calorie
Breakfast		
1 small serving Peachy Popover* 1 oz. sliced Canadian bacon **or** lean ham, grilled 1 serving Raspberry Shake*	1 large serving Peachy Popover* 1 oz. sliced Canadian bacon **or** lean ham, grilled 1 serving Raspberry Shake*	1 large serving Peachy Popover* 1 oz. sliced Canadian bacon **or** lean ham, grilled 1 serving Raspberry Shake*
Lunch		
1 serving Cucumber Cooler* 1 serving Fruit & Cheese in a Pocket*	1 serving Cucumber Cooler* 1 serving Fruit & Cheese in a Pocket*	1 serving Cucumber Cooler* 1 serving Fruit & Cheese in a Pocket* 2 sandwich cookies
Dinner		
1 small serving Confetti Rice Pie* 1 (2-inch) iceberg-lettuce wedge 2 tablespoons Thousand Island Dressing, page 81, **or** 1 tablespoon reduced-calorie Thousand Island dressing (25 calories/tablespoon) 1 Frozen Banana Pop*	1 small serving Confetti Rice Pie* 1 (2-inch) iceberg-lettuce wedge 2 tablespoons Thousand Island Dressing, page 81, **or** 1 tablespoon reduced-calorie Thousand Island dressing (25 calories/tablespoon) 1/2 cup steamed frozen Italian-style vegetables without sauce, with 1 teaspoon diet margarine 1 Frozen Banana Pop*	1 large serving Confetti Rice Pie* 1 (2-inch) iceberg-lettuce wedge 2 tablespoons Thousand Island Dressing, page 81, **or** 1 tablespoon reduced-calorie Thousand Island dressing (25 calories/tablespoon) 1/2 cup steamed frozen Italian-style vegetables without sauce, with 1 teaspoon diet margarine 1 Frozen Banana Pop*
* Recipe follows.		

Raspberry Shake **Photo on page 107.**

Buttermilk enhances the fruit flavor without tasting like buttermilk.

**1/3 cup fresh or frozen
  unsweetened raspberries**
1-1/2 cups skim milk

1 teaspoon sugar
2 tablespoons orange juice
1/2 cup buttermilk

In a blender, combine raspberries, milk, sugar and orange juice. Process until berries are broken up and drink is frothy. Pour into a 1-quart pitcher or jar. Stir in buttermilk. Serve immediately in 2 drinking glasses. Makes 2 servings.

---

1 serving = 1 fruit, 1 milk, 125 calories

Peachy Popover

The light whole-wheat batter puffs up over the fruit.

1 tablespoon brown sugar
1/4 teaspoon ground cinnamon
1 egg
1/2 cup skim milk
1/3 cup all-purpose flour
3 tablespoons whole-wheat flour

1/8 teaspoon salt
1 tablespoon regular margarine
1 medium, fresh cling-free peach (4 per lb.),
    peeled, sliced, or 2 peach halves canned
    in extra-light syrup, rinsed, sliced

In a small bowl, combine brown sugar and cinnamon; set aside. Place a 9-inch pie pan in oven. Preheat oven to 400F (205C). In a medium bowl, beat egg with an electric mixer or whisk until light and fluffy. Beat in milk. Gradually beat in all-purpose flour, whole-wheat flour and salt. Remove hot pie pan from oven. Place margarine in pan. Return to oven until margarine melts, about 30 seconds. Rotate pan to coat bottom and side with melted margarine. Pour batter into hot pie pan. Arrange peach slices over batter. Sprinkle peaches with reserved cinnamon mixture. Bake in preheated oven until golden brown and puffy, about 25 minutes. Cut into 4 wedges. **For 1000-Calorie Menu (small serving),** serve 1 popover wedge on each plate. **For 1200- or 1500-Calorie Menus (large serving),** serve 2 popover wedges on each plate. Serve immediately. Makes 4 small servings or 2 large servings.

Variations
Substitute 1 small Rome Beauty or Golden Delicious apple (3 per pound) or 1/2 small Bartlett pear (4 per pound) for peach. Peel, core and slice apple or pear. Complete and bake as directed above. Exchanges and calories will remain the same.

---

1 small serving (1 wedge) = 1 bread, 1/4 fruit, 1/2 fat, 110 calories
1 large serving (2 wedges) = 2 bread, 1/2 fruit, 1 fat, 220 calories

---

Cucumber Cooler

Cucumbers are a natural low-calorie food with only five calories for a medium cucumber.

1/2 medium cucumber (2 per lb.), peeled
3/4 cup vegetable-juice cocktail
1 cup skim milk

2 teaspoons lemon juice
1/4 teaspoon dried dill weed
Onion salt

Cut cucumber in half lengthwise. Scoop out and discard seeds. Slice seeded cucumber into a blender. Add vegetable juice, milk, lemon juice and dill weed. Process until smooth and frothy. Pour into 2 glasses. Season with onion salt. Serve immediately. Makes 2 servings.

---

1 serving = 1 vegetable, 1/2 milk, 65 calories

1200-Calorie Breakfast, clockwise from top left: Raspberry Shake, page 105; Peachy Popover; grilled Canadian bacon; peach slice reserved from Peachy Popover; raspberry reserved from Raspberry Shake.

Fruit & Cheese in a Pocket

Chutney is a tangy, sweet condiment and a perfect complement to meat and cheese.

3/4 cup diced cooked lean ham (3 oz.)
1/4 cup shredded sharp Cheddar cheese
   (1 oz.)
1/2 small Red Delicious, McIntosh or
   Jonathan apple (3 per lb.), cored, diced

1/4 cup crushed pineapple canned in juice,
   drained
1 (6-inch) pita-bread round
1 cup shredded lettuce
1/2 cup alfalfa sprouts

Yogurt-Chutney Dressing:
1/3 cup plain low-fat yogurt
3 tablespoons reduced-calorie mayonnaise
1 tablespoon chopped mango chutney or
   other fruit chutney

1/8 teaspoon curry powder
1 tablespoon evaporated skim milk

Prepare Yogurt-Chutney Dressing; refrigerate until served. In a small bowl, combine ham, cheese, apple and pineapple. Add 1/4 cup dressing; stir to distribute. Cut pita round in half crosswise. Stuff each half with 1/2 cup lettuce, 1/2 of the ham-and-fruit mixture and 1/4 cup alfalfa sprouts. Serve immediately. Makes 2 servings.
To make Yogurt-Chutney Dressing, in a small bowl, combine yogurt and mayonnaise. Stir in chutney, curry powder and evaporated milk. Cover tightly; refrigerate until served, up to 3 days. Makes about 2/3 cup.

---

1 serving = 1 bread, 1-1/4 fruit, 2 meat, 1 fat, 300 calories
2 tablespoons dressing = 1/4 fruit, 1/2 fat, 40 calories

Frozen Banana Pops

Bananas are coated with a fruit-juice-and-yogurt mixture to keep them from darkening.

2 medium bananas (3 per lb.)
1/4 cup unsweetened orange-pineapple juice

1/2 cup plain low-fat yogurt

Peel bananas. Cut each into three pieces. Insert a popsicle stick into each piece. In a small bowl, combine juice and yogurt. Place 1 banana piece at a time into yogurt mixture. Turn to cover completely. Place on a baking sheet; freeze. When frozen solid, wrap each pop in freezer wrap. Keep frozen until ready to serve, up to 2 weeks. Makes 6 frozen pops.

---

1 pop = 1 fruit, 45 calories

Confetti-Rice Pie

Good enough that you'll hope some is left for another meal.

1 cup water
1 chicken-flavored bouillon cube
1/2 cup long-grain white rice or brown rice
1 teaspoon regular margarine
1/2 cup chopped onion

1/2 cup chopped green bell pepper
2 tablespoons beaten egg
2 cups frozen mixed vegetables
2-1/4 cups diced cooked turkey (9 oz.)

Cheese Sauce:
1 tablespoon regular margarine
2 tablespoons all-purpose flour
1/8 teaspoon dry mustard

1/2 cup canned or homemade chicken broth
1/2 cup skim milk
1/4 cup shredded American cheese (1 oz.)

Preheat oven to 350F (175C). In a medium saucepan, combine water and bouillon cube. Bring to a boil over high heat; reduce heat until water barely simmers. Crush bouillon cube with back of a spoon. Stir until bouillon cube is completely dissolved. Add rice; stir until mixture comes back to a simmer. Cover; simmer 20 to 30 minutes or until rice is tender and liquid is absorbed. In a small nonstick skillet or a skillet coated with nonstick vegetable spray, melt margarine. Add onion and bell pepper; sauté until onion is soft. Quickly stir onion mixture and beaten egg into cooked rice. Press rice mixture across bottom and up side of a 9-inch pie pan. Bake rice crust in preheated oven 10 minutes. Meanwhile, cook frozen vegetables in lightly salted boiling water or a steamer according to package directions; drain. Prepare Cheese Sauce. In a medium bowl, combine cooked vegetables, turkey and Cheese Sauce; stir gently. Turn vegetable mixture into baked rice crust. Bake 20 minutes. Let stand 5 minutes. Cut into 6 wedges. **For 1000- and 1200-Calorie Menus (small serving),** serve 1 wedge on each plate. **For 1500-Calorie Menu (large serving),** serve 2 wedges on each plate. Serve hot. Cover any leftover pie with foil. Refrigerate up to 2 days. To serve refrigerated pie, reheat covered pie in a preheated 250F (120C) oven about 15 minutes. Makes 6 small servings or 3 large servings. **To make Cheese Sauce**, in a medium saucepan, melt margarine. Stir in flour and mustard until blended. Gradually stir in broth and milk. Stirring constantly, cook over medium heat until slightly thickened. Add cheese; stir until cheese melts. Do not boil. Makes about 1 cup.

---

1 small serving (1 wedge) = 2-1/2 meat, 1 bread, 1 vegetable, 250 calories
1 large serving (2 wedges) = 5 meat, 2 bread, 2 vegetable, 500 calories

---

Day 21

1000-Calorie	1200-Calorie	1500-Calorie
Breakfast		
1/2 apple-cinnamon bagel **or** raisin English muffin, toasted, spread with 2 tablespoons Maple-Cheese Spread* 1 serving Mandarin-Orange Yogurt*	1 apple-cinnamon bagel **or** raisin English muffin, toasted, spread with 2 tablespoons Maple-Cheese Spread* 1 serving Mandarin-Orange Yogurt*	1 apple-cinnamon bagel **or** raisin English muffin, toasted, spread with 2 tablespoons Maple-Cheese Spread* 1 serving Mandarin-Orange Yogurt*
Lunch		
1 serving Seafood-Stuffed Artichokes* 2 (3'' x 2'') rye wafers 1/2 cup frozen unsweetened strawberries, raspberries or blueberries, partially thawed 1 cup (8 oz.) skim milk	1 serving Seafood-Stuffed Artichokes* 1 small dinner roll 1 teaspoon diet margarine 1/2 cup frozen unsweetened strawberries, raspberries or blueberries, partially thawed 1 cup (8 oz.) skim milk	1 serving Seafood Stuffed Artichokes* 2 small dinner rolls 2 teaspoons diet margarine 1/2 cup frozen unsweetened strawberries, raspberries or blueberries, partially thawed 1 cup (8 oz.) skim milk
Dinner		
1 serving Chicken Monterey* 1/3 cup parsleyed steamed brown rice **or** white rice 1-1/2 cups torn mixed salad greens 1-1/2 tablespoons French Dressing, page 65, **or** reduced-calorie French dressing (25 calories/tablespoon) 1 serving Champagne Jelly, page 125	1 serving Chicken Monterey* 1/3 cup parsleyed steamed brown rice **or** white rice 1/2 cup California Vegetable Medley* **or** other steamed-vegetable mixture 1-1/2 cups torn mixed salad greens 1-1/2 tablespoons French Dressing, page 65, **or** reduced-calorie French dressing (25 calories/tablespoon) 1 serving Champagne Jelly, page 125	1 serving Chicken Monterey* 2/3 cup parsleyed steamed brown rice **or** white rice 1/2 cup California Vegetable Medley* **or** other steamed-vegetable mixture 1-1/2 cups torn mixed salad greens 1-1/2 tablespoons French Dressing, page 65, **or** reduced-calorie French dressing (25 calories/tablespoon) 1 serving Champagne Jelly, page 125

* Recipe follows.

Maple-Cheese Spread

You'll enjoy this wonderfully nutty spread on toast or bagels.

**1/2 (8-oz.) pkg. Neufchâtel cheese,
   room temperature**
1 teaspoon brown sugar

1/2 teaspoon maple flavoring
2 tablespoons chopped pecans

In a small bowl, beat cheese with an electric mixer until smooth. Beat in brown sugar and maple flavoring. Stir in pecans. Cover tightly; refrigerate until served, up to 3 days. Makes about 1/2 cup.

2 tablespoons = 1 meat, 1 fat, 110 calories

Mandarin-Orange Yogurt

Excellent as a dessert or as a snack between meals.

8 oz. plain low-fat yogurt (1 cup)
2 teaspoons low-sugar orange marmalade

1/2 teaspoon orange extract
1/4 cup drained mandarin-orange sections

In a small bowl, combine yogurt, marmalade and orange extract. Carefully fold in orange sections. Cover tightly; refrigerate until ready to serve, up to 4 days. Serve in stemmed glasses. Makes 1 serving.

1 serving = 1 fruit, 1 milk, 120 calories

Seafood-Stuffed Artichokes   *Photo on page 6.*

This salad packs well for an unusual brown-bag lunch or picnic.

4 small fresh artichokes (2 per lb.)
1 small lemon (5 per lb.), sliced
2 teaspoons dried leaf tarragon
1 cup cooked small pasta shells
2 green onions, sliced

8 oz. cooked fresh shrimp (about 35 tiny shrimp),
    crab, lobster or scallops or
    1 (6-3/4-oz.) can tuna packed in water, drained
4 large red-leaf-lettuce leaves

Tarragon Dressing:
1/4 cup reduced-calorie mayonnaise
2 tablespoons buttermilk
1 teaspoon Dijon-style mustard
2 teaspoons tarragon-flavored vinegar

Pinch of dried leaf tarragon
Dash of salt
Dash of pepper

Using kitchen shears, cut sharp tips from outer leaves of artichokes. Cut off stem ends so artichokes stand level. Cut off top 1 inch of tightly closed inner leaves. Fill a 4-quart pot half full with water; bring to a boil over high heat. Add lemon, tarragon and trimmed artichokes; cover. When water comes back to a boil, reduce heat until water barely simmers. Cover; simmer 20 to 30 minutes until artichokes are tender when pierced with a fork at stem ends. Drain; discard cooking water and lemon. Invert artichokes on paper towels to drain 10 minutes. Spread inner leaves of artichokes. Pull out purple inner leaves; discard. Use a spoon to scrape out hairy chokes. Refrigerate cooked artichokes until chilled, or up to 8 hours. Prepare Tarragon Dressing. In a medium bowl, combine pasta, green onions and seafood; stir gently to distribute. Line 4 plates with lettuce leaves. Spoon 1/4 of salad mixture into center of each chilled artichoke. Place 1 filled artichoke on each lettuce-lined plate. Spoon 1/4 of dressing over each serving. Makes 4 servings.
To make Tarragon Dressing, in a small bowl, combine mayonnaise, buttermilk, mustard and vinegar. Season with tarragon, salt and pepper. Refrigerate until ready to serve, up to 2 days. Makes about 1/3 cup.

1 serving = 2 meat, 1 vegetable, 1/2 bread, 1/2 fat, 195 calories

Chicken Monterey   *Photo on cover.*

Rolled chicken breasts are stuffed with vegetables and covered with Monterey Jack cheese.

4 (4-oz.) boneless chicken-breast halves,
   skinned
1/2 teaspoon salt
1/4 teaspoon paprika
1/2 small green bell pepper (3 per lb.)
1/2 small red bell pepper (3 per lb.)
1 small zucchini (3 per lb.)

1/2 small onion (5 per lb.), sliced,
   slices halved, separated into pieces
1/2 teaspoon dried leaf basil
1 teaspoon vegetable oil
1/3 cup canned or homemade chicken broth
2 oz. Monterey Jack cheese,
   cut in 4 thin slices

Remove and discard fat from chicken breasts. Place trimmed chicken breasts, 1 at a time, between sheets of plastic wrap. Pound trimmed breasts with flat side of a meat mallet until about doubled in size. Season with salt and paprika. Cut bell peppers into thin strips. Trim ends from zucchini; cut in half crosswise. Cut each half in 6 lengthwise strips. Arrange 3 zucchini strips, 1/4 of green-bell-pepper strips, 1/4 of red-bell-pepper strips and 1/4 of onion pieces on each flattened chicken breast. Let some of each vegetable extend beyond both sides of chicken. Sprinkle each with basil. Roll meat around vegetables; secure with a wooden pick. Place a large nonstick skillet or a skillet coated with nonstick vegetable spray over medium heat. When hot, brush with oil. Add chicken rolls; brown on all sides. Add broth; reduce heat until broth barely simmers. Cover; simmer 15 minutes or until chicken is tender and no pink remains. Arrange cheese slices over chicken rolls. Cover skillet until cheese melts, about 30 seconds. Place 1 chicken roll on each of 4 plates. Makes 4 servings.

1 serving = 3 meat, 1 vegetable, 202 calories

California Vegetable Medley   *Photo on cover.*

As fresh and bright as the California sunshine!

12 oz. fresh broccoli or 1 (10-oz.) pkg.
   frozen chopped broccoli, thawed
1 (9-oz.) pkg. frozen artichoke hearts,
   partially thawed
1 tablespoon regular margarine
1/4 cup chopped onion
2 tablespoons chopped green bell pepper

2 tablespoons chopped red bell pepper or
   canned chopped pimento
1/2 teaspoon dried leaf basil
2 teaspoons lemon juice
Salt
Black pepper

Wash and trim fresh broccoli; cut into 1-inch pieces. In a large saucepan, cook fresh or frozen broccoli pieces and artichoke hearts in lightly salted boiling water until broccoli is crisp-tender, about 10 minutes. Drain; set aside. In a large nonstick skillet or a skillet coated with nonstick vegetable spray, melt margarine. Add onion, green bell pepper and red bell pepper or pimento. Sauté until onion is soft. Sprinkle basil over onion mixture. Add drained broccoli and artichoke hearts; toss to distribute. Cover; simmer until heated through, about 5 minutes. Pour vegetable mixture into a serving bowl. Sprinkle lemon juice over vegetables; toss to distribute. Season with salt and black pepper. Serve hot. Makes 6 (1/2-cup) servings.

1 serving (1/2 cup) = 1 vegetable, 1/2 fat, 50 calories

1500-Calorie Dinner, clockwise from top left: mixed salad greens; Champagne Jelly, page 125; parsleyed rice; California Vegetable Medley; Chicken Monterey.

Time-Saver Weight-Loss Menus

If food preparation time is of the essense, try one of the quick and easy Weight-Loss Menus below. These easy-to-prepare meals can be used in place of any breakfast, lunch or dinner, of the same calorie count, in the 21-day Weight-Loss Menus on the preceding pages.

1000-Calorie	1200-Calorie	1500-Calorie
	Breakfast	
1/2 cup (4 oz.) orange juice **or** 1/2 cup diced fresh fruit 3/4 cup unsweetened ready-to-eat cereal **or** 1 bread slice, toasted, with 1 tablespoon diet margarine **or** 1 teaspoon regular margarine 1 oz. sliced Canadian bacon **or** lean ham, grilled, **or** 1 egg cooked without fat 1/2 cup (4 oz.) skim milk **or** 1/2 cup plain low-fat yogurt	1/2 cup (4 oz.) orange juice **or** 1/2 cup diced fresh fruit 3/4 cup unsweetened ready-to-eat cereal **or** 1/2 cup cooked cereal 1 bread slice, toasted, **or** 1/2 bagel **or** 1/2 English muffin, with 1 tablespoon diet margarine **or** 1 teaspoon regular margarine 1 oz. sliced Canadian bacon **or** lean ham, grilled, **or** 1 egg, cooked without fat 1/2 cup (4 oz.) skim milk **or** 1/2 cup plain low-fat yogurt	1/2 cup (4 oz.) orange juice **or** 1/2 cup diced fresh fruit 3/4 cup unsweetened ready-to-eat cereal **or** 1/2 cup cooked cereal 1 bread slice, toasted, **or** 1/2 bagel **or** 1/2 English muffin, with 1 tablespoon diet margarine **or** 1 teaspoon regular margarine 1 oz. sliced Canadian bacon **or** lean ham, grilled 1/2 cup (4 oz.) skim milk **or** 1/2 cup plain low-fat yogurt
	Lunch	

Open-faced sandwich, using:
  1 white-bread or whole-wheat-bread slice
  1 oz. lean meat, fish or chicken
  1 oz. low-calorie cheese
  1 tomato slice
  1 tablespoon diet margarine **or** low-calorie mayonnaise
 	
OR
 	
Luncheon Salad:
  1-1/2 cups torn lettuce
  1 oz. lean meat, fish or chicken
  1 oz. low-calorie cheese
  1/2 tomato, cut in wedges
  1/4 medium cucumber, sliced
2 tablespoons diet salad dressing (see Index) **or** prepared reduced-calorie salad dressing (25 calories/tablespoon)
6 saltine crackers **or** 1 small dinner roll
 	
AND
 	
1 serving Quick Vegetable Soup, page 57, **or** 1/2 cup (4 oz.) vegetable-juice cocktail
1/2 medium apple, pear or orange **or** 1/2 cup diced fresh fruit **or** 1/3 cup fruit canned in juice
1 cup (8 oz.) skim milk **or** 1 cup plain low-fat yogurt
	Sandwich, using:
	  2 white-bread or whole-wheat-bread slices
	  1 oz. lean meat, fish or chicken
	  1 oz. low-calorie cheese
	  1 tomato slice
	  1 tablespoon diet margarine **or** low-calorie mayonnaise
	
	OR
	
	Luncheon Salad:
	  1-1/2 cups torn lettuce
	  1 oz. lean meat, fish or chicken
	  1 oz. low-calorie cheese
	  1/2 tomato, cut in wedges
	  1/4 medium cucumber, sliced
	2 tablespoons diet salad dressing (see Index) **or** prepared reduced-calorie salad dressing (25 calories/tablespoon)
	2 small dinner rolls **or** 2 (1-inch-thick) French-bread slices
	1-1/2 teaspoons diet margarine **or** 1/2 teaspoon regular margarine
	
	AND
	
	1 serving Quick Vegetable Soup, page 57, **or** 1/2 cup (4 oz.) vegetable-juice cocktail
	1/2 medium apple, pear or orange **or** 1/2 cup diced fresh fruit **or** 1/3 cup fruit canned in juice
	1 cup (8 oz.) skim milk **or** 1 cup plain low-fat yogurt
		Sandwich, using:
		  2 white-bread or whole-wheat-bread slices
		  1 oz. lean meat, fish or chicken
		  1 oz. low-calorie cheese
		  1 tomato slice
		  1 tablespoon diet margarine **or** low-calorie mayonnaise
		
		OR
		
		Luncheon Salad:
		  1-1/2 cups torn lettuce
		  1 oz. lean meat, fish or chicken
		  1 oz. low-calorie cheese
		  1/2 tomato, cut in wedges
		  1/4 medium cucumber, sliced
		2 tablespoons diet salad dressing (see Index) **or** prepared reduced-calorie salad dressing (25 calories/tablespoon)
		2 small dinner rolls **or** 2 (1-inch-thick) French-bread slices
		1-1/2 teaspoons diet margarine **or** 1/2 teaspoon regular margarine
		
		AND
		
		1 cup canned chicken noodle soup **or** beef noodle soup, prepared as directed
		1/2 cup (4 oz.) vegetable-juice cocktail
		1/2 medium apple, pear or orange **or** 1/2 cup diced fresh fruit **or** 1/3 cup fruit canned in juice
		1 cup (8 oz.) skim milk **or** 1 cup plain low-fat yogurt

Dinner

2 oz. cooked lean beef, ham, extra-lean ground beef, fish or chicken
1/3 cup cooked rice **or** 1/2 cup cooked noodles **or** 1 small potato (4 to 5 per lb.)
1/2 cup cooked vegetable from Vegetable Exchange List, page 136
1 tablespoon diet margarine **or** 1 teaspoon regular margarine
1-1/2 cups torn mixed salad greens
2 tablespoons diet salad dressing (see Index) **or** prepared reduced-calorie salad dressing (25 calories/tablespoon)
1/2 cup diced fresh fruit **or** 1/3 cup fruit canned in juice or extra-light syrup **or** 1/2 cup (4 oz.) fruit juice
1/2 cup (4 oz.) skim milk **or** 1/2 cup plain low-fat yogurt

2 oz. cooked lean beef, ham, extra-lean ground beef, fish or chicken
1/3 cup cooked rice **or** 1/2 cup cooked noodles **or** 1 small potato (4 to 5 per lb.)
1 cup cooked vegetable from Vegetable Exchange List, page 136
1 tablespoon diet margarine **or** 1 teaspoon regular margarine
1-1/2 cups torn mixed salad greens
2 tablespoons diet salad dressing (see Index) **or** prepared reduced-calorie salad dressing (25 calories/tablespoon)
1/2 cup diced fresh fruit **or** 1/3 cup fruit canned in juice or extra-light syrup **or** 1/2 cup (4 oz.) fruit juice
1/2 cup (4 oz.) skim milk **or** 1/2 cup plain low-fat yogurt

4 oz. cooked lean beef, ham, extra-lean ground beef, fish or chicken
1 cup cooked vegetable from Vegetable Exchange List, page 136
1 tablespoon diet margarine **or** 1 teaspoon regular margarine
1-1/2 cups torn mixed salad greens
2 tablespoons diet salad dressing (see Index) **or** prepared reduced-calorie salad dressing (25 calories/tablespoon)
1/2 cup diced fresh fruit **or** 1/3 cup fruit canned in juice or extra-light syrup **or** 1/2 cup (4 oz.) fruit juice
1/2 cup (4 oz.) skim milk **or** 1/2 cup plain low-fat yogurt

Tip *Ask your butcher to grind your meat to get ten to fifteen percent fat.*

For most people, dieting usually means eliminating desserts. Not in this diet! Desserts don't have to be rich, overly sweet and calorie laden. In fact, low-calorie desserts can be good to you! These desserts use fruits, egg whites and low-calorie dairy products that provide vitamins A and C, calcium and a small amount of protein.

Fresh fruits have a natural sweetness that need little if any added sweetener. Honey-Broiled Pineapple has a tiny bit of honey drizzled over it before broiling, but Cherry-Cloud Pudding has no added sugar. It has pitted frozen unsweetened dark sweet cherries set in a milk gelatin flavored lightly with almond extract. Caramel Baked Apples each contain about 1 teaspoon brown sugar, but are sweet enough to satisfy almost any sweet tooth.

Cappuccino Mousse and Hawaiian Soufflé are light, elegant desserts. Thanks to whipped egg whites, these desserts have the lightness of a mousse or soufflé, but with fewer calories than those made with the traditional whipped cream. Serve them to guests with pride! They'll never know the desserts are low calorie—unless you tell them.

Low-calorie frozen desserts are surprisingly rich-tasting and flavorful. The combination of fruit and yogurt or skim milk make Peachy Frozen Yogurt, page 78, and Orange Sherbet smooth-textured and fruity.

Instead of using these low-calorie desserts with your meal, enjoy them between meals for a mid-afternoon break or bedtime nightcap. Use the recipes with the menus in which they appear, or plan your own menus using the Weight-Management System, pages 126 to 143. Because these desserts are not calorie-free, be sure to include them as part of your daily calorie allotment. ∎

Orange-Blossom Wake-Up

This is a great mid-morning or mid-afternoon pick-me-up.

1 pint skim milk (2 cups)
**1/4 cup thawed frozen orange-juice
    concentrate**

1/2 teaspoon lemon juice
6 ice cubes

In a blender, combine milk, orange-juice concentrate, lemon juice and ice cubes. Process until ice is finely chopped. Pour into 4 drinking glasses. Serve immediately. Makes 4 servings.

1 serving = 1/2 milk, 3/4 fruit, 108 calories

Honey-Rum Yogurt *Photo on page 21.*

Even if you don't like yogurt, you'll like this sauce over fresh berries.

8 oz. plain low-fat yogurt (1 cup)
1/2 cup evaporated skim milk

1 tablespoon honey
2 teaspoons rum extract

In a small bowl, combine yogurt and evaporated milk. Stir in honey and rum extract. Cover tightly; refrigerate until served, up to 3 days. Makes 1-1/2 cups or 6 (1/4-cup) servings.

1 serving (1/4 cup) = 1/2 milk, 1/4 fruit, 50 calories

Fruit & Rum Yogurt

A delicious, pudding-like dessert.

1-1/2 cups plain low-fat yogurt
1/4 cup evaporated skim milk
2 teaspoons rum extract

1/4 cup Fruit Compote, page 15, or
    1/3 cup fruit cocktail canned in
    extra-light syrup, with syrup to cover

In a small bowl, combine yogurt, evaporated milk and rum extract. Fold in Fruit Compote or fruit cocktail with enough syrup to cover fruit. Cover tightly; refrigerate until ready to serve, up to 2 days. Stir before serving. Spoon into dessert dishes. Makes 2 (1-cup) servings.

1 serving (1 cup) = 1 milk, 1 fruit, 135 calories

Honey-Broiled Pineapple *Photo on page 45.*

Fresh pineapple has the best flavor, but canned pineapple is also very good.

1-1/2 teaspoons honey
4 (1/2-inch-thick) fresh pineapple rings
    or drained canned pineapple rings
    packed in juice

Preheat broiler, if necessary. In a microwave oven or a very small saucepan over low heat, warm honey. Place pineapple rings in a single layer on a baking sheet. Drizzle warm honey over pineapple. Broil about 6 inches from heat until surface is bubbly, about 3 minutes. Serve immediately. Makes 4 servings.

1 serving (1 pineapple ring) = 1 fruit, 50 calories

Lemon Yogurt

This slightly sweet, lemony sauce is excellent on fruit or served by itself.

8 oz. plain low-fat yogurt (1 cup)
1/2 cup evaporated skim milk
1 tablespoon honey

1 teaspoon grated lemon peel
1 teaspoon lemon extract
1 drop yellow food coloring, if desired

In a small bowl, combine yogurt and evaporated milk. Stir in honey, lemon peel, lemon extract and food coloring, if desired. Cover tightly; refrigerate until served, up to 3 days. Makes 1-1/2 cups or 6 (1/4-cup) servings.

---

1 serving (1/4 cup) = 1/2 milk, 1/4 fruit, 50 calories

Raspberry Sherbet   Photo on page 63.

Slightly tart and very delicious!

1 pint skim milk (2 cups)
1/4 cup sugar
1/4 cup instant nonfat milk powder
1 teaspoon vanilla extract

2 teaspoons lemon juice
2 cups partially thawed,
    frozen unsweetened raspberries

In a medium saucepan, combine skim milk, sugar and milk powder. Stir over medium heat until sugar dissolves. Stir in vanilla, lemon juice and raspberries with any juice that has formed. Pour into a blender or food processor fitted with a metal blade. Puree; strain raspberry mixture through a fine sieve to remove seeds. Freeze in an ice-cream freezer according to manufacturer's directions or still-freeze in freezer compartment of your refrigerator. To still-freeze, pour raspberry mixture into a 9-inch-square baking pan. Freeze until almost firm, about 1 hour. Spoon partially frozen mixture into a food processor fitted with a metal blade. Process until smooth. Or spoon into a large bowl; beat with an electric mixer until smooth. Return mixture to freezer. Freeze until firm, about 2 hours. To serve, let sherbet stand at room temperature 10 minutes; process or beat sherbet again. For 1 serving, scoop 1/3 cup sherbet into a sherbet glass or small dessert dish. Store unused portion in freezer in a container with a tight-fitting lid. Makes 8 (1/3-cup) servings.

Variations
Substitute 1 pint (2 cups) fresh or partially thawed, frozen unsweetened strawberries or blackberries for raspberries. Prepare as directed above. Exchanges and calories will remain the same.

---

1 serving (1/3 cup) = 1 fruit, 1/4 milk, 72 calories

Lemon Yogurt over fresh fruit

Hawaiian Soufflé

A cold soufflé with the flavors of pineapple, orange and coconut.

1 (1/4-oz.) envelope unflavored gelatin
  (1 tablespoon)
1/4 cup cold water
2 eggs, separated
1 cup skim milk
1/2 cup unsweetened pineapple juice

1/2 cup orange juice
1/2 teaspoon coconut extract
1/4 teaspoon cream of tartar
1 tablespoon plus 1 teaspoon sugar
2 tablespoons chopped macadamias or almonds

In a small bowl, combine gelatin and cold water; let stand 3 minutes to soften. In a small bowl, beat egg yolks; set aside. In a medium saucepan, heat milk over low heat until bubbles form around edge of pan. Gradually pour 1/2 cup hot milk into beaten egg yolks, stirring constantly. Stir egg-yolk mixture into remaining hot milk. Cook over medium-high heat until thickened, stirring constantly. Stir several spoonfuls of hot egg mixture into softened gelatin. Stir gelatin mixture into remaining hot egg mixture. Stir in pineapple juice, orange juice and coconut extract. Refrigerate until mixture mounds when dropped from a spoon, 30 to 45 minutes. Beat egg whites and cream of tartar with an electric mixer until soft peaks form. Gradually beat in sugar, 1/2 teaspoon at a time. Beat until glossy soft peaks form. Stir 1 large spoonful of egg-white mixture into gelatin mixture. Fold in remaining egg-white mixture until no white streaks remain. Spoon into a 2-quart soufflé dish. Cover tightly; refrigerate at least 4 hours or up to 8 hours. Serve in dessert dishes with 1 teaspoon chopped nuts sprinkled over each serving. Makes 6 (3/4-cup) servings.

---

1 serving (3/4 cup) = 1/4 meat, 1/2 fruit, 1/2 milk, 1/2 fat, 90 calories

---

Cherry-Cloud Pudding

Dark sweet cherries are so naturally sweet, they don't need sugar.

1 cup frozen unsweetened dark
  sweet cherries, pitted
1 (1/4-oz.) envelope unflavored gelatin
  (1 tablespoon)

1/4 cup cold water
1 cup skim milk
1 teaspoon almond extract

Select 2 cherries for garnish; cut each in half. Store halved cherries in freezer until needed. Thaw remaining cherries. In a small bowl, stir gelatin into cold water; let stand 3 minutes to soften. In a small saucepan, heat milk until bubbles appear around edge of pan. Gradually pour hot milk into gelatin mixture; stir until gelatin is completely dissolved. Cover tightly; refrigerate until mixture has consistency of unbeaten egg whites, 20 to 45 minutes. Whip gelatin mixture with a whisk or electric mixer until fluffy. Meanwhile, in a blender or food processor fitted with a metal blade, puree thawed cherries. To remove any small particles of cherry, pour puree through a sieve into whipped gelatin mixture. Stir in almond extract. Pour into 4 dessert bowls. Cover tightly; refrigerate at least 4 hours or up to 8 hours. Garnish each serving with a frozen cherry half. Makes 4 servings.

---

1 serving = 1/2 fruit, 1/4 milk, 50 calories

How to Make Orange Sherbet

1/Spoon frozen juice mixture into a food processor fitted with a metal blade or beat with a mixer until almost smooth. Beat again before serving.

2/Scoop 1/2 cup beaten sherbet into sherbet glasses or small dessert dishes. Store unused sherbet in a container with a tight-fitting lid.

Orange Sherbet

Easy to make in an ice-cream freezer or your refrigerator-freezer.

1 medium orange (2 per lb.)
1/4 cup unsweetened frozen
   orange-juice concentrate

1 pint skim milk (2 cups)
Orange-peel garnish, if desired

Grate orange peel, making 1 tablespoon grated peel. Juice orange. In a medium bowl, combine grated orange peel, orange juice, orange-juice concentrate and milk. Freeze orange mixture in an ice-cream freezer following manufacturer's directions, or pour into an 8-inch-square baking pan. Cover; still-freeze in freezer compartment of your refrigerator until almost firm, about 1 hour, stirring twice. Spoon partially frozen mixture into a food processor fitted with a metal blade. Process until almost smooth. Or, spoon into a large bowl; beat with an electric mixer until almost smooth. Return mixture to pan. Cover; freeze until firm, about 2 hours. To serve, let sherbet stand at room temperature 10 minutes. Process or beat sherbet again. Serve in sherbet glasses or small glass dessert dishes. Garnish with orange peel, if desired. Store unused portion in freezer in a container with a tight-fitting lid. Makes 4 (1/2-cup) servings.

1 serving (1/2 cup) = 1 fruit, 1/2 milk, 90 calories

Melon & Wine Mold

The sweetness comes from the natural sugar in grape juice.

1 (1/4-oz.) envelope unflavored gelatin
  (1 tablespoon)
1/4 cup cold water
3/4 cup boiling water
3/4 cup white-grape juice

1/3 cup white wine
1 drop green food coloring, if desired
1 cup fresh or frozen melon balls
1 fresh mint sprig, if desired
3 thin fresh melon wedges, if desired

In a medium bowl, stir gelatin into cold water; let stand 3 minutes to soften. Pour boiling water over gelatin mixture; stir until gelatin dissolves. Stir in grape juice, wine and food coloring, if desired. Pour gelatin mixture into a 4-cup mold. Cover and refrigerate until mixture has consistency of unbeaten egg whites, 20 to 45 minutes. Stir melon balls into gelatin mixture, or arrange around edge of mold. Refrigerate at least 4 hours or up to 8 hours. To unmold, invert mold onto a platter or serving plate. Wet a dish towel in hot water; wring dry. Place hot wet towel around mold. Leave 5 to 10 seconds; remove mold and cloth. Cut reserved melon balls in half. Garnish mold with mint sprig and melon wedges, if desired. Makes 6 (1/3-cup) servings.

---

1 serving (1/3 cup) = 1 fruit, 50 calories

Cappuccino Mousse   Photo on page 59.

Meringue gives the lightness usually provided by whipped cream.

1 tablespoon grated orange peel
3/4 cup boiling water
1 (1/4-oz.) envelope unflavored gelatin
  (1 tablespoon)
1/4 cup cold water
1 tablespoon plus 1 teaspoon instant-coffee
  granules

1/4 teaspoon ground cinnamon
1/4 cup sugar
1 egg white
4 thin orange slices

Place grated orange peel in a small bowl. Pour boiling water over orange peel; let steep 20 minutes. In a small bowl, stir gelatin into cold water; let stand 3 minutes to soften. Strain orange-peel mixture into a medium saucepan; discard orange peel. Stir in coffee granules, cinnamon and 2 tablespoons sugar. Bring to a boil, stirring until sugar dissolves. Stir about 1/2 cup hot coffee mixture into gelatin mixture. Pour gelatin mixture into remaining coffee mixture. Stir until gelatin is completely dissolved. Cool slightly. Cover; refrigerate until gelatin mixture mounds when dropped from a spoon, 30 to 45 minutes. In a small bowl, beat egg white with a whisk or electric mixer until foamy. Continue beating while gradually adding remaining 2 tablespoons sugar. Beat until glossy soft peaks form. Using same beaters, beat gelatin mixture until smooth. Fold egg-white mixture into beaten gelatin mixture. Spoon mousse into 4 sherbet or dessert dishes. Cover tightly; refrigerate at least 2 hours or up to 8 hours. Cut each orange slice from center through peel. Twist cut edges of peel in opposite directions, making orange twists. Garnish each serving with an orange-peel twist. Makes 4 servings.

---

1 serving = 1 fruit, 1/4 milk, 60 calories

Caramel Baked Apple   *Photo on page 93.*

Rome Beauty apples make especially pretty baked apples.

1/2 whole-wheat-bread slice
1 tablespoon diet margarine
1 tablespoon dark-brown sugar
1 tablespoon chopped pecans or walnuts

2 medium Rome Beauty apples (3 per lb.)
1/2 cup plain low-fat yogurt
1/4 teaspoon apple-pie spice

Preheat oven to 350F (175C). Break bread into pieces. In a blender or food processor fitted with a metal blade, process bread to fine crumbs. In a small skillet, melt margarine. Add brown sugar; stir until sugar melts. Add bread crumbs and nuts. Stir until crumbs begin to brown slightly; set aside. Using a vegetable peeler or knife, core apples. Cut apples in half crosswise. Place apples, cut-side down, in an ungreased 8-inch-square baking pan or shallow casserole dish. Spoon 1/4 of crumb mixture into each apple half. Cover with foil or a lid. Bake in preheated oven until apples are tender, 30 to 40 minutes. In a small bowl, combine yogurt and apple-pie spice. To serve, place 1 baked apple half on each of 4 dessert dishes. Spoon 2 tablespoons spiced yogurt over each warm apple half. Serve warm. Makes 4 servings.

1 serving = 1 fruit, 1/2 bread, 1/2 fat, 100 calories

Snow Pudding

Rennet coagulates the milk, giving a pudding-like consistency.

1 tablespoon plus 1 teaspoon low-sugar
   strawberry spread
1 pint skim milk (2 cups)
2 tablespoons sugar

1 teaspoon vanilla extract
1 rennet tablet
1 tablespoon cold water

Spoon 1 teaspoon strawberry spread into each of 4 small dessert dishes; set aside. In a small saucepan, combine milk, sugar and vanilla. Heat until warm, 110F (45C), stirring constantly. At this temperature, milk mixture will feel warm when dropped on your wrist. Do not overheat milk. In a small bowl, crush rennet tablet with back of a spoon. Stir cold water into crushed rennet; continue stirring until dissolved. Stir rennet mixture into warm milk. Immediately, while mixture is still liquid, pour equally into prepared dessert dishes. Let stand at room temperature 10 minutes, undisturbed. Cover tightly; refrigerate at least 1 hour or up to 4 hours. Makes 4 (1/2-cup) servings.

1 serving (1/2 cup) = 1/2 milk, 1/2 fruit, 75 calories

Champagne Jelly

Photos on cover and page 113.

For a special occasion, serve in champagne glasses.

1 (1/4-oz.) envelope unflavored gelatin (1 tablespoon)	1 cup unsweetened white-grape juice
1/4 cup cold water	3/4 cup pink champagne
	1 cup fresh or frozen unsweetened raspberries

In a small bowl, stir gelatin into cold water; let stand 3 minutes to soften. In a small saucepan, heat grape juice until tiny bubbles form. Stir hot juice into softened gelatin, stirring until gelatin dissolves. Stir in champagne. Refrigerate until gelatin has consistency of unbeaten egg whites, 20 to 45 minutes. Carefully stir in raspberries. Pour into a 4-cup soufflé dish or mold, or pour equally into 6 stemmed champagne glasses. Refrigerate until set, at least 2 hours. Unmold soufflé dish or mold onto a glass platter, if desired. Serve in stemmed glasses or glass bowls. Makes 6 (1/2-cup) servings.

1 serving (1/2 cup) = 1 fruit, 1/4 bread, 65 calories

Lemon Wafers

Serve these light, lemony cookies with a fruit drink or frozen dessert.

1 egg white	2 tablespoons regular margarine, melted
1/4 cup sugar	1 tablespoon lemon juice
1/3 cup all-purpose flour	1/2 teaspoon lemon extract
1/4 teaspoon grated lemon peel	

Preheat oven to 350F (175C). Line a baking sheet with foil. In a medium bowl, beat egg white with an electric mixer until foamy. Gradually beat in sugar, 1 teaspoon at a time. Beat until glossy soft peaks form. Sprinkle flour and lemon peel over beaten egg-white mixture; fold in. In a small bowl, combine margarine, lemon juice and lemon extract. Drizzle over egg-white mixture; gently fold in. Drop batter by level teaspoons 3 inches apart on foil-lined baking sheet. Using back of a spoon, spread batter into a circle about 2 inches in diameter. Bake in preheated oven until edges of cookies begin to brown. Immediately remove cookies from foil to a wire rack to cool. Repeat with remaining batter. Store cooled cookies in a container with a tight-fitting lid. Makes 24 cookies.

1 cookie = 1/4 bread, 1/4 fat, 25 calories

Weight-Management System _____ Section II

If you have reached your target weight and are ready to move on to weight maintenance, you deserve a pat on the back and a hip, hip, hurray!

You have been successful in managing your weight to this point. Managing your weight means taking off excess weight and keeping it off. Some people go through life as though they were on a weight roller coaster—up and down, up and down. Don't let that happen to you! If you have completed Section I, *Sensible-Weight-Loss Plan,* you now have your weight down. Keep it down by using my *Weight-Management System.*

Don't panic! The system is easy to learn. Using the system, you'll be able to create nutritious meals without counting calories. Your menus will include the foods you and your family enjoy, and you won't have to depend on my menus or anyone elses. You can continue to use some of the delicious recipes in this book or from other books or magazines *if* they list the food exchanges. I used the *Weight-Management System* to plan the *Sensible-Weight-Loss Menus* in Section I.

The *Weight-Management System* is made up of:
● Three weight-loss plan-a-meal guides
● A step-by-step worksheet for planning menus using the food-exchange lists and the menu guides.
● Five weight-maintenance plan-a-meal guides
● Six food-exchange lists

FOOD EXCHANGES

Twenty years ago, going on a diet meant memorizing that 1/2 cup cooked oatmeal has 67 calories, 3/4 cup Rice Krispies cereal has 81 calories, one slice whole-wheat bread has 56 calories, and so on. You had to carry a calorie counter to look up the number of calories in anything you wanted to eat. Using the food-exchanges, all you have to remember is that the oatmeal, Rice Krispies cereal and bread all count as one bread exchange.

A bread exchange is one of the six food groups or *food-exchange lists* developed by the American Diabetes Association and American Dietetic Association. They were originally developed for planning diabetic diets.

Only in the last few years have the food-exchange lists been recognized as a tool for controlling calories for weight loss. The lists were published in Exchange Lists for Meal Planning and are used in this book by permission. There are exchange lists for milk, bread, fruit, vegetable, meat and fat.

Food exchanges are a simple way of planning meals without memorizing a book. Instead of memorizing every individual food, you learn groups of foods. You don't count calories, only food exchanges. Simply learn which list a particular food belongs on and the serving size that makes an exchange.

For instance, asparagus, beets, broccoli and carrots are all in the vegetable group. Cooked and cold cereals, grits, rice and pastas are all on the bread list. Most foods are found on the food-exchange list where you would normally put them. However, there are a few exceptions. Corn, lima beans and green peas are starchy vegetables and therefore are in the bread group. Avocados have such a high fat content that they are on the fat list.

Each food-exchange list, beginning on page 134, is made up of foods that have similar nutrients and calories. Because of their similarity, you can **exchange or substitute any one food for another on the same list.** For example, if Brussels sprouts are not a family favorite, substitute green beans, summer squash or tomatoes, which are also on the Vegetable-Exchange List, page 136. You may substitute one slice of toast for 1/2 cup cooked oatmeal or substitute a four-ounce glass of orange juice for 1/2 small banana.

The advantage of this system is that as you plan menus you can choose the foods you like from each exchange list. The system also encourages using a variety of foods. You are not limited to a few "diet" foods.

The one limitation is that you can't substitute foods on one list for those on another list. A meat exchange does not substitute for a bread exchange. The calories are different and the nutrients each supply are different.

Mastering Serving Sizes—Remembering serving sizes and being able to "see" the amount you can have, takes a little time and effort, but is certainly easier than counting calories! There is a general serving size for each group, such as one cup skim milk makes one milk exchange, 1/2 cup cut-up fruit makes one fruit exchange and 1/2 cup cooked or raw vegetable makes one vegetable exchange. However, not all foods on each list have the same serving size. For example, one small apple, 12 grapes and 1/2 small banana are each one fruit exchange.

After you get used to the serving sizes, you'll think of food in terms of cups or 1/2 cups or small, medium or large pieces. The portion sizes will quickly become automatic.

PLAN-A-MEAL GUIDES

Plan-a-Meal Guides, pages 128 and 132-133, are really the core of the Weight-Management System. I have designed eight calorie-level guides, three for weight loss and five for weight maintenance. Each of the nutritionally balanced guides provides the recommended protein, carbohydrate and fat recognized as most healthful. Fifteen percent to 20% of calories are supplied as protein, 50% to 55% as carbohydrate and 25% to 30% as fat.

The guides tell you the number of exchanges from each of the six food-exchange lists to use each day. For example, the 1500-Calorie Weight-Loss Guide has more exchanges than the 1000-Calorie Weight-Loss Guide because of the difference in calories allowed.

The guides also suggest a plan for dividing the total number of exchanges into three meals each day. If you'd like a heartier lunch and a lighter dinner, or want to build snacks into your menus, see *Borrowing Exchanges,* opposite. As long as the total food exchanges from each list is not exceeded, you'll stay within your chosen calorie level.

Choosing a Plan-a-Meal Guide for Weight Loss—If you want to plan your own menus with a calorie level low enough to let you lose weight, turn back to page 5 and study the *Sensible-Weight-Loss Plan.* Follow the instructions for finding your target weight in How Much Weight Do You Need to Lose, page 6.

How Do You Lose Weight, page 8, will help you find the the number of calories you can eat each day and still lose weight. Now find the weight-loss guide on page 128 for that calorie level. Let's suppose that you can have 1200 calories each day. The 1200-Calorie Weight-Loss Guide tells you the total number of exchanges you can have as well as divides the exchanges into breakfast, lunch and dinner.

Using the guide as a framework, you can choose foods from the exchange lists and create enjoyable, low-calorie meals.

Planning a Weight-Loss Meal—The Plan-a-Meal Worksheet, page 129, shows you step-by-step menu planning. Follow through each step on the worksheet, planning one meal at a time. Study the following 1200-calorie breakfast-menu example, then plan your own. Use these steps:

Step 1: Plan a breakfast menu using the 1200-Calorie Weight-Loss Guide. If your chosen calorie level is 1000 or 1500 calories, the steps will be the same, but the exchanges will be different. A 1200-calorie breakfast gives you 1 meat, 2 bread, 1 fruit, 1/2 milk and 2 fat exchanges.

Step 2: Choose a main dish, such as Egg 'n Ham Muffins, page 90, and list the exchanges for 1 serving (1 meat, 1 bread, 1 fat).

Step 3: Select a food from the bread list, if not already part of the main dish. Egg 'n Ham Muffin provides 1 bread exchange, but 2 bread exchanges are allowed. You can add another English-muffin half spread with 1 teaspoon regular margarine or 1 tablespoon diet margarine (1 bread, 1 fat).

Step 4: No vegetable exchanges are included for breakfast. Go to Step 5.

Step 5: Add a fruit exchange to the menu. You could choose 1/2 grapefruit or 4 ounces of orange juice (1 fruit).

Step 6: Total the exchanges used and compare to the guide. One-half milk exchange is still needed to meet all of the exchanges allowed. You could complete breakfast with 1/2 cup plain yogurt made from skim milk or 4 ounces skim milk and a no-calorie beverage, such as coffee or tea.

Borrowing Exchanges—If all the food exchanges are not used in the menu you've planned, include the unused exchanges later for a snack or part of another meal. If extra exchanges are needed for your menu, you can borrow from another meal that day. For example, if you run out of fat exchanges, but need margarine for toast, borrow from lunch. Or you might want to have a fruit-and-milk shake for breakfast that uses 1 milk exchange instead of the 1/2 milk exchange allowed. Borrowing is allowed as long as the total exchanges for the day is not exceeded. *So that you don't forget what was borrowed, write it down.*

Using Your Weight-Loss Menu—If you are using the 21 Sensible-Weight-Loss Menus, pages 14 to 113, you can substitute one of your planned meals for one in the menus. Or you can substitute an entire day's menus. As you continue on your diet and plan some of your own meals, eventually you will have designed a diet that is all your own.

Recipes included in your meals must tell you the food exchanges each serving provides. All recipes in this book include exchanges. You'll find some magazines and cookbooks now give food exchanges per serving for recipes. If you want to plan a menu using one of you own recipes, ask a dietitian to calculate the food exchanges per serving for you.

You may want to include canned soup, refrigerator biscuits or even frozen entrees in some of your meals. *Food Exchanges for Packaged Foods,* page 141, gives you the exchanges and serving size to use. If you want to use products that are not included in the table, write to the manufacturer for the exchanges per serving.

Plan-a-Meal Weight-Loss Guides

1000-Calorie Guide	1200-Calorie Guide	1500-Calorie Guide
Total Daily Exchanges:		
5 meat exchanges	5 meat exchanges	7 meat exchanges
3 bread exchanges	5 bread exchanges	7 bread exchanges
2 vegetable exchanges	3 vegetable exchanges	3 vegetable exchanges
3 fruit exchanges	3 fruit exchanges	3 fruit exchanges
2 milk exchanges	2 milk exchanges	2 milk exchanges
4 fat exchanges	5 fat exchanges	6 fat exchanges
Breakfast:		
1 meat exchange	1 meat exchange	1 meat exchange
1 bread exchange	2 bread exchanges	2 bread exchanges
1 fruit exchange	1 fruit exchange	1 fruit exchange
1/2 milk exchange	1/2 milk exchange	1/2 milk exchange
1 fat exchange	2 fat exchanges	2 fat exchanges
Lunch:		
2 meat exchanges	2 meat exchanges	2 meat exchanges
1 bread exchange	2 bread exchanges	3 bread exchanges
1 vegetable exchange	1 vegetable exchange	1 vegetable exchange
1 fruit exchange	1 fruit exchange	1 fruit exchange
1 milk exchange	1 milk exchange	1 milk exchange
1 fat exchange	1 fat exchange	2 fat exchanges
Dinner:		
2 meat exchanges	2 meat exchanges	4 meat exchanges
1 bread exchange	1 bread exchange	2 bread exchanges
1 vegetable exchange	2 vegetable exchanges	2 vegetable exchanges
1 fruit exchange	1 fruit exchange	1 fruit exchange
1/2 milk exchange	1/2 milk exchange	1/2 milk exchange
2 fat exchanges	2 fat exchanges	2 fat exchanges

Plan-a-Meal Worksheet

Step 1:

Choose a weight-loss guide or maintenance guide that has the calorie level you have chosen. Start with one meal. To the right, list exchanges allowed.

Step 2:

Choose a main dish or meat. Plan a serving that provides the number of meat exchanges allowed for the meal in your guide. List all the exchanges in the serving.

Step 3:

Select a bread, rice, pasta or starchy vegetable, if not part of the main dish. Plan a serving that provides part or all of the bread exchanges allowed for the meal in your guide. Remaining bread exchanges can be used for bread or part of a dessert. List the exchanges opposite.

Step 4:

Choose a vegetable, if not part of the main dish. Plan a serving that provides part or all of the vegetable exchanges allowed for the meal. List the exchanges opposite.

Step 5:

Decide on a fruit or dessert using some of the exchanges not yet used. List the exchanges opposite.

Step 6:

Total the exchanges and compare to your guide.

Step 7:

Add milk, bread or fat exchanges as needed.

Step 8:

Round out the meal with a no-calorie beverage and free raw vegetables, page 136, as desired.

Step 9:

If all exchanges are not used, they may be used as a snack later or part of the next meal.

Step 10:

If extra exchanges are needed, borrow from another meal that day. Be sure the daily total does not exceed the number of calories the guide allows.

Exchanges Allowed:

Meat	_____	Fruit	_____
Bread	_____	Milk	_____
Vegetable	_____	Fat	_____

Menu

_____

_____

_____

_____

_____

_____

_____

_____

_____

_____

_____

_____

_____

Exchanges Used:

Meat	_____	Fruit	_____
Bread	_____	Milk	_____
Vegetable	_____	Fat	_____

_____

_____

_____

Exchanges not used: _____

_____

Extra exchanges used: _____

_____

_____

_____

Weight-Maintenance

The hardest work is over, and you've learned good eating habits as you followed the menus in Section I, *Sensible-Weight-Loss Plan,* or planned your own menus using a Plan-a-Meal Weight-Loss Guide, page 128. Dietitians and experienced dieters agree that maintaining a weight loss takes effort. Without a good plan for staying at this new weight, your lost pounds will gradually reappear. Most dieters have experienced the frustration of regaining every lost pound and sometimes adding more within a year of losing it.

As holidays, celebrations or disappointments come along, it seems impossible to keep from gaining a few extra pounds. When those times come, go back on the Sensible-Weight-Loss Menu you used before, or use the Weight-Management System to help you get those unwanted pounds off and keep them off.

The solution is to continue to use the good eating habits you've formed and to develop a plan for keeping the lost weight off.

Maintaining weight doesn't mean you have to "diet" the rest of your life. With practice in using the maintenance guides, pages 132 and 133, meal planning becomes automatic. You don't have to keep track of nutrients or calories. You'll forget your menus have a structure because everything is built into the guides.

Evaluate Your New Weight—Much like a weight-loss plan, a plan to maintain weight must include a specific calorie level. However, this time calories can be increased.

Evaluate your new weight using the same method you used to determine a target weight for the Sensible-Weight-Loss Plan, page 5. Compare your new weight to the range that corresponds to your height and frame size in Table B, Height & Weight for Men, or Table C, Height & Weight for Women, page 9. Are you in the middle of the weight range? Also compare your new weight to your weight at age 25. See page 6. Both of these comparisons can guide you in deciding if this new weight is right for you.

Probably most important, ask yourself how you feel and look. If you look and feel great, greet the new you! If you look tired and worn and feel exhausted, you probably lost weight too quickly or may have lost too much weight. You may need time to adjust to your new weight or you may need to add a few pounds.

Exercise—Continue the exercise program you followed as you lost weight. Walking, jogging, biking, swimming—whatever your chosen exercise—will help you manage your weight successfully. Exercise is as important now as it was when you were losing weight. Exercise helps control your appetite, helps you use the food you eat for energy, and helps you feel alert and energized.

You might even be ready to increase your exercise. Choose a more vigorous activity or add something like tennis to your less-strenuous exercise.

Calories Needed To Maintain Weight—Energy or caloric needs differ from person to person, but most healthy adults need about 15 calories per pound of body weight each day for normal activities. Multiply your new weight by 15 to determine the number of calories you need each day to maintain weight.

Using the same example we used on page 8, a woman who has reached her desirable weight of 110 pounds needs about 1650 calories (110 pounds x 15 calories per pound = 1650 calories). If she eats 1650 calories each day, she will maintain her present weight with only minor variations.

She can use the 1600-Calorie Maintenance Guide, page 132, and know she won't gain weight. If she should continue to lose weight, she can add an additional serving from one of the food-exchange lists.

If the calorie level you need is mid-way between two guides, try the lower-calorie guide for several weeks. If you lose more weight, go to the higher-calorie guide. If you gain weight on the lower-calorie guide, increase your activity. Other maintenance guides are for 1800, 2000, 2200 and 2400 calories.

Monitoring Weight—Some ex-dieters weigh themselves every morning like they would read a horoscope. If the scale says they haven't gained any weight, it will be a good day. If their weight is up, the day has gotten off to a bad start. It is easy to become obsessed with a scale, weighing every day, looking for weight changes. Minor variations of two to three pounds are common, and are not cause for concern.

It's best to weight only once or at most twice a week. Weighing weekly is important so extra pounds don't sneak up on you, but weighing too often can keep you continually upset. Always use the same scale, weigh the same time of day and with the same amount of clothing.

What If You gain?—When weight increases more than five pounds, it's time to take action. Don't wait until you have 10 or 20 pounds to lose again. Return to a weight-loss diet plan while there are only five pounds to lose. Give yourself two to three weeks, and you'll have your weight down again.

PLANNING MAINTENANCE MEALS

Now that you've decided on a calorie level and maintenance guide that will help you maintain, you're ready to plan some nutritious meals. Until the exchanges become automatic for you, use the Plan-a-Meal Worksheet, page 129. Make photocopies of the worksheet so you will have extra copies. Look at the worksheet as you follow the step-by-step plan below. Let's suppose that you want to plan meals that have 2000 calories per day.

Step 1: Using the 2000-Calorie Weight-Maintenance Guide, page 132, let's plan a dinner. The guide allows 4 meat, 3 bread, 2 vegetable, 1 fruit, 1/2 milk and 2 fat exchanges.

Step 2: Choose a main dish, such as Turkey Scaloppine with Asparagus, page 162, and list the exchanges for 1 serving (4 meat, 1 vegetable).

Step 3: Select a bread, rice, pasta or a starchy vegetable, if not part of the main dish. The main dish does not supply any bread exchanges, so you can add 3 bread exchanges. You could have 1 cup cooked noodles tossed with 2 tablespoons sour cream and 1/2 teaspoon poppy seeds (2 bread, 1 fat).

Step 4: Decide on a fruit or dessert. One fruit exchange is allowed for dinner. You could have a serving of Orange Sherbet, page 121 (1 fruit, 1/2 milk).

Step 5: Choose a vegetable, if not part of the main dish. The main dish supplies 1 vegetable, but 2 vegetable exchanges are allowed. Let's add a broiled tomato half sprinkled with chopped parsley (1 vegetable).

Step 6: Total the exchanges used and compare to the guide. One bread and 1 fat exchange are still needed to meet all of the exchanges allowed. Add a warm dinner roll with 1 teaspoon butter or margarine (1 bread, 1 fat).

Sources of Recipes for Maintaining Weight—Section Three, Maintenance Recipes, starts your collection of trimmed-calorie recipes with Snacks & Light Meals, Salads & Vegetables, Main Dishes and Maintenance Desserts. The exchanges per serving are listed at the bottom of each recipe so you can plan any of these into your meals and snacks. Any of the recipes from the Sensible-Weight-Loss Plan, pages 14 to 125, can also be used in your meals. Look for other recipes that give the exchanges per serving in magazines and other cookbooks. As long as exchanges are given, you can plan the recipes into your meals.

After choosing the recipes, fill in the remaining exchanges with single foods from the Food-Exchange Lists, pages 134 to 139. Or you can use packaged food from Food Exchanges for Packaged Foods, pages 141 to 143.

Be Flexible—To maintain weight for a lifetime, your plan has to be flexible. Any plan that is too rigid to adapt to special situations and celebrations or occasional treats is doomed to failure. Feeling deprived can lead to greater desire for food and eventual overeating. Its important to know that **you can eat anything. No food is forbidden, but how much and how often it is eaten must be planned.** If you indulge some day, adjust other meals that day and maybe even the day before or after to balance the extra exchanges you indulged in.

Meals are much more interesting if favorite foods can be included. For example, if sour cream or Cheddar cheese are favorites, use them as garnishes. Large amounts won't fit into the meal guide, but a small amount gives flavor without adding too many calories. Save fried chicken for a special occasion. Because it is so high in fat, make sure other foods served that day are very low in fat.

Dining out is part of nearly everyone's lifestyle. Your weight-maintenance plan shouldn't keep you from enjoying meals in restaurants or with friends. With a little practice you'll be able to look at a restaurant menu and choose those foods that are lowest in calories. If you don't know how a dish is prepared, ask your waiter. Knowing that you probably will get extra fat exchanges in your restaurant meal, balance them out with low-fat meals before and after. With practice, you'll be able to adjust other meals in your plan so a rich dinner at a fine restaurant won't create the feeling you've destroyed your maintenance plan. Eating out may mean light, lean meals the rest of the day, but sometimes it's worth it!

Once in a while you can even indulge in a fast-food hamburger or milk shake. Fat is usually the calorie culprit in fast-foods, so make choices from the menu that are lowest in fat. Exchanges for Fast Food Restaurants, page 140, gives exchanges for some common fast-foods.

Many fast-food restaurants now have salad bars. Pile your plate high with lettuce and fresh vegetables, but take small spoonfuls of potato or macaroni salad or skip them altogether because they're high in fat. Sprinkle sunflower seeds, cheese and croutons sparingly over your salad and take only 1 ladle of dressing unless a low-calorie dressing is offered. ∎

Plan-a-Meal Weight-Maintenance Guides

1600-Calorie Guide	1800-Calorie Guide	2000-Calorie Guide
Total Daily Exchanges:		
7 meat exchanges	7 meat exchanges	7 meat exchanges
8 bread exchanges	10 bread exchanges	12 bread exchanges
3 vegetable exchanges	3 vegetable exchanges	3 vegetable exchanges
4 fruit exchanges	4 fruit exchanges	5 fruit exchanges
2 milk exchanges	2 milk exchanges	2 milk exchanges
6 fat exchanges	7 fat exchanges	8 fat exchanges
Breakfast:		
1 meat exchange	1 meat exchange	1 meat exchange
3 bread exchanges	3 bread exchanges	3 bread exchanges
1 fruit exchange	1 fruit exchange	1 fruit exchange
1/2 milk exchange	1/2 milk exchange	1/2 milk exchange
2 fat exchanges	2 fat exchanges	2 fat exchanges
Lunch:		
2 meat exchanges	2 meat exchanges	2 meat exchanges
3 bread exchanges	4 bread exchanges	4 bread exchanges
1 vegetable exchange	1 vegetable exchange	1 vegetable exchange
2 fruit exchanges	2 fruit exchanges	2 fruit exchanges
1 milk exchange	1 milk exchange	1 milk exchange
2 fat exchanges	2 fat exchanges	3 fat exchanges
Dinner:		
4 meat exchanges	4 meat exchanges	4 meat exchanges
2 bread exchanges	2 bread exchanges	3 bread exchanges
2 vegetable exchanges	2 vegetable exchanges	2 vegetable exchanges
1 fruit exchange	1 fruit exchange	1 fruit exchange
1/2 milk exchange	1/2 milk exchange	1/2 milk exchange
2 fat exchanges	2 fat exchanges	2 fat exchanges
Snack:		
	1 bread exchange	2 bread exchanges
	1 fat exchange	1 fruit exchange
		1 fat exchange

Copyright 1985 Susan B. Deeming, Ph.D.

Tips for Weight Maintenance

- Avoid unplanned snacking.
- Learn to prepare flavorful dishes with as few calories as possible.
- Limit alcoholic beverages. See the box on page 13.
- You can eat anything as long as you plan the exchanges into your menu.
- Continue to exercise.
- Monitor your weight. Don't let weight get out of control. Make adjustments to your maintenance plan by going to a lower calorie level for a week or two.

- Be flexible. Rigid meal plans can lead to excessive splurges. If you go over your planned number of exchanges in a meal, eat less in another meal or the day before or after.
- Remember, you are not on a diet. Any of the foods you like can be eaten occasionally, even though the calories may be a little high.
- Be proud and pleased with yourself!

Plan-a-Meal Weight-Maintenance Guides

2200-Calorie Guide

Total Daily Exchanges:
8 meat exchanges
12 bread exchanges
3 vegetable exchanges
6 fruit exchanges
2 milk exchanges
10 fat exchanges

Breakfast:
2 meat exchanges
3 bread exchanges
2 fruit exchanges
1/2 milk exchange
2 fat exchanges

Lunch:
2 meat exchanges
4 bread exchanges
1 vegetable exchange
2 fruit exchanges
1 milk exchange
4 fat exchanges

Dinner:
4 meat exchanges
3 bread exchanges
2 vegetable exchanges
1 fruit exchange
1/2 milk exchange
2 fat exchanges

Snack:
1 fruit exchange
2 bread exchanges
2 fat exchanges

2400-Calorie Guide

8 meat exchanges
14 bread exchanges
4 vegetable exchanges
6 fruit exchanges
2 milk exchanges
11 fat exchanges

2 meat exchanges
4 bread exchanges
2 fruit exchanges
1/2 milk exchange
3 fat exchanges

2 meat exchanges
4 bread exchanges
2 vegetable exchanges
2 fruit exchanges
1 milk exchange
4 fat exchanges

4 meat exchanges
4 bread exchanges
2 vegetable exchanges
1 fruit exchange
1/2 milk exchange
2 fat exchanges

1 fruit exchange
2 bread exchanges
2 fat exchanges

Food-Exchange Lists
(milk, meat, vegetable, fruit, bread, fat)

Milk-Exchange List—Milk is an important food to include in meals because it is the leading source of calcium. In addition, it adds protein, vitamin B_2, vitamin B_{12}, folacin, Vitamin A, Vitamin D and magnesium. Adults often leave milk drinking to children, but milk is valuable for adults, too.

If you'd rather not drink milk, use it on cereal, in coffee, fruit shakes and hot drinks, or eat yogurt.

Milk-Exchange List

A milk exchange is based on 1 cup nonfat milk which provides 8 grams protein, 12 grams carbohydrate and 80 calories. If low-fat (1% or 2%) milk or whole milk or milk products are used, add fat exchanges as indicated. Read labels on yogurt and buttermilk cartons to determine if they are made from skim, low-fat or whole milk.

Nonfat Fortified Milk:
1 exchange	= 1 cup skim or nonfat milk
	= 1/3 cup nonfat dry milk powder
	= 1/2 cup canned evaporated skim milk
	= 1 cup plain yogurt made from skim milk
	= 1 cup buttermilk (no fat particles added)

Low-Fat Fortified Milk:
1 exchange	= 1 cup 1% low-fat milk (add 1/2 fat exchange)
	= 1 cup 2% low-fat milk (add 1 fat exchange)
	= 3/4 cup plain yogurt made from low-fat milk (add 1 fat exchange)

Whole Milk
1 exchange	= 1 cup whole milk (add 2 fat exchanges)
	= 1/2 cup canned evaporated whole milk
	= 1 cup plain yogurt, made from whole milk (add 2 fat exchanges)
	= 1 cup buttermilk, made from whole milk (add 2 fat exchanges)

Meat-Exchange List—The key nutrient in meat is protein, but B vitamins, iron and phosphorus are also supplied. Cooked dry beans and peas, eggs, cheese and peanut butter count as meat exchanges because they provide generous amounts of protein.

Milk Exchange: hot Coffee Mocha, page 33; plain low-fat yogurt topped with Fruit & Nut Granola, page 40.

The Meat-Exchange List is divided into three sections based on fat content: **1.** lean-meat (lean cuts of meat, poultry without skin, fish and shellfish, low-fat cheeses, dry beans and dry peas). Each of these count only as 1 meat exchange; **2.** medium-fat meats (eggs, cheese and meat with a higher fat content). To use these, you must count 1 meat exchange **and** 1/2 fat exchange; **3.** high-fat meats. These count as 1 meat exchange **and** 1 fat exchange. Two tablespoons peanut butter counts as 1 meat exchange **and** 2-1/2 fat exchanges. Obviously, if you want to lose weight, you should use lean-meat exchanges.

One meat exchange is equivalent to 1 ounce of *cooked* meat. There is about a 30% loss of weight with cooking, so plan 3 ounces of uncooked meat, poultry or fish for a 2-ounce cooked serving. Trim all fat from meat and remove poultry skin before cooking. Cook meats without adding oil for browning, if possible. Use a nonstick skillet or a skillet coated with nonstick vegetable spray. When oil or margarine is added, use fat exchanges to account for the oil.

Meat Exchange: 3 ounces raw chicken, cooked, becomes 2 ounces cooked chicken; 3 ounces raw beef, cooked, becomes 2 ounces cooked beef.

Meat Exchange, clockwise from center top: 1 large egg; 1 ounce cheese containing less than 5% butterfat (Cheddar-type, jack, mozzarella); 2 tablespoons creamy or chunky peanut butter; 1/4 cup dry or low-fat cottage cheese; 1 ounce Neufchâtel cheese; 1/4 cup cottage cheese; 3 tablespoons freshly grated or dry Parmesan cheese.

Meat-Exchange List

1 lean-meat exchange equals the measurement given and provides 7 grams protein, 3 grams fat and 55 calories.

Lean-Meat Exchanges (Count 1 meat exchange)

1 oz. Beef:	Baby beef, chipped beef, chuck, flank steak, tenderloin, plate ribs, plate skirt steak, top round, bottom round, rump, spare ribs, tripe
1 oz. Lamb:	Leg, rib, sirloin, loin chops, shank, shoulder
1 oz. Pork:	Whole rump, center shank, center cut smoked ham
1 oz. Veal:	Leg, loin, rib, shank, shoulder, cutlets
1 oz. Poultry:	Skinless chicken, turkey, Cornish hen, Guinea hen, pheasant
1 oz. Fish:	Any fresh or frozen fish
1/4 cup	Canned salmon, tuna, mackerel, crab or lobster
1 oz. or 5	Clams, oysters, scallops, shrimp
3	Sardines, drained
1 oz.	Cheeses containing less than 5% butterfat
1/4 cup	Cottage cheese, dry or low-fat
1/2 cup	Cooked dried beans or peas (add 1 bread exchange)

Medium-Fat-Meat Exchanges
(Count 1 meat exchange and 1/2 fat exchange)

1 oz. Beef:	Lean ground beef (15% fat), canned corned beef, corned bottom round, rib eye
1 oz. Pork:	Loin chops, shoulder arm (picnic), shoulder blade, Boston Butt, Canadian bacon, boiled ham
1 oz.	Liver, heart, kidney, sweetbreads
1/4 cup	creamed cottage cheese
1 oz.	Mozzarella cheese, ricotta, farmer's cheese, Neufchâtel cheese
3 tablespoons	Grated Parmesan cheese
1	Large egg

High-Fat-Meat Exchanges
(Count 1 meat exchange and 1 fat exchange)

1 oz. Beef:	Brisket, corned beef brisket, ground beef or hamburger (more than 20% fat), ground chuck, rib roast, rib, club or T-bone steaks
1 oz. Lamb:	Breast
1 oz. Pork:	Spare ribs, country-style ribs, ground pork, country-style ham, deviled ham
1 oz. Veal:	Breast
1 oz. Poultry:	Capon, domestic duck, goose
1 oz.	Natural Cheddar-type cheeses
1 oz. slice	Cold cuts
1 small	Frankfurter

Peanut Butter
(Count 1 meat exchange and 2-1/2 fat exchanges)

2 tablespoons	Peanut butter, smooth or chunky

Vegetable Exchange: Crisp Cocktail Vegetables, page 150; 1/2-cup serving gives 1 vegetable exchange.

Vegetable-Exchange List—Vegetables and fruits are the leading sources of vitamins A and C. Many are good sources of potassium. Some provide folacin and others supply vitamin B_6. Fiber is an added plus in all vegetables. Serve vegetables raw or cooked, but be sure to count fat exchanges if oil, butter or margarine is added in cooking.

Be sure to choose one vegetable or fruit that is high in vitamin C each day. A vegetable or fruit high in vitamin A should be eaten at least three times a week. See Vegetable-Exchange List below, and Fruit-Exchange List, opposite.

Some vegetables have such a high water content that their calorie level is very low when eaten raw. **You can eat as much raw lettuce, spinach, cucumber and radish as you like without counting any exchanges.** Make salads, snacks and plate garnishes of these vegetables.

Free uncooked vegetables can be eaten in any quantity and at any time. Below, clockwise from lower left: spinach, romaine lettuce, green-leaf lettuce, red-leaf lettuce, endive, parsley, French cornichons, radishes, cucumbers.

Vegetable-Exchange List

1 vegetable exchange is 1/2 cup cooked or raw vegetable and provides 5 grams carbohydrate, 2 grams protein and 25 calories. Vegetables high in vitamins A or C are labeled.

Asparagus[C]	Rhubarb
Alfalfa sprouts	Rutabaga[C]
Bean sprouts	Sauerkraut
Beets	String Beans, green or yellow
Broccoli[AC]	Summer squash
Brussels sprouts[C]	Tomatoes[C]
Cabbage[C]	Tomato juice[C]
Carrots[A]	Turnips[C]
Cauliflower[C]	Vegetable-juice cocktail
Celery	Zucchini
Eggplant	
Green pepper	The following raw vegetables may be used
Greens:[AC]	as desired:
Beet	Chicory
Chard	Chinese cabbage
Collard	Cucumber
Dandelion	Endive
Kale	Escarole
Mustard	Lettuce
Spinach	Parsley
Turnip	Pickles, dill
Mushrooms	Radishes
Okra	Watercress
Onions	

Starchy vegetables are found in the Bread-Exchange List.

Fruit-Exchange List—Fruits are valuable sources of vitamins A and C and some supply good amounts of potassium and folacin. Fruit exchanges provide carbohydrate for energy and their natural sweetness makes them a good snack or light dessert to finish a meal.

Raw, cooked or dried fruits all count as fruit exchanges. Frozen or canned fruit count the same as raw fruit as long as no sugar is added in preserving. Fruit canned in juice or extra-light syrup also count as fruit exchanges, but the number of exchanges for the same serving size is different, see Food Exchanges for Packaged Foods, page 141.

Sweeteners, including table sugar, brown sugar, honey and syrups, have carbohydrate and calorie levels similar to fruit and count as fruit exchanges. When used in desserts or on fruit, sweeteners add extra fruit exchanges. If you want to use artificial sweeteners, see page 10.

Be sure to choose one vegetable or fruit high in vitamin C each day and one that is high in vitamin A at least three times a week. See Vegetable-Exchange List, opposite left, and Fruit-Exchange List, opposite right.

Fruit-Exchange List

1 fruit exchange equals the measurement given and provides 10 grams carbohydrate and 40 calories. Fruits high in vitamins A or C are labeled.

Apple	1 small	Kiwi fruit	1/2 medium
Apple juice	1/3 cup	Mango[AC]	1/2 small
Applesauce,		Melon:	
unsweetened	1/2 cup	Cantaloupe[AC]	1/4 small
Apricots, fresh[A]	2 medium	Honeydew[C]	1/8 medium
Apricots, dried[A]	4 halves	Watermelon	1 cup
Banana	1/2 small	Nectarine[A]	1 small
Berries:		Orange[C]	1 small
Blackberries	1/2 cup	Orange juice[C]	1/2 cup
Blueberries	1/2 cup	Papaya[C]	3/4 cup
Raspberries[C]	1/2 cup	Peach[A]	1 medium
Strawberries[C]	1/2 cup	Pear	1 small
Cherries	10 large	Persimmon[A]	1 medium
Cider	1/3 cup	Pineapple	1/2 cup
Dates	2	Pineapple juice	1/3 cup
Fig, fresh	1	Plums	2 medium
Fig, dried	1	Prunes	2 medium
Grapefruit[C]	1/2	Prune juice	1/4 cup
Grapefruit juice[C]	1/2 cup	Raisins	2 tablespoons
Grapes	12	Tangerine[C]	1 medium
Grape juice	1/4 cup		

Cranberries may be used as desired if no sugar is added.

Fruit Exchange: Fruits high in Vitamins A and C, clockwise from top left: oranges[C], grapefruit juice[C], honeydew melon[C], nectarines[A], peaches[A], papaya[C], persimmons[A], lemons[C], strawberries[C], dried apricots[A], raspberries[C], limes[C], grapefruit[C], cantaloupe[AC], orange juice[C]. Not shown: fresh apricots[A], mangos[AC], tangerines[C].

Bread Exchange, clockwise from top left: 1 slice rye, pumpernickel, white and whole-wheat bread; 1/2 English muffin; 1/2 cup bran flakes; 1/2 bagel; 2 graham crackers; 1 (6-inch) flour tortilla; 1 small potato; 1/3 cup corn; 1/2 cup green peas; 1/2 cup cooked pasta; 5 saltine crackers; 3 (3-1/2" x 2") rye wafers.

Bread-Exchange List—Bread exchanges are important sources of carbohydrate that give you energy as well as B vitamins and minerals. Whole-grain breads and cereals, bran-containing products and dried beans are also good sources of fiber. Extra starchy vegetables, such as corn, potatoes, fresh peas and winter squashes, are included as bread exchanges because they have as much carbohydrate per serving as breads.

Bread exchanges are easy to include in meals, but watch out for the butter or margarine usually put on them. One small potato counts as 1 bread exchange, but when butter or margarine is melted over the top, you've added fat exchanges. Some baked goods, such as muffins, biscuits and pancakes, have more fat in them than other breads or cereals. See the bottom of the following list for some prepared foods.

Bread-Exchange List

1 bread exchange equals the measurement given and provides 15 grams carbohydrate, 2 grams protein and 70 calories.

Bread	
White, whole-wheat, rye, pumpernickel, cracked-wheat, raisin	1 slice
Bagel	1/2 small
English muffin	1/2
Plain dinner roll	1 small
Hot-dog bun	1/2
Hamburger bun	1/2
Dried bread crumbs	2 tablespoons
Tortilla	1 (6-inch)
Cereal	
Bran flakes	1/2 cup
Other ready-to-eat unsweetened cereals	3/4 cup
Puffed cereal, unfrosted	1 cup
Cereal, cooked	1/2 cup
Grits, cooked	1/2 cup
Rice or barley, cooked	1/2 cup
Pasta, cooked (spaghetti, noodles, macaroni)	1/2 cup
Popcorn, hot-air-popped, no added fat, large kernel	3 cups
Cornmeal, dry	2 tablespoons
Flour	2-1/2 tablespoons
Wheat germ	1/4 cup
Bulgur, dry uncooked	2 tablespoons
Crackers	
Arrowroot	3
Graham, 2-1/2-inch squares	2
Matzoh, 6" x 4"	1/2
Oyster	20
Pretzels, 3-1/8" x 1/8"	25
Rye wafers, 3-1/2" x 2"	3
Saltines	6
Soda, 2-1/2-inch squares	4
Dried Beans, Peas & Lentils:	
Beans, peas, lentils, cooked	1/2 cup
Baked beans, no pork, canned	1/4 cup
Starchy Vegetables:	
Corn	1/3 cup
Corn on the cob	1 small
Lima beans	1/2 cup
Parsnips	2/3 cup
Peas, green, canned or frozen	1/2 cup
Potato, white	1 small
Potato, mashed	1/2 cup
Pumpkin	3/4 cup
Winter squash, acorn or butternut	1/2 cup
Yam or sweet potato	1/4 cup
Home-Prepared Foods:	
Biscuit, 2-inch diameter (add 1 fat exchange)	1
Corn bread, 2" x 2" x 1" (add 1 fat exchange)	1
Corn muffin 2-inch diameter (add 1 fat exchange)	1
Crackers, round butter type (add 1 fat exchange)	5
Muffin, plain, small (add 1 fat exchange)	1
Pancake, 5-inch diameter (add 1 fat exchange)	1
Potato or corn chips (add 2 fat exchanges)	15
Potatoes, French fries (add 1 fat exchange)	8
Waffle, 5" x 1/2 " (add 1 fat exchange)	1

Fat-Exchange List—Fats add the rich flavors of cream, butter and oils that make meals so satisfying. Without some fat, flavors seem flat and shallow. But fats also add up calories quickly! They have more calories per gram than other foods. Measure fats added to meals carefully. Even a little bit extra can mean a lot of extra calories. Besides carrying flavors, fats supply some fat-soluble vitamins and the essential fatty acid known as linoleic acid.

Because of their high-caloric value, foods on this list have small serving sizes. *One teaspoon* of regular margarine, butter or mayonnaise counts as 1 fat exchange. If you use reduced-calorie imitation margarine, called *diet margarine,* or reduced-calorie imitation mayonnaise, *1 tablespoon* equals 1 fat exchange. For other foods reduced in fat, see Food Exchanges for Packaged Foods, page 141.

Fat Exchange, clockwise from top left: 6 small walnuts; 1/8 (4-inch-diameter) avocado; 1 teaspoon mayonnaise; 1 teaspoon butter or regular margarine; 1 tablespoon cream cheese; 1 tablespoon diet margarine; 1 bacon strip fried crisp; 5 small ripe olives; 20 Spanish peanuts.

Fat-Exchange List

One fat exchange equals the measurement given and provides 5 grams fat and 45 calories. Fat content of foods is saturated, monounsaturated or polyunsaturated. To reduce the risk of heart disease, it is recommended that polyunsaturated fats be used if possible. Monounsaturated fats have neither a positive nor a negative effect on heart disease. Be sure to read labels. The fat content of unmarked foods is saturated.

Avocado, 4-inch diameter**	1/8	Oil	
Bacon, fried crisp	1 strip	corn, cottonseed, safflower, soy,	
Bacon fat	1 teaspoon	sunflower*	1 teaspoon
Butter	1 teaspoon	olive, peanut**	1 teaspoon
Cream, light (half & half)	2 tablespoons	Olives**	5 small
Cream, sour	2 tablespoons	Salad Dressings:	
Cream, heavy (whipping cream)	1 tablespoon	Commercial French dressing***	1 tablespoon
Cream cheese	1 tablespoon	Commercial Italian dressing***	1 tablespoon
Lard	1 teaspoon	Mayonnaise type***	2 teaspoons
Margarine, soft, tub or stick***	1 teaspoon	Salt pork	3/4-inch cube
Margarine, regular stick	1 teaspoon		
Mayonnaise***	1 teaspoon		
Nuts:			
Almonds**	10 whole		
Pecans**	2 large whole		
Peanuts**:			
Spanish	20 whole		
Virginia	10 whole		
Walnuts*	6 small		
Other**	6 small		

Based on material in the booklet *Exchange Lists For Meal Planning;* Copyright 1976 American Diabetes Association, Inc. and The American Dietetic Association in cooperation with National Institute of Arthritis, Metabolism and Digestive Diseases; the National Heart and Lung Institute; National Institutes of Health, Public Health Service, US Department of Health, Education and Welfare.

* polyunsaturated
** primarily monounsaturated
*** polyunsaturated (Food is polyunsaturated only when made from corn, cottonseed, safflower, soy or sunflower oil.)
For diet margarine or imitation mayonnaise, see page 142.

Exchanges for Fast-Food Restaurants

	Calories	Exchanges
Burger King®		
Hamburger	310	2 meat, 2 bread, 1 vegetable, 1 fat
Whopper®	670	3 meat, 3 bread, 1 fruit, 4-1/2 fat
Whopper Jr.®	370	2 meat, 2 bread, 1 vegetable, 1 fat
Fries, regular	210	1-1/2 bread, 2 fat
Shake	340	1 milk, 4 fruit, 2 fat
Dairy Queen®		
Cone, small	140	1/4 milk, 1 fruit, 1/2 bread, 1 fat
Cone, regular	240	1/2 milk, 1/2 bread, 2-1/2 fruit, 1-1/2 fat
Shake, small	490	1-1/4 milk, 6 fruit, 2-1/2 fat
Sundae, small	190	1/2 milk, 2-1/2 fruit, 1 fat
Dilly Bar	210	1/2 milk, 2 fruit, 2-1/2 fat
Jack-in-the-Box®		
Hamburger	276	1-1/3 meat, 2 bread, 1 fat
Jumbo Jack	485	3 meat, 3 bread, 3-1/3 fat
Taco, regular	191	1 meat, 1 bread, 1-1/2 fat
Breakfast Jack Sandwich	307	2 meat, 2 bread, 1-1/3 fat
Kentucky Fried Chicken®		
Original Recipe®		
1 breast half	199	2 meat, 1/2 bread, 1 fat
1 thigh	257	2-1/2 meat, 1/2 bread, 2 fat
1 drumstick	117	1-1/2 meat, 1/4 bread, 1/2 fat
Extra Crispy®		
1 breast	286	2 meat, 1 bread, 2-1/2 fat
1 thigh	343	3 meat, 1 bread, 3 fat
1 drumstick	155	1-1/2 meat, 1/2 bread, 1 fat
Long John Silver's®		
1 Fish with batter	202	1-1/2 meat, 3/4 bread, 1-1/2 fat
1 Chicken Planks	104	3/4 meat, 1/2 bread, 3/4 fat
3 Battered Shrimp	141	3/4 meat, 2/3 bread, 1-1/4 fat
3 Breaded Oysters	180	3/4 meat, 1 bread, 1-1/4 fat
2 Hush Puppies	145	1-1/4 bread, 1-1/3 fat
Clam Chowder (6 oz.)	128	1/2 milk, 2/3 bread, 1 fat
Baked Fish with Sauce	151	4-2/3 meat
Seafood Salad	386	1-1/4 meat, 1 bread, 1 vegetable, 5 fat
McDonald's®		
Hamburger	255	1-1/2 meat, 2 bread, 1 fat
Cheeseburger	307	2 meat, 2 bread, 1-1/2 fat
Quarter Pounder®	424	3 meat, 2 bread, 2-1/2 fat
Big Mac®	563	3 meat, 2-1/2 bread, 5 fat
Egg McMuffin®	327	2 meat, 2 bread, 2 fat
Fries, regular	220	1-3/4 bread, 2 fat
Shake, chocolate	383	1-1/4 milk, 5 fruit, 2 fat
Wendy's		
Hamburger, single	470	3 meat, 2-1/4 bread, 3-1/2 fat
Chili, small	230	2-1/3 meat, 1-1/2 bread
Frosty	390	1 milk, 4 fruit, 3 fat

Nutritional information in this table is based on information from the restaurants. It is current as of publication date. For the most up-to-date information, write to the restaurant headquarters.

Exchanges for Packaged Foods

Food	Serving	Calories	Exchanges
Soups			
Campbell's Soup Company[1]			
Campbell's Condensed Soups, prepared with water:			
Chicken Noodle	8 oz.	70	1/2 bread, 1/2 fat
Chicken with Rice	8 oz.	60	1/2 bread, 1/2 fat
Chicken Vegetable	8 oz.	70	1/2 bread, 1/2 fat
Bean with Bacon	8 oz.	150	1-1/2 bread, 1 fat
Beef broth	8 oz.	15	no exchanges
Chicken broth	8 oz.	35	1/2 bread
Tomato	8 oz.	90	1 bread, 1/2 fat
Cream of Chicken	8 oz.	110	1/2 meat, 1/2 bread, 1 fat
Cream of Mushroom	8 oz.	100	1/2 bread, 1-1/2 fat
Minestrone	8 oz.	80	1 vegetable, 1/2 bread, 1/2 fat
Campbell's Condensed Soups, prepared with milk:			
Tomato	8 oz.	170	1/2 milk, 1 bread, 1/2 fat
Clam Chowder, New England	8 oz.	160	1/2 meat, 1/2 bread, 1/2 milk, 1/2 fat
Cream of Potato	8 oz.	110	1/2 bread, 1/4 milk, 1 fat
Thomas J. Lipton, Inc.[1]			
Lipton Cup-a-Soup Instant Soup®, prepared with water:			
Chicken Noodle with Meat	6 oz.	45	1/2 bread, 1/4 fat
Beef-Flavored Noodle	6 oz.	45	1/2 bread, 1/4 fat
Spring Vegetable	6 oz.	45	1-1/3 vegetable, 1/4 fat
Cream of Chicken	6 oz.	80	2/3 bread, 1 fat
Cream of Mushroom	6 oz.	80	2/3 bread, 1 fat
Meat & Cheese			
Swift[1]			
Sizzlean Pork Breakfast Strips	2 strips	70	1/2 meat, 1 fat
Oscar Meyer[1]			
Bologna	1 slice	75	1/2 meat, 1 fat
Kraft[2]			
American Cheese	1 oz.	110	1 meat, 1 fat
Light n' Lively®	1 oz.	70	1 meat
Part Skim Mozzarella	1 oz.	80	1 meat, 1/2 fat
Borden[2]			
Skim American	1 oz.	70	1 meat, 1/2 fat
Lite Line®	1 oz.	50	1 meat
Meal Accompaniments			
Ore-Ida[1]			
Golden Fries	3 oz.	110	1-1/4 bread, 1 fat
Tater Tots, plain	3 oz.	160	1-1/3 bread, 1-2/3 fat
Golden Grain Macaroni Company[1]			
Rice-a-Roni®, Chicken	1/6 pkg.	130	2 bread
Rice-a-Roni®, Beef	1/6 pkg.	130	2 bread
Noodle Roni Parmesano®	1/5 pkg.	130	1-1/2 bread, 1/2 fat
General Mills, Inc.[1]			
Betty Crocker®			
Fettuccini Alfredo, prepared as directed	1/4 pkg.	220	1 bread, 2/3 milk, 2 fat
Noodles Romanoff, prepared as directed	1/4 pkg.	230	1 bread, 2/3 milk, 2 fat
Potato Buds®, prepared as directed	1/2 cup	130	1 bread, 1 fat
Potatoes Au Gratin, prepared as directed	1/2 cup	150	1-1/2 bread, 1 fat
General Foods Corporation[1]			
Stove Top® Stuffing			
Mix made with butter	1/2 cup	180	1-1/2 bread, 2 fat

Exchanges for Packaged Foods (cont.)

Food	Serving	Calories	Exchanges
Breads and Rolls			
Pillsbury Company[1] (also see Snacks & Desserts)			
Hungry Jack® Pancake Mix			
Buttermilk Complete pancakes)	3 (4-inch)	180	2-1/2 bread
Buttermilk Biscuits	2	100	1-1/2 bread
Hungry Jack® Flaky Biscuits	2	170	1-1/2 bread, 1-1/2 fat
Crescent Rolls	2	200	1-1/2 bread, 2 fat
Sara Lee[1]			
All Butter Croissants	1	170	1-1/4 bread, 1-3/4 fat
Pepperidge Farm, Inc.[1]			
Pepperidge Farms®			
Very Thin Whole-Wheat Bread	2 slices	90	1 bread, 1/3 fat
Pepperidge Farms®			
Very Thin Multi-Grain Bread	2 slices	80	1 bread
Pepperidge Farms®			
Seasoned Croutons	1/2 oz.	70	2/3 bread, 1/2 fat
Snacks & Desserts			
General Mills, Inc.[1]			
Nature Valley®			
Granola Oats 'n Honey Bar	1	110	1 bread, 1 fat
Dole®[1]			
Strawberry or Pineapple Fruit Sorbet	4 oz.	120	3 fruit
Frozen Fruit 'n Juice			
Bar, orange, pineapple, or strawberry	1 bar	70	1-1/2 fruit
Pillsbury Company[1]			
Banana Quick Bread Mix	1/2 loaf	150	1 bread, 1 fruit, 1 fat
Date Quick Bread Mix	1/2 loaf	160	1 bread, 1-1/2 fruit, 1/2 fat
Salad Dressings & Spreads			
Kraft			
Reduced-Calorie Dressings:			
Light n' Lively®[2]			
Reduced-Calorie Mayonnaise	1 tbsp	40	1 fat
S & W Fine Foods[1]			
Nutradiet® Reduced-Calorie Dressings:			
Italian No-Oil	1 tbsp	2	no exchanges
Thousand Island	1 tbsp	25	1/2 fat
French Style	1 tbsp	18	1/3 fruit
Blue Cheese	1 tbsp	25	1/4 fruit, 1/3 fat
Nabisco Brands, Inc.[1]			
Fleishman's® Diet Margarine	1 tbsp	50	1 fat
Fruits, Jams & Syrups			
Del Monte Corporation[1]			
Del Monte Lite Fruit:			
Peach Halves in extra-light syrup	1/3 cup	35	1 fruit
Apricot Halves in extra-light syrup	1/3 cup	40	1 fruit
Fruit Cocktail in extra-light syrup	1/3 cup	35	1 fruit
Pear Halves in extra-light syrup	1/3 cup	35	1 fruit
Dole®[1]			
Pineapple in juice			
Chunks or crushed	1/3 cup	45	1 fruit
Slices	1 slice	35	1 fruit
Aunt Jemima®			
Lite Pancake Syrup[2]	2 tbsp	50	1-1/4 fruit

Food	Serving	Calories	Exchanges
J. M. Smucker Company®			
Smucker's® Low Sugar Spread	2 tsp	16	1/2 fruit
Dairy Products & Substitutes			
Dannon Company[1]			
Dannon Fruit Yogurt	8 oz.	260	1 milk, 1 bread, 2 fruit, 1/2 fat
General Mills, Inc.[1]			
Yoplait® Custard-Style™ Yogurt, Fruit flavors	6 oz.	190	3/4 milk, 1/2 bread, 1-1/2 fruit, 1 fat
Carnation Company [1]			
Coffee-mate®	1 tbsp	33	1/2 fat
Darigold[2]			
Dari Lite®			
Sour Half and Half	1/4 cup	80	1/4 milk, 1-1/4 fat
General Foods Corporation[1]			
Birdseye® Cool Whip	1 tbsp	14	1/3 fat
Vegetables			
Pillsbury Company[1]			
Green Giant®			
Broccoli in Cheese Sauce	1/2 cup	70	1-1/2 vegetable, 1/2 fat
Cauliflower in Cheese Sauce	1/2 cup	60	1/2 bread, 1/2 vegetable, 1/2 fat
Peas in Cream Sauce	1/2 cup	100	1/2 bread, 1 vegetable, 1 fat
General Foods Corporation[1]			
Birdseye® Stir-Fry Vegetables:			
Japanese-Style	3.3 oz.	30	1 vegetable
Chinese-Style	3.3 oz.	30	1 vegetable
Birdseye® International Vegetables with Seasoned Sauces:			
Italian-Style	3.3 oz.	110	1/2 bread
New England-Style	3.3 oz.	130	1 vegetable, 1/2 bread, 1-1/2 fat
Birdseye® Combination Vegetables:			
Broccoli with Water Chestnuts	3.3 oz.	30	1 vegetable
Green Peas & Pearl Onions	3.3 oz.	70	1 vegetable, 1/2 bread
Dinners			
Stouffer Foods Corporation[1]			
Stouffer's Lean Cuisine®			
Beef & Pork Cannelloni with Mornay Sauce	9-5/8 oz.	260	2 meat, 1 bread, 1/2 milk, 1/2 vegetable, 1 fat
Chicken à l'Orange with Almond Rice	8 oz.	280	3 meat, 1 bread, 1 fruit, 1 vegetable
Chicken & Vegetables with Vermicelli	12-3/4 oz.	260	2-1/2 meat, 1-1/2 bread, 1 vegetable
Chicken Chow Mein with Rice	11-1/4 oz.	250	1-1/2 meat, 2 bread, 1 vegetable
Filet of Fish Divan	12-3/8 oz.	270	3 meat, 1/2 bread, 1/2 milk, 1/2 vegetable
Filet of Fish Florentine	9 oz.	240	3 meat, 1 vegetable, 1/2 milk
Oriental Beef with Vegetables & Rice	8-5/8 oz.	260	2 meat, 2 bread
Spaghetti with Beef & Mushroom Sauce	11-1/2 oz.	280	1-1/2 meat, 2 bread, 2 vegetable
Zucchini Lasagna	11 oz.	260	2-1/2 meat, 1-1/2 bread, 1 vegetable
Armour Food Companies[1]			
Classic Lite® Dinners from Armour			
Chicken Burgundy	11.25 oz.	230	3 meat, 1 bread
Seafood, Natural Herbs	11.5 oz.	240	2 meat, 2 bread
Sliced Beef with Broccoli	10.25 oz.	280	3 meat, 2 bread
Turf and Surf	10 oz.	260	3 meat, 1 bread
Turkey Parmesan	11 oz.	260	3 meat, 1 bread, 1 vegetable
Veal Pepper Steak	11 oz.	280	3 meat, 2 bread

[1]Nutritional information based on information provided by manufacturer.
[2]Nutritional information based on product nutritional label.

Nutrition information in this table is current as of publication date. For the most up-to-date information, write to the manufacturer.

Weight-Maintenance Recipes _____ Section III

Curried-Chicken & Ham Muffins, Ginger-Fruit Bars or Chicken Primavera hardly sound or taste like reduced-calorie foods. These recipes and many more that follow show you cooking techniques that can make "trimmed" dishes with all the flavor and pizazz you desire. These recipes aren't "diet" food but do have controlled calories. Family or guests will never guess such delicious food is good for them too.

Weight-maintenance recipes, pages 144 to 172, are only a beginning for your weight-maintenance program. Collect other recipes that give the exchanges and calories. They will give you choices as you plan meals. Examine diabetic cookbooks for good ideas, but you will probably find them too restrictive. Remember, you are not "dieting" just eating wisely.

Snacks & Light Meals

Snacking can be an obstacle to maintaining your weight loss, but not when nutritious snacks are included in your meal plan. If you have always enjoyed a light mid-afternoon or before-bed snack, you can go back to enjoying it now that you have reached your target weight. Make it a part of your daily plan.

Make your own snack foods. Most commercial snack foods are high in fat and that means extra calories. A 1-ounce bag of potato chips or corn chips has 160 calories and accounts for 3 fat exchanges. Add 2 tablespoons of a sour-cream dip and the snack totals 220 calories and 4 fat exchanges. Four sandwich cookies have 200 calories and two fat exchanges. See page 141 for exchanges and calories of other commercial snacks.

These snack recipes contain less fat and have satisfying crunchiness and good flavor so often expected in a snack. Bagel chips, made by thinly slicing and toasting rye bagels or pumpernickel bagels, are the perfect dippers for Curry-Cheese Dip. Six bagel chips give you 1/2 bread exchange and 48 calories. And nothing goes better with Cucumber

Dip than warm pita wedges. Cut a six-inch pita-bread round into 10 wedges. Heat before serving. Six pita wedges equal 3/4 bread exchange and 55 calories. You won't even miss the potato chips and corn chips.

Make some of these snacks ahead to have available when you need a snack break. Some, such as Garlic & Herb Spread and Chewy Pretzels with Mustard Dip, are good party appetizers. Puffy Baked Tuna Sandwich or Zucchini Tart will make a light meal for lunch or fill in when a larger meal would be too much.

While losing weight, it is important to eat regular meals and to eat all the foods included in the diet. However, with weight maintenance, it is more important to follow your appetite as long as it doesn't lead you to exceed your daily calorie limit. Eat regularly, but if a full dinner seems too heavy, try a light meal. Hot Chili Buns—a French-roll boat filled with chili—and Chicken-Dumpling Soup are two light luncheon dishes that are filling without being high in calories. ∎

Chewy Pretzels with Mustard Dip

The whole family will love this snack.

1 loaf frozen whole-wheat-bread dough
   or white-bread dough
2 tablespoons baking soda

1 egg
1 tablespoon water
Coarse salt or kosher salt

Mustard Dip:
1 tablespoon bottled reduced-calorie
   mayonnaise

2 tablespoons prepared mustard
1 tablespoon buttermilk

Thaw frozen bread dough according to package directions. Prepare Mustard Dip; refrigerate until served. Lightly grease 2 large baking sheets; set aside. Cut dough crosswise into 4 equal pieces. Cover 3 pieces with plastic wrap. Cut remaining piece into 4 equal pieces. Roll each piece into a 12-inch rope. Cross ends of 1 rope about 3 inches from tips. Press dough together where rope crosses. Lift loop over so it touches rope ends. Gently press loop to ends. Repeat with remaining dough. Preheat oven to 400F (205C). In a 4-quart pot, bring 2 quarts water and baking soda to a boil. Meanwhile, in a small bowl, beat egg and 1 tablespoon water until blended; set aside. Reduce heat until water barely simmers. Carefully place 4 or 5 pretzels at a time into simmering water. When pretzels rise to top, turn over. Simmer 30 seconds longer. Using a slotted spoon, remove pretzels from water. Place on greased baking sheets. Brush with reserved egg mixture. Sprinkle with salt. Bake in preheated oven until well browned, about 15 minutes. Immediately remove from baking sheets; cool on wire racks. For each serving, serve 1 warm or cold pretzel with 1 teaspoon dip. Pretzels can be stored at room temperature in a plastic bag or in a container with a tight-fitting lid, up to 7 days. To crisp stored pretzels, warm in a preheated 300F (150C) oven 3 to 5 minutes. Makes 16 servings. **To make Mustard Dip,** in a small bowl, combine mayonnaise and mustard. Stir in buttermilk. Spoon into a container with a tight-fitting lid. Cover tightly; refrigerate until served, up to 5 days. Makes about 1/4 cup.

---

1 pretzel = 1 bread, 80 calories
1 teaspoon dip = 5 calories

Curried Popcorn & Cereal Mix

If between-meal snacks appeal to you, this one will become a favorite.

8 cups hot-air-popped popcorn
2 cups bite-sized shredded-wheat cereal
1 cup dry-roasted peanuts
2 tablespoons regular margarine

1 teaspoon paprika
1/4 teaspoon garlic powder
1/2 teaspoon curry powder
1/2 cup golden raisins

Preheat oven to 250F (120C). In a large bowl, combine popcorn, cereal and peanuts; toss to distribute. Set aside. In a small saucepan, combine margarine, paprika, garlic powder and curry powder. Stir over medium heat until margarine melts. Drizzle over popcorn mixture; stir to coat evenly. Spread mixture in 2 ungreased 13'' x 9'' baking pans. Bake in preheated oven 30 minutes, stirring every 10 minutes. Cool in pans on wire racks, 15 minutes. Add 1/4 cup raisins to each pan; stir to distribute. When thoroughly cooled, store in a large container with a tight-fitting lid up to 1 week. For each serving, pour 1/2 cup into a small bowl. Makes about 11 cups.

---

1 serving (1/2 cup) = 1/2 bread, 1 fat, 80 calories

Garlic & Herb Spread

Use as a snack or party appetizer.

1/2 (8-oz.) pkg. Neufchâtel cheese,
  room temperature
1/2 cup low-fat cottage cheese
1 small garlic clove, minced
1/2 teaspoon Beau Monde seasoning

1 teaspoon chopped fresh parsley
1/2 teaspoon red-wine vinegar
1/4 teaspoon fines herbs
24 (3" x 1-7/8") rye wafers

In a medium bowl, beat Neufchâtel cheese with an electric mixer until fluffy. In a blender, puree cottage cheese; stir into Neufchâtel cheese. Stir in garlic, Beau Monde seasoning, parsley, vinegar and fines herbs. Spoon into a container with a tight-fitting lid; cover tightly. Refrigerate at least 6 hours. Serve with rye wafers. For each serving, spoon 2 tablespoons spread into a small bowl. Serve with 3 rye wafers. Makes about 1 cup.

2 tablespoons spread = 1/2 meat, 1/2 fat, 50 calories
3 rye wafers = 1 bread, 67 calories

Reduced-Calorie Dips

Cucumber Dip

1 medium cucumber (2 per lb.), peeled
1/2 teaspoon salt
3/4 cup low-fat cottage cheese
8 oz. plain low-fat yogurt (1 cup)

1 tablespoon chopped fresh parsley
1/2 teaspoon dried dill weed
1/4 teaspoon white pepper

Cut cucumber in half lengthwise. Using a spoon, scrape out and discard seeds. Shred seeded cucumber halves; spread shredded cucumber on a clean cloth. Sprinkle with salt; let stand 30 minutes. Bring ends of cloth together. Squeeze moisture out of cucumber shreds; set drained cucumber shreds aside. In a blender, puree cottage cheese. Pour pureed cottage cheese into a container with a tight-fitting lid. Stir in yogurt, parsley, dill, white pepper and drained cucumber shreds. Cover tightly; refrigerate until served, up to 2 days. Makes about 2-1/2 cups.

1/4 cup dip = 1/4 milk, 1/4 meat, 38 calories

Curry-Cheese Dip

1/2 (8-oz.) pkg. Neufchâtel cheese,
  room temperature
1/2 cup low-fat cottage cheese
1/2 teaspoon curry powder

1/8 teaspoon garlic powder
1/4 cup shredded extra-sharp Cheddar cheese
  (1 oz.)
1 green onion, sliced

In a medium bowl, beat Neufchâtel cheese with an electric mixer until light and fluffy. In a blender, puree cottage cheese; stir into beaten Neufchâtel cheese. Stir in remaining ingredients. Spoon into a container with a tight-fitting lid. Cover tightly; refrigerate at least 4 hours or up to 3 days. Makes about 1-1/4 cups.

2 tablespoons dip = 1/2 fat, 52 calories

Country Vegetable Soup

Serve with a salad or sandwich for a filling lunch.

1 (10-3/4-oz.) can condensed chicken broth
1 qt. water (4 cups)
1 chicken-flavored bouillon cube
1 beef-flavored bouillon cube
2 teaspoons vegetable oil
1/2 cup chopped onion

2 medium carrots (6 per lb.), peeled, sliced
2 celery stalks, sliced
1 cup dried split green peas
1/4 teaspoon dried leaf basil
1 bay leaf
1/2 cup uncooked broken thin noodles

In a 4-quart pot, combine broth, water and bouillon cubes. Bring to a boil over high heat; reduce heat until water barely simmers. Crush bouillon cubes with back of a spoon. Stir until bouillon cubes are completely dissolved. Meanwhile, in a nonstick 10-inch skillet or a skillet coated with nonstick vegetable spray, heat oil. Add onion, carrots and celery; sauté until onion is soft. Stir sautéed vegetables into broth mixture. Add dried peas, basil and bay leaf. Bring back to a simmer. Cover; simmer until peas are tender, about 30 minutes. Discard bay leaf. Add noodles; simmer 5 to 7 minutes longer or until noodles are al dente or just tender to the bite. Ladle 1 cup soup into each of 6 soup bowls or mugs. Serve hot. Makes about 6 servings.

---

1 serving (1 cup) = 1 bread, 1 meat, 1 vegetable, 141 calories

---

Chicken-Dumpling Soup

Add a ham sandwich and a salad of raw vegetables to complete the meal.

2 cups water
2 chicken-flavored bouillon cubes
1 medium carrot (6 per lb.), peeled, sliced
1/4 cup chopped celery leaves

1/4 teaspoon dried leaf thyme
1 (3-oz.) boned, skinned chicken-breast half
1 (14-1/2-oz.) can regular-strength
  chicken broth

Herb Dumplings:
1/2 cup all-purpose flour
1/2 teaspoon baking powder
1/8 teaspoon salt

1/8 teaspoon fines herbs or dill weed
1/3 cup low-fat cottage cheese
1/4 cup low-fat milk (1%)

In a 4-quart pot, combine water and bouillon cubes. Bring to a boil over high heat; reduce heat until water barely simmers. Crush bouillon cubes with back of a spoon. Stir until bouillon cubes are completely dissolved. Add carrot, celery leaves and thyme; bring back to a simmer. Meanwhile, remove fat from chicken. Add trimmed chicken to bouillon mixture; bring back to a simmer. Cover; simmer 15 minutes or until chicken turns opaque. Use a slotted spoon to remove cooked chicken. When cool enough to handle, dice cooked chicken. Strain cooking liquid; discard carrot and celery leaves. Return strained liquid to pot; skim any fat from surface. Add broth and diced chicken. Prepare Herb Dumplings. Drop dumpling batter, about 2 tablespoons at a time, into simmering soup, making 8 dumplings. Cover; simmer until dumplings are firm and dry inside, about 15 minutes. Ladle 1 cup soup and 2 dumplings into each of 4 soup bowls. Makes 4 servings.
To make Herb Dumplings, in a medium bowl, combine flour, baking powder, salt and fines herbs or dill weed. Add cottage cheese and milk; stir only until combined. Makes 8 dumplings.

---

1 serving (1 cup soup, 2 dumplings) = 1 bread, 1-1/2 meat, 135 calories

---

Zucchini Tart

Serve as a snack, light meal or appetizer.

1 whole-wheat-bread slice
2 tablespoons grated Parmesan cheese
2 eggs
1/2 cup low-fat milk (2%)
1/4 teaspoon salt
1/4 teaspoon pepper
1/8 teaspoon dried leaf basil

1/8 teaspoon dried leaf oregano
2 medium zucchini (2 per lb.)
1 teaspoon regular margarine
3 oz. cooked ham, diced (3/4 cup)
1/2 cup chopped onion
2 tablespoons chopped fresh parsley

Tear bread into several pieces. In a blender, process bread pieces making fine crumbs. Pour bread crumbs into a small bowl. Stir in cheese; set aside. In a medium bowl, beat eggs until blended. Stir in milk, salt, pepper, basil and oregano; set aside. Preheat oven to 350F (175C). Trim ends from zucchini. Cut zucchini into 1/4-inch-thick slices. In a large nonstick skillet or a skillet coated with nonstick vegetable spray, melt margarine. Add sliced zucchini; sauté until tender, about 5 minutes, stirring frequently. Arrange sautéed zucchini in an ungreased 10-inch quiche pan or 9-inch pie plate. Sprinkle ham, onion and parsley over zucchini. Pour egg mixture over zucchini. Sprinkle crumb mixture over top. Bake in preheated oven about 30 minutes or until a knife inserted off center comes out clean. Let stand 5 minutes; cut into 4 wedges. Place 1 wedge on each of 4 plates. Makes 4 servings.

1 serving (1 wedge) = 2 vegetable, 1 meat, 1 fat, 150 calories

Puffy Baked Tuna Sandwich

Prepare and refrigerate these in the morning, then bake for an easy supper.

1 (6-3/4-oz.) can tuna packed in water,
   drained
1/2 cup low-fat cottage cheese
1 green onion, sliced
1 tablespoon bottled reduced-calorie
   Italian salad dressing
2 eggs

1 cup low-fat milk (2%)
1/8 teaspoon salt
1/8 teaspoon pepper
1 tablespoon Dijon-style mustard
6 thin whole-wheat-bread or
   white-bread slices
Paprika

Preheat oven to 350F (175C). In a small bowl, combine tuna, cottage cheese, green onion and salad dressing; set aside. In a medium bowl, beat eggs until blended. Stir in milk, salt, pepper and mustard; set aside. Cut crusts from bread slices. Using a nonstick 8-inch-square baking pan or a baking pan coated with nonstick vegetable spray, arrange 4 trimmed bread slices in each corner of pan. Cut 2 (2-inch) circles from each of 2 remaining bread slices; set aside. Use crusts and rest of cut bread slices for another purpose. Spoon about 1/3 cup tuna mixture onto center of each bread slice in pan. Place 1 bread circle on top of each tuna mound. Gently press down on bread circles, flattening tuna mixture slightly. Pour egg mixture over sandwiches. Lightly sprinkle paprika over top of each sandwich. Refrigerate at least 30 minutes or overnight. Preheat oven to 350F (175C). Bake in preheated oven 35 to 45 minutes or until a knife inserted in bottom bread portion comes out clean. Let stand 5 minutes. Cut between sandwiches. Using a wide metal spatula, place 1 sandwich on each of 4 plates. Cut each sandwich into fourths; serve warm. Makes 4 servings.

1 serving = 2 meat, 1-1/2 bread, 1/4 milk, 240 calories

Curried-Chicken & Ham Muffins

Serve this open-faced sandwich with grapes and wedges of fresh melon for a light supper.

1 cup canned or homemade chicken broth
1 tablespoon cornstarch
3/4 to 1 teaspoon curry powder
2/3 (3-oz.) pkg. Neufchâtel cheese, diced
3 oz. cooked chicken or turkey,
  diced (3/4 cup)

3 oz. cooked ham, diced (3/4 cup)
2 cups broccoli flowerets,
  cut in bite-sized pieces
4 raisin English muffins, split
2 tablespoons sliced almonds

In a small bowl, combine 1 tablespoon broth and cornstarch. Stir until cornstarch dissolves. Pour remaining broth into a medium saucepan. Stir in cornstarch mixture. Season with curry powder. Stirring constantly, cook over medium-high heat until thickened. Stir in cheese until melted. Stir in chicken or turkey and ham. Reduce heat until mixture barely simmers. Cover; simmer 5 minutes, stirring occasionally. In a medium saucepan or steamer, steam broccoli until crisp-tender. Drain thoroughly. Meanwhile, toast muffins; keep warm. Carefully stir cooked broccoli into curry mixture. Place 2 toasted muffin halves on each of 4 plates. Spoon about 1/2 cup curried mixture over top of each serving. Sprinkle each serving with 1/4 of sliced almonds. Makes 4 servings.

1 serving = 3 meat, 2 bread, 1 vegetable, 305 calories

Crisp Cocktail Vegetables   *Photo on page 136.*

A nutritious snack or appetizer or addition to a tossed green salad.

2 cups 1/4-inch-thick peeled-carrot slices
2 cups 1/4-inch-thick celery slices
1 cup pickling onions (8 oz.), peeled,
  or 1 cup frozen small boiling onions
1 cup cauliflowerets

1 medium, green or red bell pepper
  (2-1/2 per lb.), cut in 1-inch squares
1 cup broccoli flowerets
2 garlic cloves, crushed
1 tablespoon olive oil

Cocktail Marinade:
3 cups water
1 cup white-wine vinegar
2 tablespoons mustard seeds

1/4 teaspoon hot-red-pepper flakes
1 teaspoon coarsely ground black pepper
2 teaspoons salt

In a nonstick wok or extra large skillet or a wok or skillet coated with nonstick vegetable spray, combine carrots, celery, onions, cauliflower, bell pepper, broccoli and garlic. Drizzle olive oil over vegetables. Cook over medium-high heat, stirring and turning vegetables constantly until vegetable colors brighten, 3 to 5 minutes. Spoon stir-fried vegetables into a large container with a tight-fitting lid. Do not cover; set aside to cool. Prepare Cocktail Marinade; pour over cooled vegetables. Cover tightly; turn container several times to coat vegetables. Store in refrigerator 3 days, inverting container at least once each day. For each serving, use a slotted spoon to remove 1/2 cup desired vegetables from container. Store unused vegetables in refrigerator up to 3 weeks. Makes about 8 cups.
To make Cocktail Marinade, in a large bowl, combine all marinade ingredients; stir until salt dissolves. Makes about 1 quart.

1/2 cup = 1 vegetable, 25 calories

How to Make Hot Chili Buns

1/Split sandwich rolls in half horizontally. Pull soft center from each half roll leaving a 1/2-inch shell.

2/Ladle about 3/4 cup chili mixture into each hollowed-out half roll. Top each with a cheese triangle. Bake until cheese melts.

Hot Chili Buns

Store the leftover chili in the refrigerator and use for tomorrows lunch.

8 oz. extra-lean ground beef
  (10% to 15% fat)
1/2 cup chopped onion
1 garlic clove, minced
1 tablespoon all-purpose flour
1/4 teaspoon ground cumin

1 to 2 teaspoons chili powder
1/2 cup canned condensed beef broth
1 (15-oz.) can pinto beans, drained, rinsed
3 (5" x 3" x 2") sandwich rolls
2 reduced-calorie American-cheese
  slices (1-oz.)

In a large nonstick skillet or a skillet coated with nonstick vegetable spray, brown beef. Use a fork to break up beef. Push cooked beef to side; remove and discard drippings. Add onion and garlic. Sauté until onion is soft. In a small bowl, combine flour, cumin and chili powder. Sprinkle flour mixture over meat; stir until blended. Stir in broth. Bring to a boil, stirring constantly. Stir in beans. Reduce heat until mixture barely simmers. Cover; simmer 10 minutes. Preheat oven to 350F (175C). Split sandwich rolls in half horizontally. Pull soft center from each roll half leaving a 1/2-inch shell. Ladle about 3/4 cup chili mixture into each hollowed-out roll half. Place on an ungreased baking sheet, filling-side up. Cut each cheese slice in half diagonally. Reserve 1 half slice for another purpose. Cut each remaining cheese triangle in half diagonally, making 6 triangles. Place 1 triangle over chili in each roll. Bake until cheese melts. Place 1 filled roll on each of 6 plates. Serve hot. Makes 6 servings.

1 serving = 2-1/2 bread, 1-1/2 meat, 1/2 fat, 276 calories

Salads are a dieter's delight. They're crisp, cool and full of vitamins, minerals and fiber. Lettuce and other greens are so low in calories, you can eat as much as you like.

They are also filling. If you slip and overindulge on one meal or want to eat a meal out, balance your calorie intake by having a low-calorie main-dish salad at another meal.

Salads and vegetables also round out meals, adding color, crispness and interesting shapes. Szechuan Noodle Salad, made with curly ramen-type-soup noodles, is sure to bring compliments. Kids love the funny noodles.

While salad ingredients can be low-calorie, most regular salad dressings are not! One tablespoon of regular salad dressing has at least 75 calories. There are two ways to control calories from salad dressings. One way is to limit the amount of dressing used on a salad to one tablespoon. Or you can trim calories from dressings by making your own and changing the ratio of oil to vinegar.

Some oil is needed in a dressing. Without it, the tangy vinegar and flavorful spices will slide off the salad ingredients. Regular dressings usually have three or four parts of oil to one part vinegar. The salad dressings in this chapter and in the Weight-Loss Menus, have a one-to-one ratio of oil to liquid. The liquid is part vinegar and part water or wine so the dressings are not too tart. This maintains the tart flavor and coating ability while cutting calories. Water, fruit juice, wine or tomato juice are added to give volume.

Some dressings are thickened with a small amount of dry pectin. Pectin, a natural product from fruits, is used in making jams and jellies. It comes dry or as a liquid, but they cannot be substituted for one another. Dry pectin is available in 1-3/4-ounce packages in the canning section of most supermarkets. Because you use only a small amount, be sure to fold the top of the package tightly and store it in a cool, dry place. Pectin adds no flavor of its own, but thickens dressing so it clings to salad ingredients. ∎

Stir-Fried Vegetables Deluxe

Oriental stir-frying gives vegetables a crisp, fresh taste.

1/4 teaspoon salt
1/8 teaspoon pepper
1/8 teaspoon sugar
1/2 teaspoon cornstarch
1/2 cup canned or homemade chicken broth
1 large carrot (5 per lb.), peeled

1 tablespoon vegetable oil
1 garlic clove, minced
1/2 medium onion (4 per lb.), coarsely chopped
1/2 cup sliced celery
1 cup cauliflowerets
1 cup sliced zucchini or yellow crookneck squash

In a small bowl, combine salt, pepper, sugar, cornstarch and 1/4 cup broth; set aside. Using a vegetable peeler, cut wide strips the length of carrot. Roll up carrot strips. Place in iced water; set aside. In a wok or large skillet, heat oil. Add garlic, onion, celery and cauliflower. Stir-fry 30 seconds. Add reserved 1/4 cup broth. Bring to a simmer. Cover; simmer 2 minutes. Drain carrot curls on paper towels; add squash and drained carrot curls to wok or skillet. Cook 1 minute, stirring occasionally. Stir reserved cornstarch mixture; stir into vegetables. Cook until sauce thickens, stirring constantly. Serve hot. Makes 4 servings.

1 serving = 2 vegetable, 1/2 fat, 58 calories

Curried-Chicken & Papaya Salad

Chicken and fruit are both enhanced by the light curry flavor.

4 (3-oz.) skinned, boned
  chicken-breast halves
1 cup water
1 chicken-flavored bouillon cube

1 (8-oz.) can sliced water chestnuts, drained
2 green onions, sliced
1 medium papaya (1 per lb.), peeled
4 red-leaf-lettuce leaves

Curry Dressing:
2 tablespoons bottled reduced-calorie
  mayonnaise
2 tablespoons buttermilk

1/2 teaspoon prepared mustard
1/4 to 1/2 teaspoon curry powder
Dash of onion salt

Trim fat from chicken; set aside. In a medium saucepan, combine water and bouillon cube. Bring to a boil; reduce heat until water barely simmers. Crush bouillon cube with back of a spoon. Stir until bouillon cube is completely dissolved; add trimmed chicken. Bring mixture back to a simmer; cover. Simmer until chicken is tender when pierced with a fork, about 15 minutes. Prepare Curry Dressing; refrigerate until served. Remove cooked chicken from bouillon; set aside to cool. Use cooking liquid for another purpose. Dice cooked chicken. In a medium bowl, combine diced chicken, water chestnuts and green onions. Pour dressing over chicken mixture; stir to coat. Refrigerate at least 1 hour or up to 8 hours. Cut papaya crosswise into 8 rings; remove and discard seeds. Place 1 lettuce leaf on each of 4 salad plates. Place 2 papaya rings on each lettuce-lined plate. Spoon 1/4 of chicken salad over papaya rings on each plate. Makes 4 servings.
To make Curry Dressing, in a small bowl, combine mayonnaise, buttermilk and mustard. Stir in curry powder and onion salt. Refrigerate until served, up to 5 days. Makes about 1/4 cup.

Variation
When papaya is unavailable or the price is high, substitute 1 (5-inch-diameter) cantaloupe, peeled, cut in rings or wedges. Exchanges and calories will remain the same.

---
1 serving = 2 meat, 1-1/2 fruit, 1/2 fat, 195 calories
1 tablespoon dressing = 1/2 fat, 14 calories

Dilled Carrots & Broccoli

Freeze dill in the summer when its fresh and use it as needed all year.

1-1/2 teaspoons regular margarine
3 medium carrots (6 per lb.), peeled,
  cut in 1/4-inch-thick slices
2 tablespoons dry white wine or canned or
  homemade chicken broth
1/2 medium onion (4 per lb.), cut in strips

1 cup fresh broccoli flowerets or
  thawed frozen cut broccoli
1/8 teaspoon salt
Dash of pepper
2 teaspoons chopped fresh dill weed or
  1/2 teaspoon dried dill weed

In a large nonstick skillet or a skillet coated with nonstick vegetable spray, melt margarine. Add carrots; sauté 1 minute. Add wine or broth. Cover; simmer 5 minutes. Add onion and broccoli to sautéed carrots. Sprinkle with salt, pepper and dill; toss to distribute. Cover; simmer 5 minutes or until vegetables are crisp-tender. Makes 4 servings.

---
1 serving = 2 vegetable, 1/4 fat, 60 calories

Mixed Sweet-Pepper Salad

Sweet bell peppers are now available in purple, yellow, orange, red and green.

1 medium, green bell pepper (3 per lb.)
1 medium, yellow bell pepper (3 per lb.)
1 medium, red bell pepper (3 per lb.)
1 medium, purple bell pepper (3 per lb.)

1 medium, red onion (3 per lb.)
10 large ripe olives
1/2 cup crumbled feta cheese (2 oz.)

Oregano-Wine Dressing:
2 tablespoons red-wine vinegar
2 tablespoons olive oil
1 teaspoon beaten egg
1 tablespoon red wine

1/8 teaspoon dried leaf oregano
1/8 teaspoon salt
Dash of pepper

Prepare Oregano-Wine Dressing; refrigerate until served. Slice bell peppers crosswise into thin rings. Blanch bell-pepper rings by dropping into boiling water 15 seconds; remove with a slotted spoon. Quickly cool in cold water; drain on paper towels. Place blanched bell-pepper rings in a medium bowl. Slice onion; separate into rings. Cut olives into lengthwise quarters. Add onion rings and olive quarters to blanched bell-pepper rings. Shake dressing. Drizzle dressing over bell peppers; toss gently. Refrigerate until served. To serve, toss salad; sprinkle feta cheese over top. Serve on salad plates. Makes 4 servings.
To make Oregano-Wine Dressing, in a blender, combine vinegar, olive oil and egg. Process about 5 seconds or until mixture is thick and creamy. Add remaining ingredients. Process 5 seconds longer. Pour into a container with a tight-fitting lid; cover tightly. Refrigerate until served, up to 3 days. Shake before serving. Makes about 1/3 cup.

---

1 serving = 1-1/2 vegetable, 2 fat, 130 calories
1 tablespoon dressing = 1-1/4 fat, 51 calories

Blue-Cheese Mousse

Blue cheese has such a full flavor that only a small amount is needed.

1 (1/4-oz.) envelope unflavored gelatin
  (1 tablespoon)
1/4 cup cold water
1 cup canned condensed chicken broth
1/2 cup low-fat cottage cheese

2 tablespoons crumbled blue cheese
1/2 cup plain low-fat yogurt
1/8 teaspoon white pepper
6 red-leaf-lettuce leaves
1 medium cucumber (2 per lb.), thinly sliced

In a small bowl, stir gelatin into water; let stand 3 minutes to soften. In a small saucepan, bring broth to a boil. Stir about 1/4 cup hot broth into softened gelatin. Add gelatin mixture to remaining hot broth. Stir until gelatin dissolves completely; cool to room temperature. In a blender, puree cottage cheese and blue cheese. Pour cheese mixture into a medium bowl. Stir in yogurt. Stirring constantly, slowly add gelatin mixture. Stir in white pepper. Pour gelatin mixture into 6 (6-ounce) molds or ramekins. Refrigerate until firm, at least 4 hours or up to 24 hours. Arrange 1 lettuce leaf on each of 6 salad plates. Arrange 1/4 of cucumber slices on each lettuce-lined plate, slightly overlapping in a circle, leaving center open about 2-1/2 inches. Run a knife around edge of each mold. Dip molds, 1 at a time, to depth of contents, into warm water, about 5 seconds. Carefully invert 1 mold onto center of each plate. Makes 6 servings.

---

1 serving = 1 meat, 60 calories

How to Make Radish-Mushroom Salad

III

1/Mound marinated mushrooms on centers of lettuce-lined plates. Arrange marinated radishes around mushrooms.

2/Top each serving with sieved eggs and chives or green-onion tops. Drizzle each salad with 1 teaspoon dressing.

Radish-Mushroom Salad

Serve this attractive salad in place of a tossed green salad.

6 oz. fresh mushrooms, thinly sliced (2 cups)
2 cups thinly sliced red radishes
8 to 12 Boston-lettuce leaves or
**   butter-lettuce leaves**

1 egg, hard cooked, sieved
1 tablespoon plus 1 teaspoon chopped chives
**   or green-onion tops**

Lemon Dressing:
2 tablespoons lemon juice
2 tablespoons plus 2 teaspoons vegetable oil
1 teaspoon beaten egg
1 small garlic clove, crushed

1/4 teaspoon salt
1/2 teaspoon sugar
Dash of pepper
1/4 teaspoon ground cumin

Place mushrooms and radishes in separate small bowls. Prepare Lemon Dressing; drizzle equally over mushrooms and radishes. Arrange lettuce leaves on 4 salad plates. Mound coated mushrooms equally on centers of lettuce-lined plates. Arrange 1/4 of coated radishes around mushrooms on each plate. Sprinkle egg and chives or green-onion tops equally over salads. Drizzle each salad with 1 teaspoon dressing that has drained from mushrooms and radishes. Serve immediately. Makes 4 servings.

To make Lemon Dressing, in a blender, combine all ingredients. Process about 5 seconds or until mixture is thick and creamy. Pour into a small container with a tight-fitting lid; cover tightly. Refrigerate until served, up to 8 days. Makes about 1/2 cup.

1 serving = 1/2 vegetable, 1 fat, 70 calories
1 tablespoon dressing = 1/2 fat, 20 calories

Szechuan-Style Noodle Salad

Sesame oil, ginger and soy sauce give this salad its spicy Oriental flavor.

1 qt. water (4 cups)
3 (3-oz.) pkgs. Oriental-flavored
    ramen-type soup mixes
1 teaspoon sesame oil

Ginger-Soy Dressing:
3 tablespoons rice vinegar
3 tablespoons vegetable oil
1 teaspoon beaten egg
2 teaspoons soy sauce
1 tablespoon dry sherry

1 cup fresh edible pea pods (6 oz.) or
    1 (6-oz.) pkg. frozen edible pea pods
3 oz. fresh mushrooms, thinly sliced (1 cup)
1 celery stalk, sliced diagonally

1/2 teaspoon sugar
1 small garlic clove
1/2 teaspoon shredded fresh gingerroot
1/8 teaspoon salt
1/4 teaspoon pepper

Prepare Ginger-Soy Dressing; refrigerate until served. In a large saucepan, bring 1 quart water to a boil. Stir in seasoning packet from 1 soup mix. Reserve remaining seasoning packets for another use. Break noodles from all packages into 2-inch pieces. Cook in seasoned boiling water 1 minute or until noodles are al dente or just tender to the bite and have absorbed most of the water. Drain noodles; rinse with cold water to stop cooking. Drain well; pour into a large bowl. Drizzle with sesame oil; toss to distribute. Set aside. Blanch fresh or frozen pea pods in a small amount of boiling water 1 minute. Drain; cool under running cold water. Add blanched pea pods, mushrooms and celery to noodles. Pour 1/4 cup dressing over top. Serve immediately or refrigerate until ready to serve, up to 4 hours. Toss before serving. Makes 4 servings. **To make Ginger-Soy Dressing,** in a blender, combine 2 tablespoons vinegar, oil and egg. Process about 5 seconds or until thick and creamy. Add remaining vinegar and remaining ingredients. Process 5 seconds longer. Pour into a container with a tight-fitting lid; cover tightly. Refrigerate until served, up to 3 days. Stir before serving. Makes about 1/2 cup.

---
1 serving = 1 bread, 1 vegetable, 1-1/2 fat, 160 calories
1 tablespoon dressing = 1 fat, 49 calories

Stuffed Rolled-Ham Salad

Serve with warm crusty rolls or muffins for a light supper or lunch.

8 oz. ricotta cheese (1 cup)
2 tablespoons bottled reduced-calorie
    mayonnaise
1 tablespoon lemon juice
1 green onion, chopped
2 tablespoons canned diced green chilies
1/4 cup finely chopped green bell pepper

1 small tomato (4 per lb.), peeled, chopped
2 tablespoons shredded sharp Cheddar cheese
4 curly salad-bowl lettuce leaves
8 (1-oz.) cooked lean ham slices
8 cherry tomatoes, if desired
4 ripe olives, if desired
4 fresh parsley sprigs, if desired

In a medium bowl, combine ricotta cheese, mayonnaise, lemon juice, green onion, green chilies, bell pepper, tomato and cheese. Place 1 lettuce leaf on each of 4 salad plates; set aside. Place ham slices on a flat surface. Spoon 1/4 of cheese mixture onto each ham slice. Roll ham slices around filling. Place 2 ham rolls, seam-side down, on each lettuce-lined plate. Garnish each plate with 2 cherry tomatoes, 1 olive and a parsley sprig, if desired. Refrigerate until served, up to 2 hours. Makes 4 servings.

---
1 serving = 3 meat, 1 vegetable, 1 fat, 235 calories

Cabbage Salad with Sherried French Dressing

Cabbage is an excellent source of vitamin C.

1 (1-lb.) cabbage head
1/2 cup julienned red bell pepper
1/2 cup julienned green bell pepper

1/4 cup chopped fresh parsley
2 green onions, sliced

Sherried French Dressing:
2 tablespoons rice vinegar
1 tablespoon water
1-1/2 teaspoons dry sherry

2 tablespoons vegetable oil
3/4 teaspoon sugar
1/4 teaspoon salt

Prepare Sherried French Dressing; refrigerate until served. Remove outer cabbage leaves, reserving 6 unblemished leaves. Thinly shred remaining cabbage, making about 4 cups. In a large bowl, combine shredded cabbage, bell peppers, parsley and green onions. Shake dressing; pour over salad. Stir gently to distribute dressing. Cover; refrigerate at least 1 hour to let flavors blend. Line a salad bowl with reserved cabbage leaves. Spoon salad into lined bowl. Makes 6 servings.
To make Sherried French Dressing, in a small container with a tight-fitting lid, combine all ingredients. Cover tightly; shake vigorously. Refrigerate up to 3 days. Shake before serving. Makes about 1/3 cup.

1 serving = 1 vegetable, 1 fat, 65 calories
1 tablespoon dressing = 1 fat, 43 calories

Marinated-Vegetable Salad

Look for baby corncobs in the gourmet section of the supermarket or a specialty food store.

1 (8-oz.) can baby corncobs,
   if desired, drained
1/2 medium zucchini (3 per lb.)
12 oz. fresh bean sprouts (4 cups)

1 (12-oz.) jar pickled mixed vegetables,
   including carrots, cauliflower
   and celery, drained
1 (5-oz.) jar pickled cocktail onions, drained

Sweet & Sour Dressing:
2 tablespoons rice vinegar
1 tablespoon vegetable oil
1 tablespoon regular ketchup
1/2 teaspoon beaten egg

1/2 teaspoon Worcestershire sauce
1/4 teaspoon sugar
1/8 teaspoon salt
1/8 teaspoon ground ginger

Prepare Sweet & Sour Dressing; refrigerate until served. If using baby corncobs, cut 6 cobs into 1-inch pieces. Reserve remaining corncobs for another purpose. Using a crinkle cutter or knife, thinly slice zucchini. In a large bowl, combine corncob pieces, zucchini pieces, bean sprouts, mixed vegetables and onions. Drizzle dressing over top. Refrigerate up to 4 hours. To serve, stir gently. Makes 4 servings.
To make Sweet & Sour Dressing, in a blender, combine 1 tablespoon vinegar, oil and ketchup. Process about 5 seconds or until mixture is thick and creamy. Add remaining vinegar and remaining ingredients. Process 5 seconds longer. Serve immediately or pour into a container with a tight-fitting lid; cover tightly. Refrigerate up to 4 hours. Stir before serving. Makes about 1/4 cup.

1 serving = 2 vegetable, 55 calories
1 tablespoon dressing = 2/3 fat, 36 calories

Broiled Vegetable Kabobs

Serve these delightful vegetable kabobs with broiled fish or meats.

2 small (1-1/2-inch-diameter)
  new potatoes (10 per lb.)
1 medium zucchini (2 per lb.)
4 small yellow crookneck squash (4 per lb.)
1 small green or red bell pepper (4 per lb.)
4 (1-inch-diameter) boiling onions, peeled
4 large fresh mushrooms

4 cherry tomatoes
2 teaspoons olive oil or other vegetable oil
2 teaspoons lemon juice
1/8 teaspoon salt
Dash of black pepper
1/4 teaspoon fines herbs

Scrub potatoes gently with a brush. Cook potatoes in a small amount of boiling water until barely tender, about 12 minutes. Cool under running cold water to stop cooking. Place in a large bowl. Cut zucchini crosswise into 4 equal pieces; add to potatoes. Cut crooked necks from yellow squashes, leaving round bulbs. Reserve squash necks for another purpose. Cut bell pepper into 1-inch squares. Add bulb portions of crookneck squashes, bell-pepper squares, onions, mushrooms and tomatoes to cooked potatoes. Drizzle oil over vegetables; stir carefully to coat. Sprinkle lemon juice, salt, black pepper and fines herbs over vegetables. Stir again; let stand 15 minutes to let flavors develop. Preheat broiler or grill. Press 1 piece of each vegetable, except tomatoes, onto 4 (10-inch) skewers. Pack vegetables closely together on center of skewer. Broil or grill vegetables, 6 inches from heat, until lightly browned, about 5 minutes. Add 1 tomato to end of each skewer. Turn skewers over. Broil or grill 2 to 3 minutes longer. Makes 4 servings.

---

1 serving (1 kabob) = 1 bread, 1 vegetable, 1/2 fat, 116 calories

---

Broccoli in Creamy Mustard Sauce

Also serve this piquant sauce over green beans or asparagus or as a dip for artichoke leaves.

1 lb. fresh broccoli

Creamy Mustard Sauce:
1 egg yolk, beaten
1/2 cup skim milk
1 tablespoon prepared mustard
1-1/2 teaspoons regular margarine

2 teaspoons all-purpose flour
1 teaspoon lemon juice
1/8 teaspoon salt
Dash of white pepper

Trim heavy stalks from broccoli; discard heavy stalks. Cut broccoli into 3- to 4-inch-long spears, making stalks about 1/2 inch in diameter. Steam broccoli spears until crisp-tender; keep hot. Meanwhile, prepare Creamy Mustard Sauce; keep hot. Arrange 1/2 of cooked broccoli spears on a serving plate with all tops at 1 edge of plate and stems at center of plate. Arrange remaining broccoli spears with tops at opposite edge and with stems overlapping in center of plate. Pour sauce over stems. Serve immediately. Makes 4 servings. **To make Creamy Mustard Sauce,** in a small bowl, combine egg yolk, milk and mustard; set aside. In a small saucepan, melt margarine. Stir in flour until smooth. Gradually stir egg mixture into flour mixture. Stirring constantly, cook over medium heat until sauce thickens. Stir in lemon juice, salt and white pepper. Serve hot. Makes about 1/2 cup.

---

1 serving = 1 vegetable, 1/4 meat, 1/2 fat, 70 calories

Main Dishes

Main dishes usually contain a protein food, such as poultry, fish or cooked dried beans. Chicken skin contains lots of fat and should always be removed. Use only lean cuts of beef and pork and remove any visible fat from all meats. Have the butcher weight your meat for you or use a small food scale at home so you can limit meat servings to three or four ounces.

Serving meats with vegetables adds color and flavor and increases their appeal. A single serving of Turkey Scaloppine with Asparagus or Chicken Primavera looks too generous to be calorie-trimmed. It's the vegetables that create the illusion.

Combination main dishes that include rice or pasta also make a serving appear more than adequate. Halibut with Red Pepper & Yellow Squash, tossed with spinach noodles,

can be served with a salad and warm bread to make a meal fit for any occasion.

Cooked dried beans are a good source of carbohydrate and protein, with fiber as an added bonus. Beans are a good food to help keep down calories from fat and to increase calories from carbohydrate. Include cooked dried beans, potatoes, whole grains and cereals in your maintenance meal plans.

Cook beans with a small amount of lean meat to add flavor without adding much fat. In Black-Bean Picadillo, strips of beef simmer with black beans until both are tender and the flavors blend. Serve the bean mixture rolled in a warm tortilla with a spicy salsa, dairy sour half and half and fresh lime juice. ■

Marsala Steak with Mushrooms

Close your eyes as you eat this and you'll imagine you're at the Ritz!

**4 (5-oz.) beef round eye round steaks,
   1/4 inch thick
Dash of salt
Dash of coarsely ground pepper
1 tablespoon vegetable oil
1/4 cup canned or homemade beef broth**

**1/3 cup Marsala or dry sherry
Pinch of dried leaf basil
1 teaspoon cornstarch
1/3 cup water
4-1/2 oz. fresh mushrooms, thinly sliced
   (1-1/2 cups)**

Place steaks between 2 pieces of plastic wrap. Pound with flat side of a meat mallet until almost doubled in size. Season lightly with salt and pepper. In a large skillet with a nonstick surface or a skillet coated with nonstick vegetable spray, heat oil. Add flattened steaks; brown on both sides. Remove steaks; keep warm. Add broth, Marsala or sherry and basil to drippings in skillet. Bring to a boil, stirring to loosen any bits that cling to skillet. Reduce heat until mixture barely simmers. Cover; simmer 1 minute. In a small bowl, combine cornstarch and water. Stir cornstarch mixture into skillet. Stirring constantly, cook until sauce thickens. Stir in mushrooms. Return cooked steaks to skillet, turning to coat steaks with sauce. Cover; simmer 3 minutes longer or until steaks are hot. Place 1 steak on each of 4 plates. Top each steak with about 2 tablespoons mushrooms and sauce. Makes 4 servings.

1 serving = 4 meat, 1/2 vegetable, 235 calories

Chicken Primavera

Cheese melts over the chicken and vegetables, making a rich sauce.

1/4 cup all-purpose flour
1/4 teaspoon salt
1/4 teaspoon paprika
4 (5-oz.) pieces cut-up frying chicken
  breasts, thighs or combination,
  skinned
1 tablespoon vegetable oil
1 garlic clove, minced
1/2 teaspoon dried leaf basil

1/2 cup canned or homemade chicken broth
1 medium zucchini (3 per lb.),
  cut in julienne strips
2 medium carrots (6 per lb.), peeled,
  cut in julienne strips
4 green onions, cut in julienne strips
1/3 cup shredded mozzarella cheese or
  provolone cheese (1-1/2 oz.)

In a small bowl, combine flour, salt and paprika. Roll chicken pieces in flour mixture. Shake off excess. In a medium nonstick skillet or a skillet coated with nonstick vegetable spray, heat oil. Add coated chicken pieces; brown on all sides. Add garlic, basil and broth. Reduce heat until mixture barely simmers. Cover; simmer 15 minutes. Remove chicken pieces; keep warm. Stir zucchini and carrots into pan drippings. Cover; simmer until vegetables are crisp-tender, about 5 minutes. Stir in green onions. Place cooked chicken pieces over vegetables. Sprinkle cheese over chicken and vegetables. Cover; simmer until cheese melts, about 3 minutes. To serve, spoon 1/4 of vegetable mixture onto each of 4 plate; top each serving with 1 chicken piece. Makes 4 servings.

1 serving = 3 meat, 2 vegetable, 250 calories

Easiest-Ever Tuna Casserole

Packed with protein and calcium, this is a super supper for nonmilk drinkers.

6 oz. uncooked spiral macaroni or
  elbow macaroni (about 1-1/2 cups)
1 egg
1/2 teaspoon salt
1/2 teaspoon dry mustard
1/4 teaspoon white pepper
8 oz. low-fat cottage cheese (1 cup)

1/3 cup dairy sour half and half
1/3 cup low-fat milk (1%)
1 cup shredded sharp Cheddar cheese (4 oz.)
1 (6-3/4-oz.) can tuna packed in water,
  drained
1 cup partially thawed frozen
  tiny green peas

Preheat oven to 350F (175C). Cook macaroni in lightly salted boiling water according to package directions until al dente or just tender to the bite, 5 to 7 minutes. Pour macaroni into a sieve; rinse with hot water. Drain well. Place rinsed macaroni in a 2-quart casserole with a lid; keep hot. In a medium bowl, beat egg with salt, mustard and white pepper. Stir in cottage cheese, sour half and half, milk and 1/2 of Cheddar cheese. Reserve remaining Cheddar cheese to sprinkle over top. Stir egg mixture into cooked macaroni. Break tuna into chunks. Carefully stir tuna and peas into macaroni mixture. Sprinkle reserved Cheddar cheese over top. Cover; bake in preheated oven 45 minutes. Remove cover; bake 10 minutes longer or until lightly browned. Serve hot in casserole or spoon equally onto 6 plates. Makes 6 servings.

1 serving = 3 meat, 2 bread, 299 calories

Turkey Scaloppine with Asparagus

Tender, succulent turkey cutlets are lightly sauced and very tasty.

12 fresh or canned asparagus spears
4 (4-oz.) turkey cutlets
Dash of salt
Dash of pepper
1 tablespoon vegetable oil

1/2 cup canned or homemade chicken broth
2 teaspoons lemon juice
Pinch of dried leaf tarragon
1 tablespoon all-purpose flour

Cut off tough ends of fresh asparagus spears; discard stem ends. Cook trimmed fresh asparagus in a small amount of lightly salted boiling water until crisp-tender; drain. Cut cooked fresh or canned asparagus into 1-inch pieces; set aside. Place turkey cutlets between pieces of plastic wrap. Pound cutlets with flat side of a meat mallet until flattened slightly. Season cutlets with salt and pepper. In a large nonstick skillet or a skillet coated with nonstick vegetable spray, heat oil. Add flattened cutlets; brown on both sides. Remove browned cutlets; keep warm. In a small container with a tight-fitting lid, combine broth, lemon juice, tarragon and flour. Cover tightly; shake vigorously until no lumps remain. Slowly stir flour mixture into skillet. Stirring constantly, cook over medium heat until mixture thickens. Return browned cutlets to skillet, turning to coat cooked cutlets with sauce. Reduce heat until sauce barely simmers. Cover; simmer 2 minutes or until cutlets are hot. Arrange asparagus pieces over cutlets; simmer 1 minute longer. To serve, place 1 turkey cutlet on each of 4 plates. Spoon sauce equally over servings. Makes 4 servings.

Variation
Substitute thinly cut boneless veal for turkey cutlets. Prepare as directed above. Exchanges and calories will remain the same.

---

1 serving = 4 meat, 1 vegetable, 220 calories

Hungarian Goulash

Look for hot paprika in a specialty food store if you like spicy foods.

1 lean bacon slice, diced
1 lb. boneless lean pork loin, trimmed
   of fat, cut in 1/2-inch cubes
1/2 cup chopped onion
1 tablespoon plus 1-1/2 teaspoons
   all-purpose flour

1 tablespoon sweet paprika
1/2 teaspoon hot paprika, if desired
1 (10-1/2-oz.) can condensed beef broth
1/2 cup water
1 (1-lb.) cabbage head, shredded (4 cups)
1 (8-oz.) can sauerkraut, drained

In a large skillet, fry bacon until crisp; drain on paper towels. Brown pork cubes in bacon drippings. Add onion; sauté until onion is soft. In a small bowl, combine flour, sweet paprika and hot paprika, if desired. Sprinkle paprika mixture over pork mixture. Stir 1 minute. Gradually stir in broth and water. Stir until mixture comes to a boil. Reduce heat until mixture barely simmers. Cover; simmer until pork is tender, about 45 minutes. In a large pot, bring 1/2 cup water to a boil. Add cabbage; return water to a boil. Partially cover pot; cook cabbage until crisp-tender, about 10 minutes. Drain off water. In a sieve, rinse sauerkraut under running hot water. Stir rinsed sauerkraut into cooked cabbage. Stir several minutes over medium-high heat until all moisture evaporates. Pour pork mixture over cabbage and sauerkraut; stir to distribute. Reduce heat until mixture barely simmers; simmer 10 minutes, stirring occasionally. Serve hot. Makes 4 servings.

---

1 serving = 3 meat, 2 vegetable, 230 calories

How to Make Mexican Meatball Stew

1/Make meatballs by pressing about 1 tablespoon turkey mixture around each olive.

2/Ladle stew into soup bowls or mugs. Top each serving with a tortilla chip.

Mexican Meatball Stew

Slightly spicy and very good!

8 oz. ground turkey
1/2 cup fresh bread crumbs
1/2 teaspoon salt
1/8 teaspoon pepper
1/2 teaspoon ground cumin
1/8 teaspoon dried leaf oregano
12 pimento-stuffed green olives
1 (15-oz.) can dark-red kidney beans, drained

1 cup Enchilada Sauce from Green-Chili
  Enchiladas, page 98, or
  1 (10-oz.) can enchilada sauce
1/2 cup canned or homemade beef broth
1 cup drained canned or thawed frozen
  whole-kernel corn
1 tablespoon cornmeal
4 tortilla chips

Preheat oven to 350F (175C). In a medium bowl, combine turkey, bread crumbs, salt, pepper, cumin and oregano. Make 12 meatballs by pressing about 1 tablespoon turkey mixture around each olive. Place stuffed meatballs on a nonstick 15'' x 10'' jelly-roll pan or a jelly-roll pan coated with nonstick vegetable spray. Bake in preheated oven 15 minutes or until meat is no longer pink. Meanwhile, in a medium saucepan, combine kidney beans, enchilada sauce, broth and corn. Bring to a boil over medium-high heat, stirring frequently. Gradually stir in cornmeal; stirring constantly, cook until stew thickens. Add baked meatballs. Reduce heat until mixture barely simmers; simmer stew 5 minutes. Ladle 1/4 of stew into each of 4 soup bowls or mugs. Top each serving with a tortilla chip. Makes 4 servings.

1 serving = 2-1/2 bread, 2 meat, 1 fat, 331 calories

South-American Beans & Hominy

Serve with a fresh fruit salad and a steamed green vegetable.

8 oz. extra-lean ground beef
   (10% to 15% fat) or 8 oz. ground turkey
1/2 medium onion (4 per lb.), chopped
1 garlic clove, minced
1/2 teaspoon salt
1/8 teaspoon black pepper
1 tablespoon all-purpose flour

3/4 cup canned or homemade beef broth
1 (15-oz.) can dark-red kidney beans,
   drained
1 (15-oz.) can golden hominy, drained
1 cup chopped green or red bell pepper
1/2 teaspoon dried leaf basil

In a large nonstick skillet or a skillet coated with nonstick vegetable spray, brown meat until no longer pink, using a fork to break up meat. Remove any drippings. Stir onion and garlic into cooked meat. Cook 1 minute, stirring frequently. Sprinkle salt, black pepper and flour over meat mixture. Add broth to meat mixture. Stirring constantly, cook over medium-high heat until mixture comes to a boil. Carefully stir in kidney beans, hominy, bell pepper and basil. Bring back to a boil; reduce heat until mixture barely simmers. Cover; simmer until heated through, about 15 minutes, stirring occasionally. Makes 6 servings.

---

1 serving = 2 meat, 2 bread, 1 vegetable, 270 calories

Black-Bean Picadillo

This rich-flavored South-American black-bean dish is served in a warm tortilla.

1-1/2 cups dried black beans
1 (8-oz.) boneless beef round steak,
   trimmed of fat
Chunky Salsa, page 68, if desired
1 (10-1/2-oz.) can condensed beef broth
1-1/2 cups water
1 tablespoon olive oil
1 medium onion (4 per lb.), chopped

1 garlic clove, minced
1 dried hot red pepper
1 bay leaf
1/3 cup tomato sauce
1/4 cup sliced pimento-stuffed green olives
8 (6-inch) corn tortillas, warmed
4 lime wedges
1/4 cup dairy sour half and half, if desired

Place beans in a large saucepan. Add water to cover by about 2 inches. Bring to a boil; boil 2 minutes. Remove from heat. Cover; let stand 1 hour. Meanwhile, to aid in slicing, freeze steak until firm, about 30 minutes. Prepare Chunky Salsa, if desired; refrigerate until served. Drain beans, discarding water. Return beans to pan. Add broth and 1-1/2 cups water; set aside. Cut partially frozen steak diagonally across the grain in thin strips. In a large skillet, heat olive oil. Add steak strips; cook until meat is no longer pink, stirring occasionally. Add onion and garlic; cook until onion is soft. Stir steak mixture into soaked beans. Add red pepper and bay leaf. Bring mixture to a boil over medium-high heat; reduce heat until mixture barely simmers. Cover; simmer until beans and steak are tender, about 1-1/2 hours. Remove and discard red pepper and bay leaf. Stir in tomato sauce and olives. Simmer, uncovered, until most of liquid has evaporated. To serve, spoon 1/8 of picadillo onto each warmed tortilla. Squeeze a little lime juice over picadillo; roll up. Place 2 rolled tortillas onto each of 4 plates. Top each serving with 1/4 cup Chunky Salsa or 1 tablespoon sour half and half, if desired. Makes 4 servings.

---

1 serving (2 filled tortillas without Chunky Salsa or dairy sour half and half) = 3 meat, 3 bread, 3/4
  fat, 400 calories
1/4 cup Chunky Salsa = 1/2 vegetable, 14 calories
1 tablespoon dairy sour half and half = 1/3 fat, 20 calories

Halibut with Red Pepper & Yellow Squash

A colorful dish that takes only minutes to prepare.

8 oz. uncooked spinach noodles
  (about 4 cups)
1 teaspoon regular margarine
1/4 cup plus 2 tablespoons canned or
  homemade chicken broth
1 tablespoon vegetable oil
1 lb. halibut steak or other firm-textured
  fish, cut in 1-inch cubes

1/2 teaspoon dried rosemary
1 tablespoon raspberry vinegar or
  red-wine vinegar
1 medium, red bell pepper (2-1/2 per lb.)
4 small yellow crookneck squash (4 per lb.)

In a large saucepan, cook spinach noodles in lightly salted boiling water until al dente or just tender to the bite, 5 to 7 minutes; drain. Return drained cooked noodles to saucepan. Add margarine and 2 tablespoons broth; keep warm. In a large nonstick skillet or a skillet coated with nonstick vegetable spray, heat oil. Add fish. Stirring gently, sauté until fish turns opaque but is still firm when pierced with a fork. Crush rosemary between palms of your hands; sprinkle over fish. Stir in vinegar and remaining 1/4 cup broth. Reduce heat until mixture barely simmers. Cover; simmer 5 minutes. Meanwhile, cut bell pepper in 2'' x 1/4'' strips. Cut squash in crosswise slices. Remove cooked fish from skillet; keep warm. Stir bell pepper strips and sliced squash into pan drippings. Cover; simmer 3 minutes. Return fish to skillet. Simmer 2 minutes longer or until fish just begins to flake when pierced with a fork. To serve, spoon 1/4 of cooked noodles onto each of 4 plates. Spoon 1/4 of fish mixture over each serving. Makes 4 servings.

---

1 serving = 2 meat, 2-1/2 bread, 2 vegetable, 370 calories

Seafood Creole

Based on a Cajun favorite.

1 tablespoon vegetable oil
1/2 cup chopped onion
1 garlic clove, minced
1/2 cup chopped celery
1/2 cup diced green bell pepper
1 medium tomato (3 per lb.), peeled, chopped
1 (8-oz.) can tomato sauce
1/2 cup canned or homemade chicken broth
1/4 teaspoon salt
1/2 teaspoon sugar

1 bay leaf
1/4 teaspoon dried leaf thyme
1/8 to 1/4 teaspoon red (cayenne) pepper
1 (8-oz.) pkg. fresh or thawed frozen cod,
  halibut or pollock
8 oz. uncooked, deveined, shelled medium shrimp
  (about 18), scallops or shucked oysters
2 cups cooked long-grain white rice or
  brown rice

In a large nonstick skillet or a skillet coated with nonstick vegetable spray, heat oil. Add onion, garlic, celery and bell pepper; sauté until onion is soft. Stir in tomato, tomato sauce, broth, salt, sugar, bay leaf, thyme and red pepper. Bring to a boil over medium-high heat; reduce heat until mixture barely simmers. Cover; simmer 15 minutes. Meanwhile, cut fish into 1-inch cubes. Add fish cubes and shrimp, scallops or oysters to vegetables. Cover; simmer 7 minutes longer. Remove and discard bay leaf. To serve, spoon 1/4 of soup into each of 4 bowls. Top each serving with 1/2 cup cooked rice. Makes 4 servings.

---

1 serving = 3 meat, 2 bread, 1 vegetable, 360 calories

One good way to avoid overindulging in gooey, calorie-laden desserts is to have them only when eating with friends or in a restaurant. Be sure your serving is a small one. At home, don't make a strawberry cheesecake unless you are having guests and there won't be any left.

By changing the type and the amount served, dessert can be a fairly regular addition to meals. Use fruit instead of sugar to add sweetness. Fruit not only adds natural sweetness and flavor, but also vitamins and some minerals that are not found in sugar. Strawberry Sorbet will satisfy a sweet tooth without overindulgence.

Enjoy Finnish Apple Cake or Blueberry Cake with a clear conscious. Both are sponge cakes that have less sugar and fat than conventional cakes. The apples and blueberries make frosting unnecessary.

Cookies and milk that are a part of your weight-maintenance plan can be served as a snack. Honey-Sugar Cookies are thin, crisp cookies with only 35 calories per cookie. Store them in the freezer so they are not so readily available. Thaw a few at a time and serve with fruit. ■

Ginger-Fruit Bars

These spicy and chewy cookies are low in fat.

2 cups sifted all-purpose flour
1/2 teaspoon baking powder
1/4 teaspoon baking soda
1/4 teaspoon salt
1 teaspoon ground ginger
1/2 teaspoon ground cinnamon
1/4 cup vegetable shortening

1/3 cup lightly packed brown sugar
1/4 cup molasses
2 eggs
1/2 cup plain low-fat yogurt
1 teaspoon grated orange peel
1/2 cup cut-up dried apricots, peaches,
    apples, raisins, or combination

Snow-White Icing:
1-1/2 cups sifted powdered sugar
Pinch of salt

Preheat oven to 350F (175C). In a sifter, combine flour, baking powder, baking soda, salt, ginger and cinnamon. Sift into a medium bowl; set aside. In a large bowl, combine shortening, brown sugar and molasses; beat until fluffy. Separate 1 egg, placing egg white in a medium bowl; set aside for icing. Add egg yolk and remaining egg to shortening mixture. Beat until blended. Stir in yogurt and orange peel. Add flour mixture, stirring only until blended. Stir in dried fruit. Spoon dough into a nonstick 15'' x 10'' jelly-roll pan or a jelly-roll pan coated with nonstick vegetable spray. Spread dough evenly. Bake in preheated oven about 20 minutes or until lightly browned and firm to the touch. Cool in pan 30 minutes. Prepare Snow-White Icing. Drizzle over cooled cookies. Cut into 3'' x 1'' bars. Makes about 50 bars.
To make Snow-White Icing, add powdered sugar and salt to reserved egg white. Beat with an electric mixer until icing is smooth. Makes about 1/2 cup.

1 cookie = 1/2 bread, 1/4 fruit, 1/4 fat, 58 calories

Fresh-Fruit Tart

Less than 200 calories per serving, but delicious enough for a special occasion.

2 eggs, separated
1/3 cup sugar
1/2 teaspoon grated lemon peel
1/2 teaspoon lemon extract
1/3 cup sifted cake flour
1/2 teaspoon baking powder

1/8 teaspoon salt
4 cups fresh whole or sliced strawberries;
    sliced kiwifruit, peaches or nectarines;
    whole blueberries or seedless grapes;
    pitted plums; or melon balls; or combination

Orange Glaze:
1/4 cup sugar
1 tablespoon plus 1 teaspoon cornstarch
3/4 cup orange juice

1 tablespoon orange-flavored liqueur,
    if desired

Preheat oven to 375F (190C). Use a nonstick 12'' x 8'' tart pan with removable bottom or a nonstick 11'' x 7'' baking pan or spray a tart pan or baking pan with nonstick vegetable spray; set aside. In a medium bowl, beat egg yolks until thick and lemon colored. Gradually beat in 1/4 cup sugar. Beat in lemon peel and lemon extract. In another medium bowl, using clean dry beaters, beat egg whites with electric mixer until foamy. Gradually beat in reserved sugar 1 teaspoon at a time until glossy soft peaks form. Fold egg-white mixture into egg-yolk mixture. In a sifter, combine cake flour, baking powder and salt. Sift flour mixture over egg mixture. Carefully fold in. Spoon batter into prepared pan. Bake in preheated oven 12 to 15 minutes or until lightly browned. Cool in pan at least 1 hour; remove from pan to a platter or tray. Prepare Orange Glaze. Arrange fruit attractively on cooled cake. Spoon glaze over fruit. Refrigerate until ready to serve, up to 24 hours. Makes 6 servings.

To make Orange Glaze, in a small saucepan, combine sugar and cornstarch. Stir in orange juice. Stirring constantly, bring to a boil over medium heat; boil 1 minute. Remove from heat; stir in liqueur, if desired. Cool orange sauce to room temperature, stirring occasionally. Makes about 3/4 cup.

---

1 serving = 1-1/2 bread, 1-1/2 fruit, 1/2 fat, 187 calories

Strawberry Sorbet

Sorbet is a smooth, frozen mixture of fruit juice or puree and sugar syrup.

1/2 cup sugar
1/4 cup water
2 pints fresh strawberries

2 tablespoons lemon juice
1/2 cup orange juice

In a small saucepan, combine sugar and water. Stir over medium heat until sugar dissolves; cool to room temperature. In a blender or food processor fitted with a metal blade, puree strawberries, sugar mixture, lemon juice and orange juice. Pour puree into a 13'' x 9'' baking pan. Still-freeze in freezer compartment of your refrigerator until almost firm, about 1 hour. Spoon partially frozen mixture into a food processor fitted with a metal blade. Process until smooth. Or, spoon into a large bowl; beat with an electric mixer until smooth. Return mixture to pan. Freeze until firm, about 2 hours; then process or beat again. To serve, let sorbet stand at room temperature 10 minutes. Process or beat sorbet again. Spoon or scoop 1/2 cup strawberry sorbet into each dessert dish. Serve immediately. Return any remaining sorbet to freezer. May be stored in a container with a tight-fitting lid up to 6 weeks. Makes 8 (1/2-cup) servings.

1/2 cup sorbet = 2 fruit, 160 calories

Honey-Sugar Cookies

Enjoy these thin crisp cookies as snacks or as dessert with fruit.

1/3 cup vegetable shortening
1/4 cup plus 2 tablespoons sugar
1 tablespoon plus 1-1/2 teaspoons honey
1 egg

1 tablespoon skim milk
1/2 teaspoon vanilla extract
2 cups sifted all-purpose flour
1/2 teaspoon salt
1 teaspoon baking powder

Preheat oven to 350F (175C). In a medium bowl, beat shortening, sugar and honey until light and fluffy. Beat in egg, milk and vanilla. In a sifter, combine flour, salt and baking powder; sift over honey mixture. Beat until blended. Divide dough into thirds. On a lightly floured board, roll out 1/3 of dough at a time about 1/8 inch thick. Cut each portion into about 20 (2-inch) circles. Place dough circles on ungreased baking sheets. Bake in preheated oven until edges are lightly browned, about 5 minutes. Immediately remove from baking sheet; cool on a wire rack. Store leftover cookies in a plastic bag at room temperature or freeze for later use. Freeze up to 3 months. Makes 60 cookies.

---

2 cookies = 1/2 bread, 1/2 fat, 70 calories

Finnish Apple Cake

This family favorite of a Finnish friend will make you feel like you're celebrating.

3/4 cup plus 2 tablespoons sugar
1/2 teaspoon ground cinnamon
1/4 teaspoon ground nutmeg
4 eggs, separated
1 teaspoon almond extract

3/4 cup sifted cake flour
3/4 teaspoon baking powder
1/4 teaspoon salt
2 medium Rome Beauty apples or
   other cooking apples (3 per lb.)

Honey-Almond-Yogurt Topping:
3/4 cup plain low-fat yogurt
2 teaspoons honey

1/4 teaspoon almond extract

Preheat oven to 375F (190C). In a small bowl, combine 2 tablespoons sugar, cinnamon and nutmeg; set aside. In a medium bowl, beat egg yolks with an electric mixer until yolks are thick and lemon colored. Gradually beat in 1/2 cup sugar, scraping bowl often; beat until mixture is light and fluffy. Beat in almond extract; set aside. In another medium bowl, beat egg whites with clean beaters until foamy. Gradually beat in remaining 1/4 cup sugar, 1 tablespoon at a time. Beat until glossy soft peaks form. Fold beaten egg whites into egg-yolk mixture. In a sifter, combine cake flour, baking powder and salt. Sift 1/2 of flour mixture over egg mixture; gently fold in. Repeat with remaining flour mixture. Pour batter into a nonstick 15'' x 10'' jelly-roll pan or a jelly-roll pan coated with nonstick vegetable spray. Spread batter evenly in pan. Peel and core apples; thinly slice. Arrange apple slices over cake batter. Sprinkle cinnamon mixture over apple slices. Bake in preheated oven 12 to 15 minutes or until top of cake springs back when lightly pressed. Cool slightly in pan on a wire rack. Prepare Honey-Almond-Yogurt Topping. Cut warm cake into 10 equal pieces. To serve, drop 1-1/2 tablespoon topping in a dollop on each cake serving. Cover leftover cake with plastic wrap. Store at room temperature up to 3 days. Refrigerate topping up to 3 days. Makes 10 servings.
To make Honey-Almond-Yogurt Topping, in a small bowl, combine all ingredients. Makes about 3/4 cup.

---

1 cake serving with 1-1/2 tablespoons topping = 1/2 meat, 1 bread, 2 fruit, 170 calories
1-1/2 tablespoons topping = 1/4 milk, 19 calories

How to Make Peaches with Orange-Yogurt Cream

1/Refrigerate until gelatin mixture has consistency of unbeaten egg whites, about 45 minutes.

2/Spoon sliced fruit into stemmed glasses or dessert bowls. Top with yogurt mixture. Decorate with orange slices.

Peaches with Orange-Yogurt Cream

Orange liqueur adds delightful flavor and keeps the peaches from darkening.

1 (1/4-oz.) envelope unflavored gelatin
   (1 tablespoon)
1/4 cup water
3/4 cup freshly squeezed orange juice
1 teaspoon grated orange peel
1/4 cup sugar
3/4 cup plain low-fat yogurt

1/4 cup whipping cream
3 medium, fresh peaches or
   nectarines (3 per lb.)
1 tablespoon Grand Marnier or
   other orange-flavored liqueur
1/2 small orange (4 per lb.), thinly sliced

In a small bowl, stir gelatin into water; let stand 3 minutes to soften. In a small saucepan, combine orange juice, orange peel and sugar. Stirring occasionally, bring to a boil over medium heat. Stir about 1/4 cup hot orange-juice mixture into gelatin mixture. Stir until gelatin dissolves. Stir gelatin mixture into remaining hot orange-juice mixture; cool to room temperature. In a medium bowl, stir yogurt until smooth. Stirring constantly, slowly pour gelatin mixture into yogurt. Refrigerate until gelatin mixture has consistency of unbeaten egg whites, about 45 minutes. Beat cream until stiff peaks form; set aside. With same beaters, beat gelatin until foamy. Fold whipped cream into beaten gelatin mixture; set aside. Peel peaches; slice peeled peaches or unpeeled nectarines into a medium bowl. Sprinkle liqueur over peach slices or nectarine slices; stir to coat. Spoon sliced fruit into 4 stemmed glasses or dessert bowls. Pour yogurt mixture equally over fruit, covering fruit completely. Refrigerate until yogurt mixture is set. Decorate each serving with an orange slice. Makes 4 servings.

1 serving = 2 fruit, 1/2 milk, 1 fat, 180 calories

Blueberry Cake

This tasty casserole cake is similar to a cobbler.

2 eggs, separated
1/4 cup plus 2 tablespoons sugar
1 teaspoon vanilla extract
1/3 cup sifted all-purpose flour

1/8 teaspoon salt
3 cups fresh blueberries or
    thawed, drained, frozen blueberries
2 cups Orange Sherbet, page 121, if desired

Preheat oven to 375F (190C). Lightly grease a shallow 2-quart casserole dish with regular margarine. In a medium bowl, beat egg yolks until thick and lemon colored. Gradually add 3 tablespoons sugar, beating constantly. Stir in vanilla; set aside. In another medium bowl, beat egg whites with clean beaters until foamy. Gradually beat in remaining 3 tablespoons sugar, 1 teaspoon at a time, until glossy soft peaks form. Fold egg-whites mixture into egg-yolk mixture. In a sifter, combine flour and salt. Sift over egg mixture; fold in. Pour about 1/2 of batter into greased casserole. Spread blueberries over batter. Drop remaining batter by spoonfuls over blueberries. Bake in preheated oven 30 to 35 minutes. Cut warm cake into 8 equal portions. To serve, spoon 1 portion into each of 8 dessert dishes. Serve warm, topping each serving with 1/4 cup Orange Sherbet, if desired. Makes 8 servings.

---

1 cake serving = 1 bread, 1 fruit, 1/2 fat, 135 calories
1/4 cup Orange Sherbet = 1/2 fruit, 1/4 milk, 45 calories

Metric Chart
Comparison to Metric Measure

When You Know	Symbol	Multiply By	To Find	Symbol
teaspoons	tsp	5.0	milliliters	ml
tablespoons	tbsp	15.0	milliliters	ml
fluid ounces	fl. oz.	30.0	milliliters	ml
cups	c	0.24	liters	l
pints	pt.	0.47	liters	l
quarts	qt.	0.95	liters	l
ounces	oz.	28.0	grams	g
pounds	lb.	0.45	kilograms	kg
Fahrenheit	F	5/9 (after subtracting 32)	Celsius	C

Liquid Measure to Milliliters

1/4 teaspoon	=	1.25 milliliters
1/2 teaspoon	=	2.5 milliliters
3/4 teaspoon	=	3.75 milliliters
1 teaspoon	=	5.0 milliliters
1-1/4 teaspoons	=	6.25 milliliters
1-1/2 teaspoons	=	7.5 milliliters
1-3/4 teaspoons	=	8.75 milliliters
2 teaspoons	=	10.0 milliliters
1 tablespoon	=	15.0 milliliters
2 tablespoons	=	30.0 milliliters

Liquid Measure to Liters

1/4 cup	=	0.06 liters
1/2 cup	=	0.12 liters
3/4 cup	=	0.18 liters
1 cup	=	0.24 liters
1-1/4 cups	=	0.3 liters
1-1/2 cups	=	0.36 liters
2 cups	=	0.48 liters
2-1/2 cups	=	0.6 liters
3 cups	=	0.72 liters
3-1/2 cups	=	0.84 liters
4 cups	=	0.96 liters
4-1/2 cups	=	1.08 liters
5 cups	=	1.2 liters
5-1/2 cups	=	1.32 liters

Fahrenheit to Celsius

F	C
200—205	95
220—225	105
245—250	120
275	135
300—305	150
325—330	165
345—350	175
370—375	190
400—405	205
425—430	220
445—450	230
470—475	245
500	260

Index